"A compelling account by a disti
uphold the rule of law in a part of
Always attuned to humanity, Dean ᴦ .... us on a journey that can
be harrowing or humorous, but leaves readers with a profound appreciation
of the devastating consequences when a society values vendettas more than
victims, and power more than precedent."

—Jeffrey Amestoy, former Vermont Supreme Court chief justice and
author of *Slavish Shore: The Odyssey of Richard Henry Dana Jr.*

"This book provides a fascinating insight into the minutia of international
justice. Judge Pineles' account highlights the many challenges faced by those
tasked with actually implementing ambitious mandates, and the difficulties
inherent in navigating both bureaucracy and political interests at both local
and international levels."

—Aidan Hehir, University of Westminster, London, and coeditor of *Kosovo
and Transitional Justice: The Pursuit of Justice After Large-Scale Conflict*

"My EULEX [European Union Rule of Law Mission in Kosovo] colleague
Judge Dean Pineles came to Kosovo with the training, education, and
experience of an outstanding judge and had an immediate impact on his
Kosovar and international colleagues. Judge Pineles sought out and was
assigned to some of the most important cases that came before EULEX
judges. This book is a good, educational, and sometimes hilarious account
of his and our time in Kosovo. A great read that brought back many good
memories about the work and the wonderful people of Kosovo."

—Judge Charles Smith III, international criminal judge, Kosovo Special
Chambers, The Hague, Netherlands

"What an interesting life Dean Pineles has lived. Commissioner of labor and
industry, governor's counsel, and Vermont trial judge were enough to make
a career, but after those jobs Judge Pineles became an international criminal
judge, hearing cases of war crimes and human organ trafficking in Kosovo
and providing training on rule of law and jury trials. His is a life of service

and dedication, and he reveals himself in this memoir as a good man and a good judge."

—Paul Gillies, author of *The Law of the Hills: A Judicial History of Vermont*

"The memoir authored by Judge Pineles provides marvelous insight into his pathway to the noble work he performed as a principled advocate for international rule of law in post-conflict and developing countries. As is evident from the memoir, it is intuitive that a true democracy depends upon even-handed jurisprudence. However, introducing and sustaining best practices for criminal justice is not an easy task in an environment where those concepts were unknown and, perhaps, unwelcome to some segments of society.

Moreover, as suggested by the memoir, the process is sometimes made more difficult by intersecting bureaucracies and less than noble motivations. Yet Judge Pineles's navigation from taxi driver during law school to an intrepid judge on foreign territory is remarkable, because the adventures and challenges that he confronted in international settings reflect jurisprudential courage, notwithstanding periodic risks to his safety. Judge Pineles and his work set a high bar for those who work in the international rule of law field, and his story should be read for the important lessons that it teaches."

—Michael Cuniff, international rule of law practitioner (Kosovo, Serbia, Bosnia, Ukraine, Pakistan, and Ethiopia)

"Dean Pineles offers a delightful, entertaining account of his career in the international arena, where he worked to build rule of law in a variety of countries as they emerged from dictatorship or conflict. Anyone who reads this will gain an appreciation for how challenging, and how rewarding, this work can be."

—Clint Williamson, third United States ambassador-at-large for war crimes

"It is extremely rare in the annals of international jurisprudence and war crime prosecutions to get an international justice's perspective; as a consequence, this compelling memoir by Judge Pineles, who was on the ground in Kosovo, is required reading for anyone trying to understand how international criminals are held accountable."

—Philip Kearney, international prosecutor and author of
Under the Blue Flag: My Mission in Kosovo

"Judge Pineles's book opens a door to the world of international criminal and humanitarian law and allows us a view of not only the issues, but the people who attempt to make this system work. The development of the rule of law is a still a delicate balancing act that doesn't lend itself to binary judgements and suppositions, contrary to popular thought. But more importantly, Pineles's memoir allows us a nuanced view behind the robes for a deeper understanding of the people who work in this sector and often have to navigate through discontent on all sides."

—Bronwyn Jones, American journalist in Kosovo

"Dean Pineles provides a road map to a world now at the epicenter of conflict. Russia's invasion of Ukraine in 2022 makes Pineles's personal story all the more valuable as a way to understand the places and characters at the center of this conflict. His journey as a Vermont lawyer working globally to strengthen the rule of law should give us all hope that even in war ravaged nations, good people—like Pineles—are helping to make the world better."

—David Goodman, Vermont author, journalist, and radio and podcast host

"Pineles combs his experience as a judge for the European Union Rule of Law Mission in Kosovo (EULEX) for two and a half years to illuminate the way international law and justice actually develop–or stall—in a war-affected country like Kosovo. In theory, an international juridical organization like EULEX should move ahead even on sensitive cases, whereas a purely local court or panel could get mired by political influence. As Pineles explains, the reality can be quite different. Justice can be frustrated by turf battles, bureaucracy, incompetence, lack of political will when needed, poor communication, and even corruption. Anyone interested in justice in the

Balkans—or interested in utilizing international panels in post-conflict settings—should read this book."

—Edward P. Joseph, Balkans expert and lecturer and senior fellow, Johns Hopkins School of Advanced International Studies

"Judge Pineles's memoir is a journey through a dangerous forest of uncertain trails and trials, searching for that pinnacle of democracy: the rule of law. It includes a near career-ending event when, as the Vermont governor's legal counsel, he recommended taking into custody the children of a secretive religious community based on allegations of mental and physical abuse, an event etched into Vermont's legal and cultural history. Pineles subsequently survived a very contentious judicial confirmation process and became a respected Vermont trial judge, inoculated with the wisdom and humility that came from this intense personal ordeal.

Twenty-one years later, after a successful judicial career, Judge Pineles began another career as an international rule of law adviser in Russia, Kazakhstan, and Georgia. Then, after rigorous screening by the European Union Rule of Law Mission in Kosovo, he was selected to be an international criminal judge, helping to improve justice in that tortured land. He finds it a maelstrom of complex social, international, cultural, ethnic and political forces. He recounts many of his cases, including his meticulous fact-finding, and by ignoring these perilous forces he demonstrates how the rule of law should be implemented. Nevertheless, some of these cases have bizarre outcomes which undermine his best efforts. These are compelling accounts. They demonstrate a vigorous mind that brings to life important events. A reader seeking understanding of the frailty of democracy mediated by thoughtful judicial process will find this journey intriguing."

—Kimberly Cheney, former vermont attorney general and author of
A Lawyer's Life to Live

"This is the inside story of justice delayed and frequently denied in post-war countries, despite the best efforts of skilled prosecutors and jurists deployed to advance the rule of law and justice for all persons.

The incendiary politics and conflicted policies of the international community are exposed during the trial of the high-profile Medicus case, an indictment against organ trafficking in the Balkans that shocked the conscience of Europe and beyond—with EU institutions and the governing elite willing to concede the defeat of justice, in the name of regional stability."

—Jonathan Ratel, *Medicus* chief prosecutor

Also by Dean B. Pineles

Book Chapter

Kosovo and Transitional Justice, Chapter 8, "A Critical Analysis of the Evolution of the Kosovo Specialist Chambers and the Specialist Prosecutor's Office, and the Rationale for Their Existence"

Online Articles
Balkan Insight

"'Ghost Court' Delays Justice for Kosovo War Victims"
"Kosovo's Medicus Case: Bad Omen for Rule of Law"
"War Crimes Indictments Could Wreck Kosovo-Serbia Talks"
"American Dilemma: What if Kosovo's Thaçi is Indicted?"
"Donald Trump Should Call a Serbia-Kosovo Summit"
"Trump Administration's Bet on Kosovo's Thaçi Fails to Pay Off"
"Were Prosecutors Right to Publicize Charges Against Kosovo's Thaçi?"
"Kosovo War Crimes File Leaks Deliver a Blow to Justice"
"Kosovo's Klecka War Crimes Trial Was No Joke"
"How the 'Kosovo Precedent' Shaped Putin's Plan to Invade Ukraine"
"The Controversial Legacy of Dick Marty in Kosovo"

Vermont Bar Journal:

"Life Beyond the Vermont Trial Bench: Tales from Kosovo"
"Kosovo: International Criminal Justice in Slow Motion"

Rhode Island Bar Journal:

"Georgians On My Mind: International Courtroom Drama in Rhode Island"

Op-Eds

"*Free Press* Took Unfair Swipes at Vermont Judiciary"
"Teen's Judge Chose Compassion over Despair"

Interviews

Montana Public Radio: From Vermont Lawyer to War Crimes Judge
RTV1, video interview for inclusion in Russian documentary about international human organ trafficking and the *Medicus* case

---

Screenplay

Episode 3 of Georgian TV series *Verdict*

A Judge's Odyssey

7/30/22

To Sally and Rick,
Great to see you again
and thanks for your
interest in my book.
Best wishes and stay
well.

Tom

A Judge's Odyssey

From Vermont to Russia,
Kazakhstan, and Georgia,
Then on to War Crimes &
Organ Trafficking in Kosovo

Dean B. Pineles

Rootstock Publishing

Montpelier, VT

First Printing: 2022

A Judge's Odyssey, Copyright © 2022 Dean B. Pineles

All Rights Reserved.

Release Date: July 5, 2022

Hardcover ISBN: 978-1-57869-089-3
Softcover ISBN: 978-1-57869-088-6
eBook ISBN: 978-1-57869-090-9

Library of Congress Control Number: 2021925195

Published by Rootstock Publishing
an imprint of Multicultural Media, Inc.
27 Main Street, Suite 6
Montpelier, VT 05602 USA

www.rootstockpublishing.com

info@rootstockpublishing.com

Interior and cover design by Eddie Vincent, ENC Graphic Services (ed.vincent@encirclepub.com)
Cover art credit: Shutterstock
Author photo by Gillian Randall
Front map by Tim Newcomb

Parts of chapters 15–17, 19, 23, 25, 27, 29, 34, 35, 37, and the epilogue are reprinted, with permission from the *Vermont Bar Journal*, from "Life Beyond the Vermont Trial Bench: Tales from Kosovo," Spring 2017, Volume 43, no. 1, and from "Kosovo: International Criminal Justice in Slow Motion," Spring 2020, Vol. 46, no. 1.

For permissions or to schedule an author interview, contact the author at: pineles@pshift.com.

Printed in the USA

I wish to dedicate this memoir to Violet, my six-year-old granddaughter, who brings sunshine into my life every time she bursts into my office. Her energy, creativity, wit, laughter, joyfulness, and strong will give me hope for future generations. My fervent hope is that she will grow up and thrive in a world more committed to peace and the rule of law. I also hope that when Violet is older, she takes interest in this memoir to learn more about Grandpa Dean.

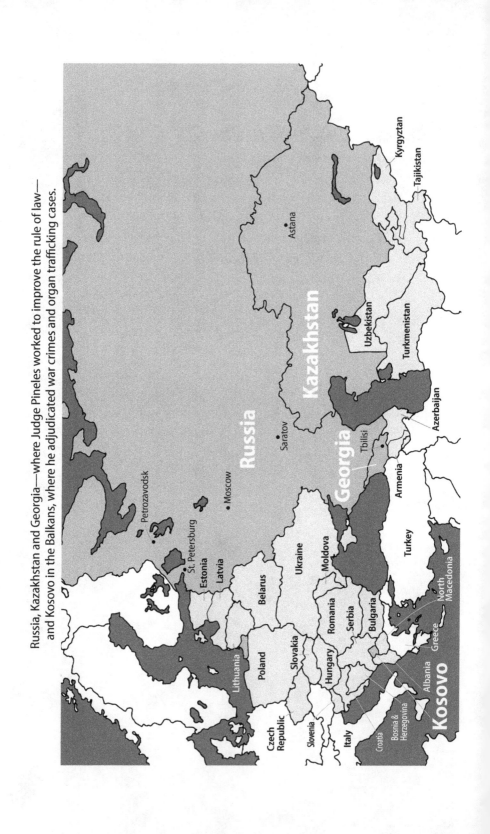

Russia, Kazakhstan and Georgia—where Judge Pineles worked to improve the rule of law—and Kosovo in the Balkans, where he adjudicated war crimes and organ trafficking cases.

Table of Contents

Preface

"He was a man endowed with keen judgment whom neither threats, nor honors could sway."
—Inscription on the headstone of Governor Simon Bradstreet, Salem, Massachusetts (1603–1697)

My mother Barbara traced her ancestry back to Simon Bradstreet and his wife Anne Dudley Bradstreet, who arrived in colonial Massachusetts from England on the *Arbella* in 1630. Simon served in many governmental positions during his long life, including as governor of Massachusetts Bay Colony on two separate occasions (1679–86 and 1689–92), and was highly respected for his public service, diplomatic skills, business acumen, hard work, honesty, and integrity.

He was one of few people with the courage to oppose spectral (ghostly) evidence leading to the execution of many poor souls convicted of witchcraft during the Salem Witch Trials in the early 1690s. Anne Bradstreet (1612–72) was America's first English poet, and Bradstreet Gate at Harvard is named in her honor.

Simon Bradstreet. Photo courtesy of Thomas Crane Public Library, Quincy, Massachusetts.

My middle name is Bradstreet and I'm proud of my heritage; Simon and Anne helped settle America. I've been inspired by their lives throughout my career and hope they would be proud of my public service and my willingness to step out of my comfort zone, take risks, and explore new horizons as they did (albeit in the extreme) back in the early 1600s.

This book is a memoir of my experiences as a lawyer and judge in Vermont, which led to my work as an international rule of law judge, primarily in Georgia and Kosovo where I served long-term residential assignments, but also in Russia and Kazakhstan where I served short-term assignments.

Each of these countries was transitioning from some form of upheaval. Russia, Kazakhstan, and Georgia, all former Soviet republics, were still transitioning from the breakup of the Soviet Union and establishing themselves as independent countries. Georgia was the victim of a Russian invasion in August 2008; Kosovo was developing a Western-style democracy following the disastrous war with Serbia in the late 1990s.

Establishing the rule of law is the underpinning of a healthy democratic society, and is extremely important work. It can be satisfying and rewarding as a result of an occasional success story, but can also be extremely frustrating, with failures, unexpected emergencies, turf battles, duplication of efforts, corruption, local resistance, and personality conflicts. The work, as you will see, did not proceed in a smooth, linear fashion.

Working and living in cultures far different from our own produces a never-ending inventory of personal anecdotes which I have included throughout this book. Here is a brief sampling of the international experiences I cover:

During my first trip to Russia, in 1996, I learned about local conviviality the hard way. And I learned about the allure of rock and roll music, while fearing an international incident.

In Kazakhstan in 2006, which I'd thought was a poor, backwater, post-Soviet country, it seemed like I'd been dropped into a Disney set.

While in Georgia in 2008–09, turf battles greatly impeded my work as a jury trial expert, but not from Georgian sources as you might imagine, rather from fellow Americans.

In August 2008, Americans were evacuated from Tbilisi, Georgia, to Yerevan, Armenia, during an international military crisis as the Russians invaded Georgia.

In October 2008, I escorted a group of Georgian judges to Boston, Massachusetts, and Providence, Rhode Island, to observe the American legal system in action. We were invited to observe a jury trial in Providence. The outcome was shocking.

In August 2010, a notorious loan shark was murdered in his office in Prizren, Kosovo, during the holy month of Ramadan. A man who owed the loan shark a substantial amount of money was charged with the murder. The case went to trial a year later, in August 2011, but the trial did not end the matter. Instead, the ancient Albanian Code of Kanun intervened, calling for blood revenge.

In the summer of 2011, two Kosovo Liberation Army (KLA) soldiers went on trial in Prizren, having been charged with a war crime for terrorizing Serbian civilians years earlier, in 1998, during the war between Kosovo and Serbia. The courtroom drama was riveting, as the SWAT team maintained order.

In the fall of 2011, in a case followed closely by the international media, ten former members of the KLA, including a popular politician, went on trial in Pristina, the capital of Kosovo, for war crimes against Serbian prisoners of war. But the prosecution's key witness—a former guard at the detention facility, who was in the witness protection program—became unavailable just before the trial started, creating a procedural and evidentiary nightmare.

Also in the fall of 2011, several Kosovo medical doctors and government officials went on trial for human organ trafficking and organized crime. The case would last for nineteen months, into 2013—one of the longest and most complex cases in Kosovo legal history—gaining international media attention. Unbelievably, nearly a decade later, the case is still in the courts.

Before the war between Kosovo and Serbia, in 1998–99, a Kosovo lawyer had an active law practice representing people who had been injured in car accidents, but many of the claims remained unresolved when the war broke out. After the war, when he became a municipal judge, he concocted an elaborate scheme to bilk his former clients and their insurance company out of more than 1.5 million euros (over $2 million at the time). His case went to trial in 2012, and the house of cards came tumbling down.

Introduction

I was born in 1943 and grew up in Hamilton, Massachusetts, less than an hour from Boston, on the North Shore. My childhood was very enjoyable. We lived in a pleasant neighborhood, I walked to school, where I did well; I had two younger sisters to harass, lots of friends, visited my grandparents often, went to the beach, and played sports. We were not wealthy, but lived a comfortable middle-class life.

My dad, Bernie, attended Carnegie Tech and MIT. He worked hard, first as a chemist with United Shoe Machinery Corporation in Beverly (now long gone), where he earned certain patents; then in various management positions; and finally as a principal in an international management company, Pineles International. I was intrigued by his global travels and often mused about the possibility of someday doing the same.

My mom was a typical post-war 1940s–60s stay-at-home housewife, and was very smart, friendly, pretty, and talented. She kept the household running and was a great mother, but as I grew older I came to understand that she was frustrated at not being able to use her many talents outside the home, always catering to my father's needs and wishes, as was common during that era.

My parents instilled in me a strong work ethic. When I was ten or eleven, I started a paper route which grew to around fifty customers and lasted about three years. I saved over $1,000, which was a fortune for a kid in those days. I attended Hamilton High School my freshman and sophomore years, where I was a good student and played basketball, making the varsity team my sophomore year. I scored 21 points and the winning basket against our archrivals Manchester in a gym full of screaming fans. And I always worked during the summers.

My parents sent me to Mount Hermon School, with my approval, for my final two years of high school. Mount Hermon is a boarding school in western Massachusetts, where my dad graduated in 1937. The money I earned from my paper route was used to offset my tuition. I was a decent student, and played three varsity sports: cross-country in the fall, basketball in the winter, and track in the spring. I was inducted into the Mount Hermon Hall of Fame as a member of the cross-country team, which was undefeated my senior year. Mount Hermon had a mandatory work program for students, so I worked in the bakery my junior year and on the campus crew my senior year, getting up before dawn for each job.

One night during the spring of my junior year, I engaged in a prank that could have gotten me expelled. After dark, while the senior prom was in full swing at the gym, a friend and I snuck down to the working farm on campus and filled two pillowcases with piglets, which we then released into the gym, causing mayhem. We escaped unnoticed, and the piglets were later returned to the farm unharmed. This incident became part of campus lore, and was even discussed at my fiftieth reunion.

During this time, I was introduced to a tall, willowy young woman named Kristina (also known as Kitty) Stahlbrand, who lived in Boxford, a couple of towns over, and who was also in boarding school, at Abbot Academy (now Phillips Andover). We connected immediately and have been together ever since. Kristina's father was from Sweden and her family traveled regularly to Sweden and other European countries. Kristina would regale me about her international travels and I would dream about adventurous travel with her someday.

Following graduation, in 1961, I enrolled at Brown University. I lived in a dorm my freshman year, got acceptable grades, participated on the varsity track team, and learned to enjoy a cold beer. Sophomore year I joined a fraternity, Phi Gamma Delta, which was great fun (think Fiji Island parties), good camaraderie, and lots of mischief, all of which is memorialized by a Fiji owl tattoo on my hip. I still went to class and studied hard, continued with the varsity track team as a high jumper (6'6" before the Fosbury Flop revolutionized the event), and worked at student jobs my whole time at Brown. I graduated in 1965 with a degree in history.

Practice session. Photo courtesy of the author.

During the summer between my junior and senior years, my lifelong friend and I traveled extensively throughout Western Europe in a VW Bug. This was an eye-opening experience for a kid who'd never been anywhere, triggering a wanderlust that endures to this day.

I then enrolled in Boston University Law School in a class of about two hundred with only three women. This was during the height of the very unpopular Vietnam War, and my primary motivation for going to law school was to secure another three years of deferment from my local draft board. I always worked part-time during law school; one of my jobs, my clear favorite, was driving a taxi in Boston, mostly on weekends. "Take me to the airport, and step on it," always resulted in a good tip.

Kristina and I were married on May 28, 1967, after my second year of law school. We lived in an unrenovated apartment in the Bay Village section of downtown Boston, in the house where Edgar Allen Poe was born.

The wedding ceremony was held in the same church where, a decade earlier when I was serving as an acolyte, I had fainted dead away at the altar on Easter Sunday while the minister was preparing the sacrament. The service was interrupted while the minister and others dragged me into an anteroom where I recovered. I had locked my knees, something I learned later in the army never to do when standing straight up for lengthy periods, like standing at attention.

I graduated with a Juris Doctor degree in 1968, that terrible year in American history with the assassinations of Martin Luther King Jr.

Joyous day! The author and his bride on their wedding day. Photo courtesy of the author.

and Bobby Kennedy, and the turmoil surrounding the Vietnam War. That summer I took the Massachusetts Bar Exam, a stressful rite of passage.

I was now listed 1-A at my draft board in Hamilton, having been deferred through college and law school. I opted for Infantry Officer Candidate School, thinking naively that the war might be over before I finished my year-long training. Shortly after the Bar Exam, I boarded a bus in Boston—destination Fort Dix, New Jersey—for basic training.

At a mail call several weeks later, my name was called and I had a letter from the Massachusetts Board of Bar Examiners. My hands were shaking as I opened it, but then I saw the word "Congratulations," which was all I needed to know. During Christmas leave, before reporting to Fort Benning, Georgia, for OCS, I attended a swearing-in ceremony at the Massachusetts Supreme Judicial Court and became a full-fledged lawyer, albeit totally inexperienced. Kristina and I then took a short ski vacation to Stowe, Vermont, and fell in love with the town. I then began six months of grueling training, but did well, graduating on the Commandant's List—top 10 percent out of about two hundred—as a 2nd Lieutenant, Infantry.

One of my most unpleasant experiences, among many, was getting completely lost with another officer candidate on a night compass course in a swampy snake- and mosquito-infested hellhole in nearby Alabama. While we survived the elements, it took us several hours to find our way back to the starting point, only to discover that the rest of the company had departed for Fort Benning, leaving us stranded. We were finally able to find a ride back to Benning, arriving in the early-morning hours, and were greeted by one of the officers, who yelled, "Where the hell have you been? I was about to mark you AWOL and send the military police."

The war was not over and I assumed I was headed for Vietnam as an Infantry officer, but my orders sent me to Fort Belvoir, Virginia, where I was assigned to a Judge Advocate General unit, working with other young lawyers who had gone to JAG school. I spent my tour prosecuting cases, mostly AWOLs, desertions, and other military infractions, later working as defense counsel—all very good legal training.

Following my discharge in 1971, I accepted a job in Washington, D.C., with the Office of Legislative Affairs in the US Justice Department. This was the office that John Dean headed before becoming White House Counsel to President Nixon. A couple of experiences stand out: I assisted with vetting both Louis Powell and William Rehnquist when they were nominated to the United States Supreme Court, as Associate Justice and Chief Justice, respectively; and with vetting Clarence Kelly when he was nominated as FBI Director. All were confirmed by the US Senate.

At the time, the Justice Department had a program for their young lawyers which involved a six-month stint at the District of Columbia Superior Court as a Special Assistant US Attorney. This was a great assignment where I got additional on-the-ground experience as a prosecutor trying criminal cases before a jury.

One other experience of note: The White House was recruiting for a young lawyer to work on special projects and I was encouraged to go for an interview. This was during Watergate and the person who interviewed me, for whom I would be working, was a man named David Young. He asked me a series of questions about my loyalty to President Nixon, which I did not answer satisfactorily, and I was not offered the job.

Sometime later, as the Watergate scandal continued to unfold, I opened up the *Washington Post* and read that David Young had been indicted as one of the White House "plumbers" (although he was ultimately granted immunity). What would have happened if I had landed the job? Jail, or maybe a book deal? I've often thought about the different path my life could have taken, though perhaps I might not have had the experiences I'm describing in this odyssey.

Part I

Career in Vermont

Chapter 1

Legal Positions

After a couple of years at Justice, and after Kristina graduated from a master's program in German linguistics at Georgetown (she was an undergraduate at Northwestern and Columbia), we decided to return to New England to pursue our careers. I sent out résumés and got an immediate response from the Vermont Attorney General's Office, inviting me for an interview.

The job opening was in the division that represented the department of social welfare, and the department of social and rehabilitation services. I went up to Vermont for an interview with Attorney General Kim Cheney and was offered the job as an assistant attorney general. In early September 1973 we relocated to Montpelier, the state's capital.

The hallmark of my tenure in the AG's office was a case that my office mate and I took to the US Supreme Court in 1975, which involved some obscure provisions of Vermont and federal welfare and unemployment law. I wrote the brief and my colleague presented the oral argument. Although we lost the case, it was an exhilarating experience, sitting in the hallowed, ornate courtroom, presenting a case to the highest court in the land—something most lawyers never get a chance to do.

I left the AG's office in 1976 after three years, and tried my hand at private practice with a small firm in Stowe, my then-hometown. I stuck it out for a couple of years but never really enjoyed it.

During this time, Kristina, who was teaching school in Vermont, had the good fortune to spend several summers in Trier, West Germany, along the Mosel River, teaching the German language to Georgetown undergraduates. On a couple of occasions I met her at the end of her program, and we

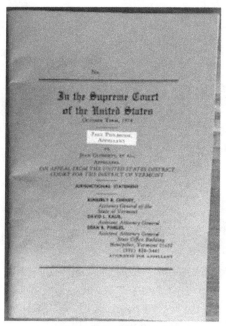

US Supreme Court brief.
Photo courtesy of the author.

traveled throughout Eastern and Western Europe. The most memorable trip was to East Germany, Czechoslovakia (as it was then known), and Hungary, all behind the Iron Curtain.

After being searched, harassed, and insulted at the border in East Germany, we were admitted and stayed with a married couple with whom Kristina had made contact, in the city of Erfurt. They did not allow us to speak about politics in their tiny apartment, for fear of being bugged, and the Stasi followed us everywhere we went. Joyless people walked the drab streets as if they had lost their souls, all under the thumb of Mother Russia and local functionaries, and all constantly wary of informers. They would wait in long lines for groceries (that often weren't available) and years for basic items like refrigerators.

The husband, who had trained as a classical musician, was relegated to working in a ball bearing factory where the end product was shipped to Russia. As a gesture of defiance, the workers occasionally made the ball bearings either slightly too big or too small, so they would be useless upon arrival. This experience informed me of the great misfortune of being in the Russian sector when Europe was carved up after World War II, and the absence of basic freedoms and the rule of law, at least as we understand it in the West.

I decided I wanted to return to work in the public sector, and enrolled in the Master in Public Administration program at the Kennedy School of Government at Harvard for the academic year 1978–79. I had time left on the GI Bill to pay the tuition. Kristina remained in Vermont to continue teaching, and working toward another master's degree (EdM) at the University of Vermont. We visited on weekends.

During that year, the Harvard campus was roiling with anti-South Africa sentiment because of apartheid, and the Kennedy School had a particular problem. My class was the first one to occupy the school's new building complex on JFK Street in Cambridge. The school had accepted a $1 million donation from the Charles Engelhard Foundation, named for and funded by a man who had made his fortune in the gold and mineral mines of South Africa during the apartheid regime. The library was to be named in his honor, which created a maelstrom on campus.

The *Harvard Crimson*, in an October 13, 1978, article, "Goldfinger Buys a Library," described Charles Engelhard as follows:

> Harvard will also be honoring Charles W. Engelhard, the man who for two decades served as the United States' largest corporate backer of the apartheid regime in South Africa. Not just any small-time mogul who has run roughshod over the political and economic rights of 18 million people, but the very epitome of US corporate complicity in apartheid. It is a situation that demonstrates philanthropy at its self-serving worst.[1]

I took one of the leadership roles on the student committee we formed to demonstrate our opposition, and after months of protest, including a one-day boycott of the Kennedy School, we were finally able to negotiate a settlement with the foundation which was ultimately acceptable to the university. This called for the foundation to forgo the naming rights and settle for a plaque in the library, but to maintain the donation. This was a good outcome that garnered considerable local media attention.

The *Boston Globe* published a front-page article on May 12, 1979, "Library Won't be Called Engelhard," which stated:

> Dean Pineles, one of the three students who negotiated the agreement with the foundation, said yesterday, "It's not an ideal solution, but a real life compromise."[2]

I was quite satisfied with this outcome that demonstrated the power of civic activism undertaken by mere students, even at an elite university like Harvard. It also demonstrated the power of money in purchasing honorifics by wealthy donors and foundations, something akin to money laundering.

Following graduation with an MPA degree in 1979, I took a public sector job as deputy commissioner and general counsel with the Vermont Health Department. I was responsible for overseeing the department's regulatory programs, such as food safety, water safety, restaurant inspections, and others, and representing the commissioner and board of health in all legal matters. This was my first experience with management responsibilities in addition to legal representation, and it prepared me well for my next job.

In March 1981, I was appointed by Republican Governor Richard Snelling to the position of commissioner of labor and industry. This was a cabinet-level position with statewide responsibility for occupational safety, workers' compensation, building code enforcement, fire prevention, wage and hour enforcement, and the safety of ski lifts.

The *Burlington Free Press* ran an editorial on March 23, 1981, which got me off to a good start, "Discard the Bad Regulations and Enforce the Good Ones," stating,

> New Vermont Commissioner of Labor and Industry Dean Pineles is the physician who may have the cure. Already the commissioner has taken a pro-business posture by promising to review 16 volumes of regulations kept by the department. And he'll do so with an eye toward cutting back rather than writing new legislation.[3]

All was not rosy. On July 3, I was notified that there had been a terrible accident on Mt. Mansfield in Stowe (the "Ski Capital of the East") the night before, involving two men who were repairing the cable on the gondola and were catapulted to the ground, one dying at the scene and one dying later in the hospital. I rushed to the scene early the next morning to assess the situation, then mobilized my inspection team.

My inspectors conducted a thorough investigation and determined that the tragic accident was caused by undersized bolts that pulled loose when tension increased on the cable. I fined the company $2,300 for three serious safety violations: using wrong-sized bolts, failing to ensure the employees had proper fall protection, and failing to ensure the employees wore hard hats.

While the amount seems paltry, it was the maximum that could be imposed under the law in effect at the time. We then undertook a comprehensive evaluation of the entire ski industry to ensure that the lifts were safe, not only for workers but for the skiing public, since skiing is a vital component of Vermont's economy. Memories of this tragic situation came flooding back in the fall of 2021, when a worker on the zip line at Mt. Mansfield was killed when he was unable to stop while traveling at eighty miles an hour. An investigation determined that a critical safety feature of the apparatus had failed because it had worn out and had not been replaced as required. In May 2022, the company was fined $23,000, also a paltry amount.

Another traumatic event occurred six months later. In late December 1981, two young volunteer firefighters perished while fighting a raging fire at the Star Hotel in Bellows Falls, Vermont. My department was responsible for enforcing the state's fire code, and the building had previously been cited for violations. We determined that the fire had started in the basement as a result of a code violation that had not been corrected (piles of trash), and that the two firefighters had not been adequately trained or properly supervised at the scene. This unfortunate matter was widely covered in the media, and I had to defend against allegations that the tragedy was the department's fault, not the building owner's.

In June 1982, Governor Snelling, in his third two-year term, appointed me his legal counsel. He was a moderate Republican and he ran the state well. He was a tough boss and did not suffer fools lightly, but I respected him greatly and enjoyed working for him. I represented him in court and before legislative committees, and acted as his liaison with several state agencies, such as human services, agriculture, and public safety (the state police). I often ran interference for some of the agency heads who preferred to speak through me rather than to the governor directly.

Examples of my legal representation include several highly publicized cases where state employees who had been fired from their jobs attempted to serve the governor with a subpoena and force him to testify either in court or before the labor relations board. I argued against these attempts as a lawyer representing a client, which was my job.

In one case, involving the controversial firing of the state's livestock director, as discussed in an article in the *Rutland Herald* on September 2, 1983, "Snelling Subpoena is Quashed," I was quoted as follows:

[Pineles told the judge] the subpoena would "open the floodgates" to people with grievances against the executive branch, causing the governor's office "irreparable harm."

"He (Snelling) would have to go around with his hands in his pockets to prevent being handed a subpoena by everyone who is disgruntled," he said.[4]

The *Barre-Montpelier Times Argus* ran a story on November 10, 1983, "Judge Quashes Snelling Subpoena," stating, "Governor Richard Snelling Wednesday successfully withstood another attempt to force him to testify in a legal dispute."[5] The article was accompanied by a picture of me with the caption, "Pineles convinced the judge."

During this time, our daughter Erika was born several weeks prematurely. She had a very rough start, and spent the first three months of her life in the neonatal ICU at the Medical Center Hospital in Burlington, Vermont, clinging to life. Kristina and I lived in Burlington at the time and, after our daily visit to the NICU, were able to walk home in about ten minutes. There were other families with very sick kids from throughout Vermont and upstate New York who had nowhere to stay.

Kristina and I, along with many other concerned members of the community, explored the possibility of starting a Ronald McDonald House in Burlington, and the idea quickly came to fruition. Governor Snelling gave the keynote address at the opening ceremony on Valentine's Day, 1984. After a tentative several months following her discharge, Erika began to thrive. She is now a women's health nurse practitioner, having graduated from the University of Vermont and Georgetown; she is married and the mother of a daughter, Violet.

Another important issue during my tenure as legal counsel was the absence of female judges on the Vermont bench. Judges in Vermont are chosen through a merit selection process and serve six-year renewable terms, subject to legislative retention. The Judicial Nominating Board is responsible for submitting the names of qualified applicants to the governor, who then interviews the candidates and makes the appointment, subject to confirmation by the state senate.

Governor Snelling appointed several attorneys to the bench, none of whom were women because none had been presented to him by the Judicial

Nominating Board. In June 1983, a group of eighty-five Vermont lawyers, about half of whom were women, sent Snelling a letter suggesting he reject any list of names submitted to him by the Board that did not contain woman candidates. The editorial writers had taken notice. The *Burlington Free Press* ran an opinion piece on June 7, titled "Judicial Board Should Name Female Candidates,"[6] and the *Brattleboro Reformer* weighed in on June 10, with an editorial, "Put a Woman on the Bench."[7]

Snelling wanted to correct the problem, and I was tasked with communicating with the Board about the urgency of becoming more aggressive in seeking female candidates. Not too long thereafter, a list from the Board was submitted to the governor which contained the name of a woman for the first time, who was then appointed by him, confirmed by the state senate, and served the state well for thirty years. Women judges soon became regular and welcomed additions to the Vermont judiciary.

Snelling decided not to run for a fourth term early in 1984, so I had to decide what to do next. At the time, Jeffrey Amestoy, who had succeeded me as labor and industry commissioner, was also mulling over his next employment. I had known Jeff from our days in the Attorney General's Office, and he and I had lunch one day where the subject of our next moves came up. I was giving serious thought to applying for a vacant judgeship, and Jeff was planning to run for attorney general in the 1984 election cycle. We both agreed that we would not encroach upon the other's plans, as uncertain as they might be.

I then notified Snelling that I was planning to apply for the judgeship. He listened carefully, and tried to talk me out of it, asking if I might be interested in becoming commissioner of public safety. I thanked him but said I would go ahead with the judicial application.

Jeff won the election and served six two-year terms as attorney general, from 1985 to 1997, and was then appointed chief justice of the Vermont Supreme Court, serving until 2004.

I submitted an application to the Judicial Nominating Board; my name was then forwarded to the governor along with several others. Following the interviews, Governor Snelling informed me that I would receive the appointment, which he announced at a press conference the next day, May 16, 1984.

I then agreed to leave the governor's office in mid-July to begin my judicial career, subject to Senate confirmation when the legislature returned in January 1985. Before I left, an event occurred which threatened to derail my confirmation and possibly end my legal career: the so-called Raid at Island Pond, which became one of the most notorious events in Vermont's legal and cultural history.

Chapter 2

The Raid at Island Pond

The Northeast Kingdom Community Church, a reclusive community of adults and children, had recently taken up residence in Island Pond, Vermont, in the far northeastern part of the state. They would not disclose any information about births and deaths, did not send their children to school, and allegedly engaged in physical abuse of their children by beating them with wooden rods, supposedly as dictated by their strict interpretation of the Bible.

These allegations first surfaced in 1982 and continued into 1983 and 1984. About eighteen children were specifically identified over time as having been abused, according to information leaked from the community, primarily from defectors. State officials made many attempts during this period to obtain information and cooperation from the elders of the church, but were repeatedly rebuffed. The state also commissioned a full psychological assessment by a respected Burlington psychologist, who reviewed all available information and materials and reached the opinion that all of the children in the community were at risk of both emotional and physical abuse.

The situation, followed closely in the media, gradually took on great importance within the Snelling administration, and involved the Governor's Office (me and others), the Human Services Agency, the Department of Social and Rehabilitation Services, the Health Department, the Attorney General's Office, the Department of Public Safety, and the Orleans County state's attorney.

In June 1984, because of the total lack of cooperation and the ongoing risk of harm to all of the children, those of us in the working group reluctantly concluded unanimously, after lengthy and intense discussions, that all options had been exhausted other than to remove the children from their homes, take them into state custody, and have them examined by doctors and social workers. An operational team was formed to accomplish these goals and placed on standby.

There was also a growing sense of urgency based on information that the children might soon be spirited away, so the date of the intervention was set for June 22. The operational team was mobilized and placed on high alert while the Attorney General's Office sought a judicial warrant to authorize the plan, which was issued on June 21, by Judge Joseph Wolchik. With the warrant in hand, the governor then made his decision approving the operation.

On the night of the 21st, dozens of state police vehicles, about ninety police officers, fifty social workers, medical personnel, and representatives from all of the offices mentioned above, including me, mobilized not far from Island Pond, where we would spend the night. Before dawn, the convoy moved out and, upon arriving in Island Pond, the troopers entered twenty residences and removed no fewer than 112 children.

By the time the kids were delivered to Newport for medical checkups and court proceedings, a different judge, Frank Mahady, had been assigned by the chief administrative judge, Thomas Hayes, to convene hearings in juvenile court and rule on the state's applications for detention orders. Mahady denied all of the applications for what he said was insufficient evidence, and the children were released back to their parents.

The event created a media firestorm, both locally and nationally. The front-page headline of the *Boston Herald* on June 23 screamed, "Troopers Crack Child Abuse Sect, 112 Kids Rescued,"[8] along with a picture of a state trooper escorting a child out of one of the residences. On the same day, the *New York Times* ran a front-page story with a photo, "Children of Sect Seized in Vermont."[9] The *Boston Globe*, on June 23, ran a story, "Vermont Seizes 112 Children From Sect,"[10] along with three front-page photos.

Locally, the *Burlington Free Press* ran two front-page stories on June 23, "At Dawn, Officials Moved In,"[11] and "Judge Blocks State."[12] In the latter story, a lawyer appointed to represent three of the children responded harshly:

> He said there was a "conspiracy between the judiciary and the state to violate the civil rights of these people . . . when (state

officials) break the Constitution, they're the biggest criminals on the face of the earth."

The *Times Argus* ran a headline on June 23, "Judge Sends Sect's Children Home,"[13] along with a picture and article, "From Left, Right, Lawyers Rap Raid."[14] It stated:

> Vermont lawyers said grave constitutional questions remained about the tactics used by the state to learn whether any were victims of child abuse.

State officials vigorously responded to the mounting opposition. In a front-page story, along with a photo on June 26, the *Burlington Free Press* stated:

> State officials ardently defended their incursion into the Northeast Community Church, contending Monday that the constitutional rights of small children and not those of religious extremists were foremost in their minds when they decided to launch the controversial raid.[15]

Taking kids into state custody pursuant to judicial process was hardly unusual, they argued; the only difference here was the scale of the undertaking.

On June 27, Judge Mahady issued a scathing written opinion, stating that the raid was a "grossly unlawful scheme."[16] Governor Snelling weighed in with a lengthy op-ed piece in the *Burlington Free Press* on June 30, which I contributed to, titled, "State Took Action to Protect Children and the Constitution."[17]

And so it went, back and forth, pro and con, throughout the summer and fall, with the state intent on vindicating its position and protecting the children, and the detractors intent on holding the decision makers accountable.

It has always been my understanding, based on information from someone with firsthand knowledge, that Judge Hayes, a former lieutenant governor and fierce political rival of Snelling's, had handpicked Judge Mahady expecting a specific result, which Mahady delivered. This was confirmed by

Judge Pineles takes the bench. Photo courtesy of the author.

Duncan Kilmartin, an attorney and vigorous opponent of the intervention, in an article in the *Caledonian Record* on August 5, 2017, headlined "Secrets from Island Pond's Chilling Raid."

According to Kilmartin, Judge Wolchik, who had issued the warrant for the roundup of the children, called Judge Hayes to request additional judges to handle all the juvenile hearings that would take place once the children had been delivered to court. But Hayes removed Wolchik from any further responsibility because of a purported conflict of interest, and instead said he would appoint "his own people to handle the results of the raid." Hayes then appointed Mahady—and only Mahady—to hear and decide all the cases. Kilmartin believes that this was the result of "divine intervention."[18]

I was sworn in as a district court judge on July 16, 1984, just over three weeks after the intervention; it was well known that I was one of the governor's advisers. It was awkward, to say the least, to be a newly appointed judge and at the same time under scrutiny for being part of what many people and commentators believed to be an illegal and unconstitutional raid.

As luck would have it, one of my first assignments was in Caledonia County (St. Johnsbury), the same geographic region in the Northeast Kingdom as the raid. I kept my head down and did the best I could to demonstrate my bona fides during my first six months on the bench.

Shortly after the legislature convened in January 1985, I was summoned to appear before the judiciary committee for my confirmation hearing. I had begun to establish what I hoped was a good judicial reputation, but I was questioned repeatedly and pointedly during several hearings by the committee members, including senator and former governor Phil Hoff, about the constitutionality of the raid, my role in recommending approval, and my judgment.

At the time, I was the only person from the Snelling administration who required Senate confirmation for a new position, with one exception, the former deputy attorney general who was actively involved in the Island Pond affair. He had been nominated by Snelling to be the commissioner of public safety, and was required to appear before another senate committee for confirmation; the committee members did not ask him a single question about the operation. Although some commentators claimed I was a scapegoat, I did not see it that way; people in public service have to be publicly responsible for their decisions and actions, and I was willing to do so.

The committee hearings were a painful, anxiety-ridden experience, and I was genuinely concerned that I would not be confirmed. I was reading about myself in the papers almost every day. For example, the *Times Argus* ran a front-page story with my photograph on February 20, 1985, with the headline, "Pineles Grilled On Church Raid."[19] I was also the subject of negative editorials. The *Burlington Free Press* ran an editorial on February 22, "Raid Raises Questions about Pineles' Judgment."[20]

Another editorial in the same paper, on March 14, "Raid on Sect Raises Doubts About Pineles," stated:

> What is troublesome about the Pineles appointment is that he was Snelling's legal confidant and could have advised the governor to cancel the raid on the grounds that it would violate the constitutional rights of church members. That he assented to the action raises serious questions about Pineles' judgment which could have an impact on his conduct on the bench.[21]

Then a former colleague of mine from the Snelling administration, Bill Gilbert, who himself had been legal counsel, and then secretary of administration and also a close Snelling confidant, offered to be my lawyer, pro bono, and came to my rescue. He lined up a number of prominent personalities who agreed to testify on my behalf. As the *Times Argus* put it on March 20, "Pineles Lauded by Witnesses at Confirmation Hearing," stating, "The roster of Pineles supporters reads like a Who's Who of state government, past and present."[22]

The *Burlington Free Press* ran a lengthy article on March 21, "Pineles Presents Witnesses to 'Protect My Reputation.'"[23] Witnesses included Lieutenant Governor Peter Smith, Attorney General Jeff Amestoy, a former US attorney for Vermont, a former chair of the Vermont Public Service Board, the Secretary of Human Services, the Commissioner of Health, and the Commissioner of Budget and Management. The *Free Press* wrote:

> For nearly three hours, witness after witness described the former Snelling aide as a thoughtful, patient, contemplative man, extolling him for his compassion, kindness and ongoing contributions to his community. Several of those witnesses were high-placed officials, and included one of Pineles' legal adversaries in the Island Pond court case and a harsh critic of the raid—Defender General Andrew Crane.

The *Free Press* went on to say,

> Crane said, "(I have) gone out of my way to obtain evaluations on his performance" since Pineles began serving on the bench last July. "Without exception, without a single exception, he is held in high regard. If I've heard any complaint, it is that he is too scrupulous. It's no secret that I think he made an error in judgment in respect to his decision in the Island Pond case. . . . But any reservations I might have had have been removed since his term as a judge."

This turned the tide and my nomination was finally voted out of committee favorably, 5–1, after four exhaustive hearings, then approved by the whole Senate, 25–4. The ordeal was over, and I am eternally grateful for those who came forward in my support, particularly Bill Gilbert; without them I likely would not have been confirmed. Following confirmation, I then settled in to my judicial career that lasted over twenty-one years.

The fundamental question about Island Pond lingered, and still lingers today: Was the intervention proper or not? My answer to that question at the time was quoted in the *Rutland Herald* in an article on March 21, 1984, "Support Voiced for Judge Pineles."

> "I would sit here with a heavy conscience if we had done nothing and had been faced with a dead child," Pineles said, referring to a similar case in Michigan in which the state took action after a child died of a beating. "I would rather be here defending what we did."[24]

My answer today would be much the same.

Chapter 3

Judicial Career

On the bench, I was no longer just attorney Dean Pineles, but "Your Honor," and people stood when I entered the courtroom adorned in my black robe—"All rise for the Honorable Court." These courtesies were not meant for me personally, but for the sacred institution I was now representing, one of the pillars of our democracy. It was a humbling realization, and it was now my responsibility to uphold the dignity of the court, and to make sure that others did as well.

My first day on the bench, at a busy arraignment session in a crowded courtroom, was a mixture of anticipation, anxiety, stress, and self-consciousness. These emotions flooded over me as I took the bench. Did I appear to know what I was doing? Did I have control of the courtroom? Did I display the appropriate judicial demeanor? Did I process the many cases efficiently, but with respect and patience for the litigants and their attorneys? Did I make the correct legal decisions? I managed to make it through the schedule without any glaring errors, so this was the very beginning of my developing self-confidence.

Being a judge is markedly different from being a lawyer and advocate; it's a role reversal. Lawyers are duty-bound to provide vigorous representation for their clients within the bounds of the facts, the law, and ethical considerations. They are not supposed to be impartial. Judges, on the other hand, are duty-bound to be fair and impartial, and to make rulings and decisions that are well-reasoned, dispassionate, and respectful of the positions of the parties appearing before the court regardless of the type of case. Switching from advocate to judge did not come easily and required training, discipline, and ongoing self-reflection and evaluation. It was a learning process that took time.

During my career, I presided from time to time in all of our trial court dockets: criminal, civil, juvenile, family, truancy, mental health, and drug court. I was often the only general jurisdiction judge in the county, most of them being small, and I would be responsible for all the dockets during the term of court. My favorite was criminal court, where I probably spent the majority of my career. It was an unending, relentless flow of cases and the pace was always fast—from arraignments to motion hearings, to jury trials, to sentencing hearings, to never-ending decision writing. When one case or hearing was concluded, there were dozens more waiting to be heard.

Criminal jury trials were always challenging, as they often involved very serious cases such as sexual assault and murder, and I had to be very careful with my procedural and evidentiary rulings both before and during the trials so as not to commit "reversible error" and have the case reversed by the Supreme Court on appeal. Over the years, I presided in well over one hundred jury trials, everything from drunk driving to first-degree murder.

Criminal judges in Vermont, and everywhere else in the United States, also spend a good deal of time hearing and deciding "changes of plea." A change of plea is when criminal defendants change their pleas from not guilty to guilty or no contest, usually pursuant to a plea agreement between the defense attorney and the prosecutor, which then has to be approved by the judge.

While rarely perfect, a well-constructed plea agreement can serve a multitude of purposes. First, it eliminates the need for an actual trial which can be expensive, time-consuming, and inconvenient for witnesses, not to mention the uncertainty of the outcome for both the prosecution, the victims, and the defendants—one can never predict how the jury will evaluate the evidence. Plea agreements are the lubricant that keeps the criminal court functioning; if every case went to trial the system would quickly grind to a halt.

With an agreement, the prosecution secures a conviction based on pleas of guilty or no contest to the charges (which are sometimes reduced or dismissed as part of the agreement) and the defendant knows in advance what the sentence will be, or at least the sentencing range, and much uncertainty is eliminated for both sides. The defendants generally, although not always, waive their right to appeal, so there is no risk that an appellate court might view the case differently. With a guilty plea, the defendant takes responsibility for their criminal behavior, an important goal of the criminal justice system. On the down side, plea agreements are often viewed as coercive, with the prosecutor having the upper hand.

Probably the most difficult part of the job was imposing the sentence in serious criminal cases. While some cases were straightforward, others were agonizing. For example, in a rape case the courtroom could be packed with the victim's supporters and family, and likewise for the defendant. I would listen to impassioned statements from both sides, often tearful, as well as from the prosecutor and defense attorney, and finally from the defendant, before making a decision.

During my career on the bench, I dealt with many serious cases, the majority of which traveled under the radar. Occasionally there were cases so serious or outrageous, they became front-page news. I've selected just two to discuss, one involving a guilty plea, the other involving a jury trial.

The former case was that of Gregory Gabert. The case began on September 29, 1986, when Gabert grabbed a Champlain College student in Burlington, dragged her behind some bushes, and brutally raped her. He was released on bail (not by me) and committed a second rape on February 10, 1987. In that case, he tricked his way into a neighbor's home, where he beat and raped the nineteen-year-old victim after tying her friend up with a phone cord and locking her in a closet.

The horrific nature of the crimes created fear throughout the greater Burlington community. But Gabert was apprehended and, after intensive pretrial proceedings and plea negotiations, entered guilty pleas to the charges, which I accepted. I then scheduled the sentencing hearing. A *Rutland Herald* story at the time, "Rapist Gets 22–50 Years for Series of Rampages," reported:

> A Williston man who said "he had nothing to lose" by raping a woman while awaiting sentencing on another sexual assault charge was sentenced to 22–50 years in prison Friday.
>
> District Court Judge Dean Pineles, saying the crimes were "particularly brutal, humiliating and degrading," handed down the sentence . . . before a courtroom crowd packed with friends and supporters of the victims.
>
> Both rape victims recalled their assaults during the tearful

hearing, and cried throughout their testimony, as did many in the audience. The parents of one of the victims sat hugging each other while listening to their daughter speak and the mother's clenched fist shook violently while her daughter described the effects of the rape on her life.

Pineles . . . called him a predator who planned his crimes and picked vulnerable victims he could overpower. Death threats made by Gabert and the long-lasting effects of the rapes on Gabert's victims and their families were also taken into consideration in sentencing, the judge said. "You must be punished," Pineles said. "Because we have no way to guarantee that you won't do it again, I must conclude that incapacitation must be the primary goal. In order to safeguard the public a very long maximum sentence is called for."[25]

Gabert appealed his conviction and sentence, but the Vermont Supreme Court affirmed my decision in 1989. Gabert was not released from prison until 2019.

Another criminal case, perhaps one of the most notorious and outrageous in Vermont's legal history because of its seriousness and its multiple, lengthy delays, involved a Vietnam veteran named Robert Percy, who was working at a gas station in Stowe in January 1981, and kidnapped and raped a woman who had pulled in for gas (the Sue Kremelberg case). He was apprehended hours later in Connecticut, after she escaped. At the time, he was out on bail for another rape charge, that one occurring in Essex, Vermont, in December 1980 (the Susan Sweetser case).

The defendant was tried and convicted in each of these cases, which were prosecuted separately, long before my involvement. In each, however, the guilty verdicts were overturned by the Vermont Supreme Court: the Sweetser case in 1986 and the Kremelberg case in 1988. The cases were then remanded for retrials.

After further delay, I was assigned to the retrial of the Kremelberg case, now in October 1990, nearly ten years after the crime. Because of its notoriety, I ordered a change of venue from Lamoille County, where Stowe is located, to Windsor County, about seventy-five miles away. I also ordered the jury be sequestered, meaning they had to stay in a hotel with no outside contact, under constant supervision by a deputy sheriff. This was because of the incessant publicity surrounding the case, particularly about the inordinate delay.

Indeed, on September 2, 1990, the *Boston Sunday Globe* ran a lengthy story, with photos of the two women, on the front page of the New England section, entitled, "Vermont Rape Victims Kept Waiting for Justice. Two Cases have Dragged on for Nearly 10 Years."[26] It stated:

> Susan Sweetser got raped. Then Sue Kremelberg got raped. And then, both women say, came the most enduring abuse—at the hands of Vermont's criminal justice system.

On October 16, the *Burlington Free Press* began its trial coverage: "Percy Rape Trial Begins. Potential Jurors Hear Description of 10-Year-Old Case."[27] It stated:

> This trial, held in Windsor Superior Court, promises to be a long and emotional one—filled with psychiatrists, hypnosis testimony, Vietnam War stories and the victim's testimony of nine hellish hours almost a decade ago.

Both the state and the defendant were well represented—Philip Cykon and David Tartter for the state, and James Dumont for the defense.

The jury was empaneled on October 17, with three men and nine women. The next day, both sides presented their opening statements: Cykon carefully laying out the state's case to show that Percy had planned the kidnapping and rape, and was clearly in touch with reality; and Dumont conceding that Percy had kidnapped and raped Kremelberg, but was insane at the time as a result of his Vietnam experience, and was experiencing a Vietnam flashback.

As reported in the *Rutland Herald* on October 18, in a front-page article, "Insanity is Key to Defense," Dumont, with a photo, was quoted as saying, "When the evidence is closed, you'll know what it's like to have your life invaded by mental illness."[28]

The state then presented its case with several witnesses who testified about Percy's behavior leading up to the kidnapping, attempting to prove that Percy knew exactly what he was doing in Stowe, Vermont, that day, not Vietnam, and was perfectly sane.

Then Sue Kremelberg testified on the 18th. She described in detail the nine-hour ordeal of being kidnapped at gunpoint, being repeatedly raped, and finally escaping in Connecticut. As reported on the front page of the *Burlington Free Press* on October 19, along with three photos of Kremelberg, "Victim Describes Rape in Percy Case. She Says She Expected to Die."[29]

Percy's insanity defense was based on the claim that he had a flashback to his time in Vietnam while at the gas station and believed the woman needing gas was a Vietnamese woman who had betrayed his military company.

One of the defense witnesses described the horrors of Vietnam on the front page of the *Rutland Herald* on October 20, "War Stress Detailed at Rape Trial."[30] It reported:

> A veteran testified Friday that he had driven trucks with accused rapist Robert Percy in Vietnam under sleepless, hazardous conditions so stressful that "we ate speed for breakfast, smoked dope all day and took heroin at night to go to sleep."

The *Burlington Free Press* put it this way: "Witness Tells of Life in Vietnam. Percy Jury Hears of Horror, Constant Drug Use."[31] It stated:

> The jury must decide if [the witness's] testimony of decapitated bodies, the liquid fire of napalm, sniper attacks and round-the-clock drug use among Vietnam War soldiers supports or discredits Percy's insanity defense

One of the defendant's witnesses, a psychiatrist and professor emeritus at Dartmouth Medical School, then testified. He stated that he had injected Percy with sodium amytal and put him under hypnosis, and that all Percy would talk about was Vietnam when questioned about the crime, supporting the flashback theory.

The final defense witness, Dr. Lawrence Colb, was the principal investigator under a federal grant to study post-traumatic stress disorder in Vietnam veterans. As reported in the *Burlington Free Press* on October 23, "Witness Says Percy Suffered Flashback":

> "He [Percy] was sort of reliving Vietnam experiences and acted them out in violent ways," Colb said. "He was one of those individuals with a severe (post-traumatic stress disorder) complicated with the use of drugs and alcohol. I think he misperceived Mrs. Kremelberg as one of those Vietnamese women and was dangerous."[32]

Colb told the jury that Percy was insane.

The state rebutted this theory by presenting its own expert witness, Dr. Stanley Brodsky, a forensic psychiatrist. As described in the *Burlington Free Press* on October 24, "Accused Rapist is Called Sane,"

> "I believe he was fearful of the charges pending against him [in the Sweetser case]. He knew he was out on bail. He planned to jump bail, he commandeered an automobile with a gun, threatened the life of an individual. On the way, he was fully aware he was in Vermont," Brodsky said.[33]

Following closing arguments and my carefully worded jury instructions, including presumption of innocence, proof beyond a reasonable doubt, unanimous verdict, and the elements of the insanity defense, the case went to the jury for deliberation. Was Percy guilty of the horrific crimes or was he not guilty by reason of insanity?

The jury answered the question on October 25. The next day, the *Burlington Free Press* reported, "Percy Guilty Again."[34] Accompanying the story was a large photo of Sue Kremelberg with her fists raised and a broad smile on her face, exclaiming, "God. Yeah." The story noted:

> After 10 years and two trials, rape victim Sue Kremelberg embraces justice. "We get to sleep tonight," she said.

The *Rutland Herald* that same day also ran a dramatic front-page photo of Sue Kremelberg.

The front page of the Rutland Herald,
October 26, 1990.
Photo courtesy of the Rutland Herald.

The next step was the sentencing hearing on February 7, 1991. I sentenced him to a prison term of forty to sixty years. The front-page headline in the *Burlington Free Press* read, "Percy Receives 40–60 Years. Sentence Ends Tortuous 10-Year Rape Case."[35] The "Quote of the Week" in the paper's edition of February 10, 1991, read:

"I can't find a glimmer of hope here, Mr. Percy. I cannot take a risk." Vermont District Court Judge Dean Pineles on sentencing rapist Robert Percy of Elmore [Vermont] to 40 to 60 years in prison.[36]

Attorney General Jeff Amestoy vowed to devote his efforts to making changes in the criminal justice system so that sexual assault victims would never have to endure such an ordeal again. And the Supreme Court upheld the conviction in 1992. Years later, Percy died in prison.

A case like this, and all other difficult cases with sympathetic victims, put me (and I'm sure my judicial colleagues) to the test of neutrality: Could I remain scrupulously neutral in the face of compelling, heart-wrenching testimony, such as that from a rape victim? Jurors tend to have high regard for the person in the black robe sitting elevated on the bench, and a misplaced word, or even a telling facial expression, could potentially influence the jury. The proper judicial demeanor required much discipline. But I always got my chance to speak my mind at the sentencing hearings, as illustrated above.

My jury trial experience turned out to be the springboard to international work. My first international experience was in Russia in 1996, years before my retirement, and the focus was on jury trials, as you will see shortly. Up to this point, all of my international travel had been of a personal nature. But this trip to Russia instilled in me the idea that it might be possible to actually work abroad in some legal capacity, which I kept in the back of my mind for the next decade.

Other well-publicized criminal cases of mine included:

- A stranger rape at St. Michael's College.

- The robbery and beating death of an elderly man with a baseball bat.

- The rape and brutal beating of a woman left for dead by a man who secretly flattened a tire on her car and then pretended to be a Good Samaritan.

- The gunshot murder of a man who was suspected of having an affair with the shooter's wife.

- The sexual assault of several young children at a day care center by the owner's brother, in which I permitted videotaped testimony of the children for the first time in Vermont.

- The sexual assault of a five-year-old girl by a psychologist who tied her up during the crime.

- The approval by me of the "necessity defense" for protesters at the National Governor's Conference in Burlington in 1995, who were charged with disorderly conduct for protesting the upcoming execution of Mumia Abu-Jamal in Pennsylvania. The governor of Pennsylvania, who had the final authority to commute the sentence, attended the conference. (Vermont's Governor Dean, the host of the conference, was furious.)

- The sexual molestation of a child by a Catholic priest.

One of a judge's important responsibilities is protecting the dignity of the judicial institution by insisting on proper decorum, respect, and behavior in the courtroom. For the most part, this responsibility goes without saying; the vast majority of people who appear before the court are well-behaved and respectful, if not a bit nervous. Occasionally, however, someone breaches the norm.

The excerpt below is taken verbatim from a decision by the Vermont Supreme Court affirming my finding of criminal contempt during a routine court session in 2001. It was an example of profane courtroom drama.

> Defendant appeals the district court's order summarily finding him in criminal contempt based upon his profane verbal outburst during proceedings in open court. We affirm.
>
> Defendant was being arraigned in a crowded courtroom during the afternoon of May 7, 2001 on an aggravated assault charge when he interrupted the proceedings. The following exchange took place:
>
> COURT: All right, we'll enter the plea of not guilty.
>
> DEFENDANT: Whoa, whoa, wait a minute, wait a minute. What probable cause do you have? This thing was dismissed over two years ago for the same information that you supposedly found probable cause for? During the probable cause hearing, there was a Motion for Prima Facie that was entered in . . .
>
> DEFENDANT'S ATTORNEY: (Inaudible).
>
> DEFENDANT [addressing his attorney]: Man, shut the fuck up. Sit the fuck down. Now, I have the right to do that.
>
> COURT: Mr. Russell, Mr. Russell, hold on a minute.
>
> DEFENDANT: It was dismissed for prima facie motion.

COURT: Mr. Russell, hold on a minute.

DEFENDANT: The same information that you have right now and you're telling me that you have probable cause to charge me again? No new information?

COURT: I'm finding you, I am finding you in criminal contempt of Court . . .

DEFENDANT: Big fucking deal, I've been doing the last four fucking years contempt of Court, ass wipe. You ain't got fucking probable cause for jack shit. I didn't see jack shit, motherfucker.

COURT: In addition to the time you're now serving, I am sentencing you to . . .

DEFENDANT: Fucking bitch. [Referring to court personnel].

COURT: . . . 180 days consecutive . . .

DEFENDANT: Yes, sir . . .

COURT: For criminal contempt of Court.

Defendant spat in the direction of the court as he was being removed from the courtroom. The next day, the court issued an order sentencing defendant to 180 days for criminal contempt, stating that defendant had acted in a manner inconsistent with the orderly administration of justice by repeatedly and loudly using profanity toward the court, his attorney, and court staff, and by spitting in the direction of the court.[37]

The Supreme Court determined that the defendant's arguments to avoid my contempt finding were unavailing, and affirmed my decision.

Another example involved a physical attack that occurred when I was presiding over a case in mental health court. The defendant sitting in front of me, with his lawyer, had petitioned the court to release him from the state hospital, arguing that his mental health had improved and that he was now safe to be released into the community.

As I was looking down and reviewing a document, I heard a commotion and saw the person rushing toward the bench. Before I could react, he grabbed the microphone from the bench and hurled it in the direction of my head. Fortunately, the mic's cord got stuck and it crashed onto the bench, just missing me. The court officer grabbed him and escorted him out of the courtroom. He was not released.

Yet another example occurred immediately following a routine status conference in the second-floor courtroom of the historic and grand Hyde Park courthouse. The defendant was in custody wearing handcuffs and guarded by a deputy sheriff. As I was making notes, I heard the sound of shattering glass. He had flung himself out the window and landed on the ground twenty feet below, creating chaos as the deputy, along with court personnel and onlookers, flew down the stairs and rushed outside. Remarkably, he was not seriously hurt, and was retaken into custody. Sometime later, he shot and killed his ex-girlfriend's lover, then shot and killed himself.

During another routine status conference in the first-floor courtroom of the Barre courthouse involving a defendant who had been charged with rape and aggravated assault, a totally unexpected and dangerous situation arose. While waiting in the holding cell for the conference to begin, the man, who was secured with both handcuffs and leg irons, had somehow managed to loosen his leg irons. When the conference ended and he was being escorted back to the cell, he shook off the leg irons, bolted out the unlocked door and sprinted behind some buildings on the other side of the street, followed by a stunned deputy sheriff. He was soon apprehended unharmed, but speculation was that this was an attempt at "suicide by cop." He was later convicted of the underlying charges, and I sentenced him to a lengthy prison term.

In Vermont, judges rotate periodically to different courts. While I enjoyed the periodic change of location, I was almost always commuting to a courthouse which could be up to an hour away. One time, I was driving to St. Johnsbury to begin a new term of court (this was years after my first tour of duty there following the Island Pond incident). While I approached the town of Hardwick, which is in the same county, I was pulled over by a Hardwick officer and given a ticket for speeding, which was warranted. Of course, I made no mention of the fact that I was a judge on my way to the county courthouse; that would have been unethical.

Later that day, during a criminal motion hearing, the prosecutor called his next witness, who just happened to be the officer who had pulled me over. He entered the courtroom and we immediately recognized each other. If there was ever a look of shock, even panic, on a person's face, this was it. He made his way to the witness stand right next to my bench and fidgeted nervously. I then described what had happened for the record, stated that I believed I could evaluate his testimony objectively, and continued with the hearing. (I later paid the ticket.)

On another occasion, I was commuting north on a deserted section of I-89 heading to St. Albans, probably going about seventy-five. I then saw flashing lights in my rearview mirror and pulled over. The officer approached, looked at me, and said, "Aren't you Judge Pineles?" I said yes, and she responded that she was just going to give me a warning, not a ticket. I said that I wanted to be treated just like anyone else under similar circumstances. She said, "Judge Pineles, you're the boss in your courtroom, I'm the boss out here. Have a nice day." And that was the end of it.

On yet another occasion, I drove to the Washington County District Court for the first day of a new term. I entered the parking lot behind the courthouse and pulled into a space marked "Reserved for Judge." At the end of the day I found a ticket on my windshield for illegal parking. Since this was a space reserved for me, I was dumbfounded. I asked the court clerk to contact the officer who had issued the ticket and explain the situation.

He was a bit defensive and said he should have been notified in advance with the car's make and model and plate number, but was otherwise agreeable to having the ticket annulled. But he had no authority to do so; this required a decision by the city council. So I wrote a polite letter, attended a council meeting and pleaded my case, and the ticket was finally canceled.

Maintaining good health was always a challenge because of the stress of the job, and I tried to stay in good shape, both physically and mentally. But then I experienced a health scare that came out of the blue. Following a meeting in the fourth-floor library of the Burlington courthouse, I left through the fire door leading to a staircase that descended to the courtrooms and offices below. As the door closed behind me, something inexplicable happened—I fell face-first onto a large drainpipe in the corner of the stairwell, knocking myself unconscious. When I gradually came to, I was dripping with blood from a gash on my head and had no idea where I was or what had happened.

I pulled myself to a shaky standing position, pushed open the fire door and stumbled back into the library. People from the meeting were still lingering about, and were horrified to see me covered with blood and mumbling incoherently. Had I been mugged, or fainted, or suffered some kind of medical emergency like a heart attack or stroke? A court officer who was an EMT stretched me out on the floor, attempted to stanch the bleeding, called 911, and initiated the security protocol in the event I had been assaulted (which as it turned out I hadn't been).

The ambulance soon arrived, and I was taken out of the courthouse on a stretcher and rushed to the hospital, with flashing lights and siren. I spent the next two nights there, getting stitched up and undergoing every test imaginable, but a definitive diagnosis could never be determined, the most likely being syncope, or fainting. Otherwise I was fine, except for two very obvious raccoon eyes from bruising, giving me a unique appearance on the bench. The situation has never reoccurred.

One of my proudest accomplishments was starting Vermont's first drug court, located in Chittenden County (Burlington) and begun in 2002, following months of preparation. It was designed for drug-abusing parents whose children had been placed in state custody. It was an innovative and intensive program at the time, based on a therapeutic, nonjudgmental model as opposed to the traditional criminal justice model that had proven unsuccessful. The program was modestly successful (about 50 percent, the national average) at helping the parents, mostly mothers, break their drug habit and regain custody of their kids.

Presiding in family drug court also taught me the extraordinary power of addiction. While the parents would always profess an interest in becoming drug free, the drug habit would often raise its ugly head and undermine or defeat their progress. Disappointingly, the other 50 percent of participants were unable to complete the program.

On December 31, 2005, after more than two decades on the trial bench, I submitted my resignation. I loved the job and believed that I did it well, but it was time for new challenges and opportunities. My exit strategy was to become active in local affairs while I pursued international positions, having been energized by my experience in Russia in 1996.

I became an EMT with the Stowe Rescue Squad and, in addition to my regular duties, participated in a medical mission to Honduras. I also served on the local hospital's board of directors, and became a member of both the Stowe Development Review Board and the Supreme Court's Professional Responsibility Board. I also sat part-time in the trial courts and occasionally in the Supreme Court when one of the justices had a conflict.

JAMES M. JEFFORDS
VERMONT

United States Senate
WASHINGTON, DC 20510-4503

July 11, 2006

Dear Dean:

Congratulations on receiving the "2006 Shining Star Award" from KidSafe Collaborative.

You have served the Vermont community well in your twenty-one years as a Vermont trial judge. Not only have you helped in cases of child abuse and neglect, but you were able to handle and assist families involved with dealing with many other issues too.

I would like to commend you on your commitment to starting Vermont's first drug court for parents with serious substance abuse problems. This program has positively affected the lives of many people since its inception and will continue to have a positive impact well into the future.

Again, congratulations on your recent achievement. I hope this letter finds you well and enjoying Vermont's summers.

Sincerely,

Jim Jeffords

The Honorable Dean B. Pineles
1011 Stage Coach Rd.
Stowe, VT 05672

Senator Jeffords congratulates Judge Pineles. Photo courtesy of the author.

Part II

Russia and Kazakhstan

Chapter 4

Vermont Karelia Rule of Law Project

I awoke with a splitting headache. I had no recollection of where I was, how I got there, or why I felt so miserable. I pulled myself out of bed and stumbled across the room to a window which looked onto a street several stories down. The script on the buildings below appeared to be Cyrillic.

There was an open suitcase on the floor with papers scattered about. One of them had an outline of a presentation about jury trials, and my name was listed. The date printed at the top was 1996.

The circumstances of my whereabouts slowly surfaced in my addled brain. I was in a hotel in Petrozavodsk, Russia, and I was a member of a delegation of Vermont judges and lawyers. We were there to introduce Russian prosecutors to the concept of jury trials. But why did I feel so terrible? Had I been mugged? Was I ill? Was I hungover?

As I tried to gather my thoughts, a fuzzy recollection began to emerge of my sitting at a large banquet table in the hotel dining room the previous evening. This was to be our last night in Petrozavodsk after completing the formal part of our program.

I had noticed the waitstaff setting the table with slabs of an unappetizing white substance. One of our English-speaking translators explained that the substance was bacon fat intended to be ingested early in the evening so that the large quantities of vodka we would consume would be absorbed more slowly. I respectfully demurred.

Now it was all coming back to me. Those of us on the American side were expected to keep pace with our Russian counterparts as they tossed back shot after shot; it would be an insult not to, so I had attempted to do my part. Soon the effects of the alcohol set in, and in a serious way. The room had begun to spin, I began to see double, slur my words, and make silly remarks. Beyond this point I had no recollection, but I now understood why I felt so bad. This was hardly an auspicious way to begin my international rule of law work, but at least I understood the efficacy of bacon fat.

What was a Vermont trial judge doing in Petrozavodsk, Russia, a city of about 250,000 on the shores of Lake Onega in the Russian province of Karelia along the Finnish border, an overnight train ride northeast of St. Petersburg?

Shortly after the Soviet Union imploded in the early 1990s, a sister state relationship was created between Vermont and the Russian region of Karelia, spearheaded by then-governor of Vermont Madeleine Kunin, and the head of the Karelian Parliament. Out of this partnership sprung the Vermont Karelia Rule of Law Project (VKROLP), created by prominent members of the Vermont legal profession, including Justice John Dooley of the Vermont Supreme Court, and attorney Mark Oettinger.

The Project was designed to work with our Russian counterparts to implement reforms in the Russian legal system which was transitioning from the oppressive Soviet-era model to a more Western-oriented approach. Legal professionals from Vermont—judges, lawyers, law professors, court administrators, and others—traveled to "Petro," as the city came to be known, about once a year for a week or two, to present lectures, seminars, and workshops for Russian judges, lawyers, prosecutors, court staff, social workers, and others, to introduce them to American best practices.

In addition, VKROLP, in coordination with Petrozavodsk State University Law School, started the first student legal clinic, to give practical experience to students while giving legal assistance to citizens of Karelia who could not afford a lawyer. Such clinics now exist in most Russian law schools.

The program was funded by the United States Agency for International Development (USAID) through a nongovernmental organization called ARD/Checci, conveniently located in Burlington, Vermont, with which VKROLP formed a joint venture. This joint venture was the first USAID funded project to work on rule of law development in Russia.

Ironically, there had been jury trials during the days of the czars, but they were abandoned during the Soviet times, and were just now being reconsidered. The members of the Karelian legal community very much wanted to know how jury trials worked, and had sought help from VKROLP. One of the Project's early objectives was to promote and explain jury trials, and to urge their adoption in Karelia.

As part of our preparatory work, a routine jury trial I had presided over in Vermont, which involved a stolen car and which had been videotaped, was dubbed into Russian and was in circulation throughout the country, giving me movie star exposure, though I was never asked for an autograph.

In Petro, we put on a mock criminal jury trial for the Russians where I played the role of judge. Other members of our delegation each played a role in the mock trial, including prosecutor, defense counsel, defendant, or witness. The mock trial went off without a hitch, but the reaction was mixed, since we were demonstrating a trial process that would redefine and reduce the role of the prosecutors.

Under the existing inquisitorial system, judges did the questioning of witnesses based on an investigative report, while prosecutors generally sat back and waited for a conviction. Under the adversarial system involving a jury, the burden would be on the prosecutors to prove the case, likely leading to fewer convictions, an outcome the prosecutors were not enthusiastic about. On the other hand, the judges and defense lawyers were supportive of jury trials. Regardless, we had planted the seed that would later germinate in Karelia.

Our host on this occasion was the head prosecutor of Karelia, a burly man who took us to visit the local jail, although I can't fathom why, since the facility was straight out of the gulags. The main cell was crammed with at least a dozen men who hardly had enough room to turn around and who had to use a hole in the floor for a toilet. When the door to the cell was opened for us to see, the cigarette smoke was overwhelming. This was a pretrial detention facility, and the men had not yet even gone to trial.

Down the corridor was a cell containing two juveniles who were also being held in pretrial detention. The cell had a dirt floor with no beds or furniture. When the cell door was opened, the two young men could hardly pull themselves to a standing position. They said, through an interpreter, that they had been there for weeks with no progress on their cases. It was obvious that Russian criminal and juvenile justice had a long way to go.

Accompanying us on this tour was the chief judge of the Karelian Supreme

Court, who was not pleased to learn how long the prisoners and juveniles had been lodged in this jail, much longer than the two months allowed under Russian law. I don't know, but doubt, that any changes were made.

After finishing our business in Petro, a smaller group comprised of Justice Dooley, another Vermont judge, our Russian assistant Sergey, and I traveled by train, together with a legal delegation from Wyoming, to the southern Russian city of Saratov, a city of about 800,000, along the Volga River, the occasional home of Yuri Gagarin, the Russian cosmonaut and first human to travel into space.

Saratov had been a closed city until after the Soviet Union collapsed, because of its military importance, and no Westerners had been allowed to enter. The city had also been the scene of intense fighting during WWII, with 175,000 Russians killed. I would learn that WWII and the enormous sacrifices of the Russian people were never far beneath the surface of the Russian psyche, as demonstrated by the Victory Day Parade in Red Square on May 9, 2022, while the brutal war in Ukraine was continuing.

Upon arriving in downtown Saratov I was surprised to see a bustling pedestrian mall that reminded me of Burlington, Vermont. We checked in to our nearby hotel, and went to our rooms to relax and prepare for the session the following day.

A few hours later, then evening, I was not able to find my companions, so struck out on my own for something to eat. I strolled along the mall until I found a café that looked inviting. I went in and took a seat while the other patrons, who may never have seen an American in person before, watched me closely. A waitress soon appeared and helped me with the indecipherable menu. I knew the Russian word for beer—*pivo*—which broke the ice.

It was getting dark, and most of the other customers had finished their meals and gradually departed the café. Then, all of a sudden, the café was filled with the sounds of Western rock and roll music. This seemed strange but, as a fan of rock and roll, I decided to stay for a while to enjoy the music.

The waitress, a tall and attractive Russian woman, came to my table and cleared the plates. She returned momentarily, and I assumed she would present me with the check. Instead, with gestures—raising her hands, palms up—she asked if I wanted to dance. What? Here I was, in a café in Saratov, Russia, being asked to dance by the waitress.

Was this a setup of some sort? After all, Saratov had been a closed city and perhaps Westerners were viewed as tempting targets. Was she moonlighting as a prostitute? Would I somehow end up being robbed? Could this turn out to be an international incident?

These thoughts flooded through my mind as I sat there motionless, trying to decide what to do. I sensed that the locals in the café were watching intently with amusement, waiting to see if the American would take the bait.

Well, what the hell. I stood up, took off my jacket as the waitress moved a few empty tables out of the way, and we started to dance. The onlookers began to clap to the music. I will admit that I like to dance, and we rocked around the makeshift dance floor to song after song—Bob Seeger, Steve Miller, the Stones, the Beatles, and other popular Western bands—for about half an hour.

All the while, however, I worried that this might not end well. Then, abruptly, the waitress indicated that she had to leave. She went to the register, produced a check, received payment from me, and was out the door. I headed back to the hotel wondering what had just happened, and worrying that there could still be adverse consequences; but nothing ever happened.

The following morning we gathered in the conference room of a large government building where we would present another mock jury trial, this time in collaboration with the group from Wyoming. There were lots of people moving about, going in and out of offices, and walking up and down the long corridor. As we waited for our session to begin, the other Vermont judge decided to make a trip to the public restroom at the end of the hallway. She emerged a couple of minutes later, and I decided to follow suit.

In those days we wore money belts with $2,500 in US currency for expenses like hotels, meals, and transportation because we did not use the Russian banking system, such as it was. We were instructed to protect the cash with our lives. But, upon entering the restroom, I noticed a money belt sitting on the top of the toilet. I unzipped it and counted out $2,500. Fortunately, I had been the next person to use the restroom, otherwise it would have been hell to pay for my colleague, although it would have been like hitting the lottery for a local citizen—lots of hard currency in the form of US dollars.

I stuck the money belt in my jacket pocket, exited the restroom, and headed back down the hall. I sensed a commotion and saw my colleague running down the hallway at full speed, weaving in and out of other folks along the way. When she approached me she blurted out, "I left my money belt in the toilet! Did you see it? Did you see it?" I momentarily played dumb as the color drained from her face. I then slowly produced the money belt, and she heaved a great sigh of relief. "Thank you, thank you!" she uttered as we headed to the conference room, grateful that we had avoided an unpleasant incident.

The mock trial was based on a famous case involving Abraham Lincoln who, as a lawyer, had been able to undermine the prosecutor's case by showing that the purported eyewitness could not have seen the defendant committing the crime that night because it had been raining heavily, not under starlit skies.

Our presentation was well received, though those of us from Vermont never returned to Saratov. The Wyoming delegation did return, and actually created a fellowship for a Russian student to attend the University of Wyoming.

On my return to Vermont after this trip to Russia, the local *Stowe Reporter* carried an article, on March 23, 1996, titled "Vermont Judge Helps Russians Learn about Rule of Law, Justice," which was a nice tribute.

I returned to Russia many more times with VKROLP. I went for the last time in June 2010, following my residential assignment in Georgia in 2008–09, and shortly before my residential assignment in Kosovo began in early 2011.

Over the years, I was involved in lectures, workshops, and seminars on a wide variety of legal subjects including juvenile justice, child protection, domestic violence, legal ethics, bench/bar relations, and criminal procedure, among others. I was fortunate to travel to several other Russian cities in addition to Petrozavodsk and Saratov, including St. Petersburg, Moscow, Pskov, Novgorod, and Kingisepp. I also became a member of the board of directors of the Vermont Karelia Project.

Over time, the Project expanded into the much larger Russian American Rule of Law Project, which involved eleven US states that formed partnerships with eleven Russian regions, all under the direction of Justice Dooley, who'd attained rock star status among our Russian counterparts. We developed many productive working relationships, not to mention friendships.

Over the years, many legal professionals from Russia visited Vermont

Farewell banquet, Petrozavodsk. Justice Dooley, right, toasting. Photo courtesy of the author.

to observe our legal system firsthand, some attending sessions in my courtroom. My wife Kristina and I hosted several Russian colleagues at our home in Stowe, Vermont.

On one occasion, a Russian delegation of a dozen or so was invited to a party, which had become an annual event, on an island in the middle of Lake Champlain where Justice Dooley had a vacation home. It was a beautiful, warm summer day and, after volleyball and a cookout, we took a long walk with our Russian friends around the periphery of the island, high up on the cliffside. As we looked out on the shimmering lake, we saw a small sailboat anchored below. This completed the idyllic picture, and we Americans were quite pleased to be showing off such a beautiful sight.

As we got closer, the boat seemed to be rocking, which was strange because there was very little wind and no waves. A little farther along the path, we were able to look directly down upon the boat. To our surprise and amusement, we observed a couple, completely naked, *in flagrante delicto*. They heard our rustling above, abruptly ceased their fevered activity, and made a beeline for the cabin, bare butts shining in the sun. Another beautiful sight which delighted the Russians!

I have many recollections of my trips to Russia, two of which stand out in my mind because they involved Kristina, who accompanied our group to Russia on a couple of occasions.

When visiting Novgorod for a regional conference during one of our annual trips, there was a banquet

Cage for defendants on trial.
Photo courtesy of the author.

one evening for members of our delegation and representatives of the local legal profession. The banquet was held in a large turret embedded in the corner of a medieval wall circling the ancient part of the city, up several flights of stairs. As usual, there was a lavish meal accompanied by unlimited quantities of alcohol and, predictably, some of the Russians got drunk. I had learned my lesson about consuming alcohol in Russia and carefully limited my intake.

Once the band got going, a Russian judge asked Kristina to dance. She is a very attractive woman and always likes to have a good time, but she's not a heavy drinker and was perfectly sober. The dance floor was crowded and I was having a conversation with someone, so was not paying attention to the judge and my wife.

Shortly thereafter, one of my American colleagues ran up to me and said that Kristina was being groped on the dance floor. The Russian judge was pawing her, lifting her off her feet and rubbing against her in a provocative way, a predicament she was unable to break away from.

I rushed onto the dance floor to rescue my wife, tapped the Russian judge on the shoulder, and interrupted the unpleasantness. Kristina was a bit shell-shocked, but recovered quickly. While she took the incident in stride, privately she did not hide her disdain and distaste for an inebriated Russian jurist who would show such disrespect for an American colleague and his wife.

Inside the wall which circled the city were a surprising number of churches. Legend had it that if a woman wanted to become married, she would have to run around a church seven times. We considered this apocryphal, but sure enough we actually observed several young women doing exactly that.

On another trip, Kristina joined me in Petrozavodsk after she and Mark Oettinger's wife Becky visited St. Petersburg. Kristina had eaten some food in the train station before leaving for Petro, resulting in food poisoning that set in suddenly the morning after she arrived, with all its attendant problems.

Once at the courthouse where our delegation was doing business that day, the presiding judge offered her the use of an empty apartment, apparently owned by the court clerk, behind the courthouse where she could rest and recuperate. She graciously and thankfully accepted the offer. We went to the apartment, which didn't seem to be lived in, where there were a couple of beds so she was able to lie down and try to get some sleep. I returned to the courthouse.

Soon, there was a knock on the door. Kristina roused herself from bed, unlocked the door, and a doctor introduced herself in the doorway. She was impeccably dressed, with fine jewelry—a fact that would never go unnoticed by Kristina, even when ill. We learned later that the presiding judge, who did not want an international medical emergency on his watch, had called the local minister of health, who in turn had dispatched the doctor for an unusual house call.

The doctor, who spoke excellent English, did a complete exam and provided medication to calm Kristina's stomach. In the course of their discussion, the doctor asked where Kristina might have contracted the food poisoning. She explained that she'd eaten chicken in the St. Petersburg train station before leaving for Petrozavodsk. The doctor stared at her in amazement, as though she had just committed a felony, and said in a strong voice, "Never eat chicken in a Russian train station. Never." Kristina was very grateful for the treatment and advice.

After the doctor left, Kristina fell into a deep sleep. When she awoke several hours later, she needed to use the bathroom, which was located near the entrance to the apartment. She went in, leaving the door to the bathroom open. She then heard footsteps approaching down the hall leading to the apartment, and heard the giggling voices of a man and a woman. She heard a key being put in the door lock, and the door swung open. A young couple entered the apartment with intimate smiles and caresses, heading toward one of the beds. They then saw Kristina, who was seated on the john. The woman gave a shriek, and they turned and quickly scurried out of the apartment.

Suddenly, the intended purpose of the apartment became clear—it was a daytime way station for trysts and "afternoon delights."

On another trip, several of us attended a criminal jury trial in progress. The jurors were seated in the jury box, just like in the US, and the judge was presiding from the bench, just like we would see at home. We were proud of the fact that he had been one of the judges we'd trained. There was, however, a significant difference in this tableau: The defendant was secured in an iron cage, across the courtroom from where the jury was seated. This was shocking, but we learned that the cage was commonplace in Russian trials. In our opinion, such a visual completely undermined the presumption of innocence.

We also noticed that the defendant was wearing a pair of tight-fitting leather gloves. During a recess, we asked the judge about the gloves. He replied that the gloves covered up the Russian version of "fuck you" tattooed on the defendant's knuckles.

Traveling on Russian trains, which we did often, was always an adventure. We traveled first class, which meant only two persons to a cabin, while the locals sometimes traveled six to a cabin. There were many stories about Russians who may not have known each other getting into arguments or fights in the close quarters. Alcohol was usually involved. Typically, we would stock up on food and beer in the train station, then gather in one of our cabins to eat, drink, and tell stories until it was time for bed.

On our trip to Saratov, I shared a cabin with our USAID representative who was stationed in Moscow but was accompanying us to our training session. He knew the lay of the land and informed me that there had been a spate of train robberies where the modus operandi involved squirting gas under the cabin door to immobilize the occupants, then breaking down the door and making off with any valuables. I assumed he was kidding. I knew that Russia could be a little rough around the edges, but this was not the Wild West, right?

He assured me this was no joke, and to prove his point began pulling items out of his bag. First, something resembling a draft stopper—a device similar to a rolled-up towel those of us who live in cold climates would place along the bottom of a door during winter to stop the draft. This item was placed along the bottom of our cabin door to prevent infiltration of gas. Then he produced a long rod, one end of which was fastened to the inside door handle and the other end placed securely on the floor, making it impossible for the door to be forced open. Fortunately, the night passed uneventfully.

On another train ride, there were just two of us heading from Petro to Moscow, where we would catch a flight back to the US. It was dinnertime, and soon the attendant appeared with our meals and asked if we wanted beverages. My cabinmate spoke Russian and was able to understand our choices: for each of us, a pint of vodka or can of Miller Lite. Say what? Miller Lite on a Russian train? We opted for the vodka.

After we finished our meal and were relaxing with a shot or two of vodka, a couple of young men in sloppy uniforms appeared at our open door. They couldn't have been more than eighteen or twenty. They demanded to see our identification and threatened to throw us off the train because we were consuming alcohol with our door open. Consuming alcohol was a national way of life, at least among Russian men, and we were being chastised by two kids for quietly enjoying the national drink? My cabinmate smoothed things over in Russian and we shut the door, which ended the problem, even without a bribe.

The bottom fell out of the Project in 2012, when the Russian government expelled USAID from Russia, effectively terminating our program because of President Putin's disdain for foreign programs promoting democracy, legal reform, human rights, and fair elections.

It is my understanding that the right to a trial by jury is now provided in the Russian constitution for criminal cases (although not for national security cases), and that jury trials are held in all regions of the country, although I am unaware of how they function in practice.

Chapter 5

Not Your Borat's Kazakhstan

One day in early December 2006, a year after I retired from the Vermont bench, I received an urgent email from Justice Dooley, which went to everyone on his extensive mailing list, inquiring whether anyone would go to Kazakhstan, a former Soviet Republic, on behalf of an American nongovernmental organization (NGO) engaged in rule of law work there. The person would have to be a jury trial expert, in order to represent the NGO at an international conference celebrating Kazakhstan's initiation of jury trials, which were scheduled to begin shortly after the conference.

I thought this was obviously a joke, since the movie *Borat*, which stars the English actor/comedian Sacha Baron Cohen and which brutally satirizes Kazakhstan, had just come out and was playing in theaters nationwide. Indeed, Kristina and I had just seen the film. In the movie, citizens of Kazakhstan were depicted as ignorant, brutish goat herders. (The sequel was released in late 2020.)

But it was not a joke, and I agreed. I was quickly vetted by the NGO's D.C. office, and the next thing I knew I was on a plane traveling about 6,500 miles to Almaty, Kazakhstan, a city close to the borders with Kyrgyzstan and China, where the NGO's in-country office was located. However, the conference was to be held in Astana (now known as Nur-Sultan), the new capital city about 600 miles to the north, a few days later.

I had little idea what to expect, but kept thinking about one of my favorite scenes from *Borat*, where the main character (Cohen playing Borat) had just checked into a hotel in New York City and was directed to the elevator. As the elevator doors opened, he surveyed the interior, thinking it was his room, and said, "Very nice!" I wondered what my hotel room would be like.

I arrived in Almaty late at night and checked into my room, which was clean and comfortable and bore no resemblance to the interior of an elevator. When I awoke the next morning, I pulled the curtains open and experienced an utterly spectacular view of high, snowcapped mountains. The mountains seemed so close I felt like I could step out of my window onto one of the mountaintops.

Later that morning I met with a representative of the NGO, a young American attorney who would be my host. He was very cordial and helpful, and we spent the first day seeing the sights of Almaty, a typical Soviet city with many monuments to Soviet-era heroes and miles of stark apartment buildings.

It quickly became clear that the plan for my participation was still a work in progress. I would be expected to present a keynote speech at the conference—that much was clear—but might also participate in a mock trial and a workshop on jury trials with local judges. But there was ongoing uncertainty between the NGO in Almaty and Kazakh authorities in Astana. In any event, I spent the next day at the NGO's office preparing my remarks.

When it came time to leave for Astana, I learned that I and a couple of the NGO staff members would travel on Astana Airlines, rather than a safe and respected international carrier. But, wait a minute. I had always been advised that in Russia or former Soviet republics you should never fly on a domestic carrier. Indeed, Aeroflot, the Russian carrier, was sometimes referred to as Aeroflop. As Kazakhstan was a former Soviet republic, shouldn't the same cautionary advice apply? I was told not to worry. Also, there was no other way to get there.

We arrived at the airport before dawn, and I was filled with trepidation. As dawn broke I was able to see our plane at the gate. I was expecting an ancient, hand-me-down aircraft, but to my surprise and great relief it was bright and shiny and appeared to be brand-new.

The attendants were smartly dressed and multilingual, and greeted us in English. The interior of the plane was spotless, and the leather seats were wide with plenty of legroom. Once the wheels were up, the attendants came around with coffee and a selection of Western newspapers, such as the *Financial Times*. On the TV monitor, there was a clip from the Montreal

Laugh Festival. It was a delightful flight, and we arrived safely in Astana after about an hour.

Astana, which rises out of the steppes, was a sight right out of a Disney set, and contrasted dramatically with Borat's Kazakhstan. Astana had replaced Almaty as the capital city, and was basically being built from scratch along an ancient trade route.

I was put up in a beautiful five-star Turkish hotel with all the amenities one could ask for. Shortly after arrival, I and several other international attendees were given a private tour of the opulent Supreme Court palace. Along the walls of the spectacular atrium hung pictures of former Kazakh judges, with inscriptions like: "Executed in 1937," and "Rehabilitated in 1996," which recalled the purges of the Stalin era.

The conference was held in a beautiful new conference hall equipped with the latest technology. When we arrived, there were many international and local dignitaries buzzing around, along with multiple TV crews, all there to hail the introduction of jury trials.

I presented my speech through an interpreter to a large audience of judges, lawyers, court personnel, members of the media, and other international experts, extolling the virtues of American jury trials and congratulating the Kazakh leadership for taking a key step toward judicial independence. I was later told that my speech was well received.

Promoting jury trials during a workshop. Photo courtesy of the author.

I was treated like royalty by my local hosts. The evening following the conference, I was taken out to a plush restaurant by several Kazakh judges, along with a couple of other foreign dignitaries and experts. We were treated to the national dish of Kazakhstan, which was not disclosed in advance: horse meat.

The next day, we attended a workshop for judges and participated in a lively discussion about the practical aspects of jury trials, such as how to select the jurors and how to be fair and impartial to both sides.

The judges seemed ready to take on their new responsibilities, although not without some anxiety. At the end of the session, I went up on the stage where the chief judge stood and presented him with a small gift, a book of color photos of Vermont.

Jury trials commenced in 2007, shortly after the international conference, and, as I've been led to believe, continue to this day. But who can predict the future, given the massive anti-government protests and brutal government crackdown involving Russian troops in January 2022?

Part III

Georgia

Chapter 6

Landing a Job

As a result of my experiences in Russia and Kazakhstan, I wanted to engage in a longer assignment somewhere in the world where my legal and judicial expertise and experience would be useful. Perhaps naively, I felt I had the skills to make a meaningful difference wherever I might go. So, during the fall of 2007, I began a serious search for international opportunities.

Because of my involvement with the Vermont Karelia Project, which over time had developed a relationship with the American Bar Association Rule of Law Initiative (ABA ROLI), I checked its website for job opportunities. ABA ROLI has projects all over the world, so I was optimistic that something appealing might be available.

There was an opening for a legal specialist in Georgia—like Kazakhstan, a former republic within the USSR—specifically for a judge with extensive jury trial experience. The legal specialist would work with the Georgian judiciary and legal profession in an advisory and training capacity.

The Georgian Parliament was considering a sweeping proposal to amend the Soviet-style criminal procedure code to establish an American adversarial system in the criminal courts, including jury trials in serious cases for the first time. The new system was designed to enhance the independence of the judiciary and increase public confidence in the criminal justice system, which was very low.

This was a significant piece of legislation which had the support of all key Georgian and international authorities and organizations, including the Supreme Court and the reformer president, Mikheil Saakashvili, who was a vigorous advocate.

Although I knew little about Georgia, and had to consult a map to see exactly where it was, I decided to apply. I submitted an application online, emphasizing both my jury work and my international experience, and awaited a response. I seemed to fit the bill perfectly.

I heard back quickly from Donna, the ABA country director in Georgia, and was offered a one-year assignment in the Georgian capital, Tbilisi. While the position was considered pro bono, that is to say unpaid, ABA ROLI would cover all travel and living expenses.

Georgia is an ancient country in the South Caucasus, similar in size to South Carolina or West Virginia, with a population of about five million. It was the birthplace of Joseph Stalin, along with his henchman and head of the ruthless Soviet secret police, Lavrentiy Beria. In a rather remarkable example of irony, Beria's former home in Tbilisi was the headquarters of the Georgian Public Defender Service while I was there.

About 87 percent of the population are ethnic Georgians. Georgia is bordered by Russia to the north, Armenia and Turkey to the south, Azerbaijan to the east, and the Black Sea to the west. Lore has it that the Greek mythological heroes Jason and the Argonauts landed on this section of coastline. Along the border with Russia are the towering Greater Caucasus Mountains, with Mount Elbrus rising to 18,500 feet.

Tbilisi, the ancient capital city founded in the fifth century, is today populated by about 1.5 million. It spans both sides of the Kura River. Its architecture is a mix of old, new, and Soviet styles, with several broad boulevards lined with beautiful trees and stately buildings. There is a large castle overlooking the city, and the city is ringed by mountains. It is vibrant, with many good restaurants and shops, a lively arts scene, and a thriving opera house.

Georgia has diverse climatic regions, with a temperate climate in Tbilisi, in the southeast, and a Mediterranean climate along the Black Sea coast. The country is dotted with ancient monasteries, and the scenery can be spectacular. The Russian city of Sochi, where the 2014 Winter Olympics were held, is just a short way up the Black Sea coast from the disputed Georgian province of Abkazia, which claims to be independent. Georgia is a major wine producing country, as I came to appreciate.

The country experienced great turmoil after the Soviet Union collapsed, including civil war and lawlessness in the 1990s. Over time, the situation stabilized, and in November 2003, the nonviolent Rose Revolution took place, ousting President Eduard Shevardnadze, a Georgian national who had served as Soviet Minister of Foreign Affairs during the Gorbachev era and as president of Georgia from 1992 to 2003.

New parliamentary and presidential elections were called, and in 2004 Mikheil Saakashvili, who had led the revolution, was elected as president at age thirty-seven. He served in that office for two terms, until 2013, and thus was president during my tenure there. He was Western-educated (LLM, Columbia Law School), and a Western-leaning reformer who was able to reduce corruption and bring about a stable and functioning parliamentary democracy with a view toward joining the European Union and NATO, much to the displeasure of Russia.

His wife, Sandra Roelofs, was from the Netherlands, and they'd met in Strasbourg in 1993. She was a very popular figure in Georgian society, and was responsible for bringing a huge fleet of yellow buses to Georgia from the Netherlands. The yellow buses were everywhere, and the fare was dirt cheap. The equivalent of a US quarter would take you anywhere in the city.

The Georgian Supreme Court, under the leadership of Chief Justice Kublashvili, was also reform minded, and ABA ROLI had developed a very good working relationship with him and the deputy chief justice, both of whom were interested in jury trials.

Georgia is overwhelmingly Christian Orthodox. We learned that the Orthodox Church plays a prominent role in Georgian society, and the patriarch is highly regarded. While we were there, the church urged Georgian women to produce more children, and promised to bless each new child personally. This offer was viewed as a great incentive, and as time passed we noticed more and more pregnant women on the streets. The church and society at large were very conservative in cultural issues such as gay rights. Indeed, as described in the *New York Times* on May 17, 2013: "Crowd Led by Priests Attacks Gay Rights Marchers in Georgia."[38]

Chapter 7

Arrival in Tbilisi

After a brief orientation at ABA headquarters in Washington, D.C., I flew to Tbilisi in late April 2008, and spent my first week looking for an apartment and getting oriented. Kristina accompanied me, but had to return to Vermont for about six weeks to finish up her teaching responsibilities at South Burlington High School. In early June she returned with Piper, our feisty Lhasa apso we'd adopted from a shelter in Montreal. Piper turned out to be a real trouper and a valuable companion during our tenure in Georgia.

Our arrival coincided with Orthodox Easter that year. There was a church close to our hotel, and on the eve of Easter we joined the faithful gathered outside. At the stroke of midnight, the priest led the large group in a procession which circled the church several times—a moving experience.

We found an apartment we liked on Chavchavadze Avenue, one of the main boulevards of Tbilisi, and a short walk from the ABA office. It was a spacious apartment on the third floor, but it was three flights up (sixty-three stairs) with no elevator. No matter, this would be good exercise, although as time passed Kristina's knees would rebel against the climb. The apartment had a door that was virtually impenetrable against the marauding gangs during the period of instability in the early 1990s. If you didn't have several special keys, you weren't going to get in.

There was a bus stop right outside our apartment building, and we were regular riders of the ubiquitous yellow buses since we didn't have a car (nor did we want one, as I will explain shortly). The apartment was also fairly close to a health club, located about a mile away and directly across the avenue from the Iranian Embassy. Knowing of our poor relations with

Iran, I sometimes wondered if I would be kidnapped and held for ransom as I ran by.

There were several markets nearby which made food shopping convenient, as well as a wine store where we got fresh, inexpensive Georgian wine right out of the keg. We brought empty two-liter plastic bottles to the shop and filled them on the spot. Our favorite varietal was Saperavi, a dry red wine which is available in the US. There was a park close by called Children's Park, which was a good place to walk Piper, though we had to be very careful of the feral dogs that roamed about.

While the apartment was well situated, it would turn out to be incredibly noisy. It was a corner unit overlooking a complicated three-way intersection, and we quickly learned that Georgian drivers incessantly used their horns. Every situation, large or small, required the use of the horn. The constant din floating up to our kitchen made it almost impossible to have a conversation.

Georgian drivers were among the worst I have encountered in the world. I know, everyone has their worst-drivers-in-the-world stories, but I hereby nominate Georgian drivers against all others. No roadway infraction was off limits. Drivers routinely ran red lights. Drivers routinely raced up a sidewalk to get to the head of a line of traffic. Drivers routinely endangered pedestrians trying to cross the street, even with the crossing light in the pedestrians' favor—it didn't matter if it was a mother pushing a stroller or someone walking a dog, pedestrians beware.

One time I was nearly run over by a speeding driver who forced his way through an intersection while running a red light. I slammed the heel of my hand on his rear fender as he nearly clipped me. He screeched to a stop a bit farther down the road, jumped out, and ran after me. I continued across the intersection and down the opposite sidewalk. He ran up to me, shouting something in Georgian. I simply shrugged my shoulders, played dumb, and kept walking, hoping this would not lead to a physical altercation. He shouted again, something that contained the word "fuck," then ran back to his car. When people ask if I ever felt in danger in Georgia, especially after the Russians invaded, my typical answer is that the most danger I ever felt was walking from my apartment to my office, because of the insane Georgian driving habits.

Soon after arriving in Tbilisi, I hired a housekeeper named Lea on the recommendation of the ABA office. This turned out to be an excellent decision. She shopped for food, cooked delicious Georgian meals, cleaned the apartment, and washed our clothes. We really only needed her about once a week, but decided to have her come three times a week. Her husband was unemployed and there was a teenage daughter at home, so Lea supported the family and needed the income. She didn't speak much English, but that was never a problem. The tasks were pretty straightforward and didn't require much explanation.

One evening several months later, Kristina and I decided to go to a movie theater that showed English-language movies. As soon as I closed the door to the apartment, which locked automatically, I realized I had forgotten the keys. After overcoming our initial panic, I remembered that Lea had a set, so we got in touch with her by phone and explained through her daughter, who spoke some English, that we would knock on her door after the movie and get the keys.

Around 9 p.m., we went to her apartment, which was up a steep flight of outside stairs, and learned that Lea had prepared a table for us with all sorts of foods and drinks. We were honored by her hospitality, and settled in for a nice meal. Her daughter and husband were present, and we managed to carry on a very basic conversation. After eating, her husband pulled out a bottle of homemade liquor known as "chacha," which had a reputation for being lethal. The custom was to drink with the host, shot for shot, similar to the tradition in Russia which I had experienced during my trips there, particularly during my first trip in 1996.

On this occasion at Lea's residence, I was very apprehensive. I did not want to be impolite and refuse the shots, but I was wary and decided to proceed with utmost caution. He would pour the drinks, we would clink our glasses, and he would toss down the shot. On the other hand, I would sip it slowly. This went on for a while, and I felt fine. Apparently, chacha was not as bad as I'd been led to believe.

Eventually the evening ended and we got up to leave. We headed to the stairs leading to the street, but as I took my first step down, my legs went out from under me and I toppled down the stairs, head over heels, to the ground below. I pulled myself up to a wobbly standing position and seemed to be okay, but I could not get my legs to move in a coordinated fashion. Lea and her husband were mortified. After all, I was a guest in their home, not to mention Lea's employer and an American judge, and they certainly didn't want me to hurt myself.

Her husband, who was still mobile, steadied me, put his arm over my shoulders, slowly walked me home, and helped me negotiate the sixty-three stairs to our apartment. When I awoke the next morning, feeling like I was on death's doorstep, I was forced to acknowledge the lethality of chacha. I can still hear the stories about the American judge making a fool of himself.

Chapter 8

Getting Started

When I first arrived in Georgia, in late April 2008, the ABA country director, Donna, who had hired me, was no longer there. She had been promoted and reassigned to headquarters back in D.C., as the regional director for Georgia and several other countries in that part of the world.

The only other American in the Georgian office was a former federal prosecutor from California named Dan, who was also an ABA pro bono legal specialist, like me. He had been named the acting country director until a full-time replacement could be hired, and was nominally my boss. Dan had been in Georgia for several months when Kristina and I arrived. He met us at the airport and we had dinner with him and his wife that first evening.

In addition, the office consisted of about half a dozen bright, energetic Georgian attorneys and a couple of support staff, all of whom spoke excellent English. I shared an office with two female attorneys, Irina and Ira, for whom I developed a great deal of respect. They were smart, helpful, knew their way around Georgian judicial and legal systems, and had developed productive relationships with many key players and institutions, including the Supreme Court and Parliament.

They were more than willing to have me participate in projects they were working on, such as election reform and domestic violence legislation, all of which were included in the annual "work plan" approved by our federal funding agencies. Indeed, within the first couple of weeks, I found myself as the spokesperson for the office (always with a translator), holding press conferences and giving speeches on various subjects, some of which I was learning about on the fly. But I greatly enjoyed the experience.

After being in Georgia for only a couple of weeks, I represented ABA
ROLI at a press conference regarding our project, called Georgian Lawyers
for Fair Elections. The project was designed to train Georgian lawyers
of all political parties in election law, so they could respond quickly and
effectively in the event of violations during the upcoming parliamentary
elections on May 21. At the press conference, I introduced the *Election
Law Manual for Lawyers*, which was the textbook for the training sessions.

Two days later, on May 16, I was again standing before cameras at
another well-attended press conference, this time on the subject of domestic
violence, where I introduced our *Manual for Lawyers on Domestic Violence*.
The manual included a series of hypothetical cases and offered guidance to
persons and organizations that dealt with this issue, such as police, lawyers,
and judges.

The issue had slowly risen to importance in Georgian society and was
being promoted by the chief justice's wife, though Georgia was well behind
the US, perhaps in part because of the conservative Orthodox Church.
While a judge in Vermont, I'd been a member of a domestic violence task
force developing protocols for all stakeholders, such as victim's advocates,
police, and court personnel, and I had handled countless domestic violence
cases in court, so was very familiar with the subject and felt comfortable
being the ABA's representative.

In early June, when Kristina returned with Piper, she explained the
ordeal she had gone through to get Piper's papers. She'd spent days and
days completing the right forms and waiting for the necessary official
documents, right up to the last minute before her departure. When all was
said and done, no one between Burlington, Vermont, and Tbilisi, Georgia,
expressed the slightest interest in the papers, and Piper breezed through
numerous checkpoints along the way without incident.

On June 8, I was interviewed for an article in the journal of the
Georgian Bar Association on judicial reform in Georgia, to be published
in the upcoming issue. Since I was just getting started, I had to speak in
generalities, but explained that judicial reform involves a long process and
requires a commitment on the part of all key actors to create a system
that is fair to all parties, independent of political influence, and free of
corruption. But, if reform is truly legitimate rather than mere tokenism, the
public at large will have to trust the system, and such trust was lacking in

Georgia according to various studies and public opinion polls. Georgia was making progress, but had a long way to go.

Doing the interview caused me to reflect on the American judicial system. While hardly perfect, what stood out for me is the confidence and trust the average person has in our judicial framework. A common refrain when people have a serious disagreement is, "I'll see you in court."

Even though I enjoyed the work I was doing in my early weeks in Tbilisi, I'd been hired primarily as a jury trial expert to train Georgian judges in the many aspects and nuances of jury trials, and I wanted to get started right away. It turned out that Dan and another American lawyer, Roger, who was working for the US Department of Justice in Georgia, had already developed an extensive jury trial training program. I had not been informed about this project during the hiring process, and did not learn of it until after arriving in Tbilisi—an example of the left hand not knowing what the right is doing, which I would learn is not uncommon in international rule of law work.

The training program, designed not only for Georgian prosecutors and defense attorneys but also for judges, was well underway. I felt like I would fit right in, and told Dan I was ready to begin working with the judges immediately. Well, not so fast. I received a series of explanations and excuses why this would not work, but the real reason, or so I assumed, was that Dan and Roger had a strong proprietary interest in the training program and that I, a Johnny-come-lately, was not welcome despite my extensive jury experience on the judicial bench and being the only American judge in Georgia. I wasn't quite sure how to handle the situation. I was new in the country and didn't yet know my way around. I enjoyed the other work I was doing and I liked Dan, and we otherwise got along well.

I then learned that a representative from one of our US funding agencies, the Bureau of International Narcotics and Law Enforcement (INL), a bureau of the US State Department, would be in Tbilisi to discuss the training program, so I invited myself to the meeting scheduled at the ABA office the following day. It was my intent to explain that I had not been invited to participate in the training of judges.

I arrived at the appointed time only to learn that the meeting had been moved to the US Embassy, several miles out of town. No one had bothered to tell me. When I confronted Dan later in the day, he offered an excuse as to why the meeting had been moved and why I hadn't been notified, but it was obvious, at least to me, that I was purposely being cut out of the action. At that point I should have contacted Donna back in D.C., but a new country director had been hired and was en route, so I decided to wait for his arrival to pursue the matter, assuming that the situation would be easily rectified.

Garry, the new director, arrived shortly with his Russian girlfriend Svetlana (known as Sveta and now his wife). He was an American lawyer and an experienced and skillful rule of law professional, about a generation younger than I, who had recently worked in Mongolia. Soon after his arrival, Garry and I had a frank conversation about judicial training, and he understood my position clearly. From his point of view there were other important activities that had to be addressed immediately, some of which I would be responsible for, and he did not want to rock the boat so early in his tenure, so the issue was shelved for the time being.

It was obvious this was going to be a dead end, and I was ready to move on. I was disappointed, of course, but I had an ace in the hole which I felt would be even more valuable than the training program—an approved trip to the US for a select group of Georgian judges to actually observe our adversarial system and sit in on a real jury trial in progress, which I would soon begin planning.

One task I had to address immediately was the planning of an international conference in Tbilisi, on the subject of judicial independence, scheduled for July 17 and 18. The keynote speaker for the conference was to be Judge John Walker, a senior judge on the US Court of Appeals for the Second Circuit in New York, a well-respected jurist, and a member of the Bush family who had visited Georgia before and made a positive impression. There would be many other foreign dignitaries at the conference, as well as the US ambassador, and there was a great deal of logistical preparation I needed to accomplish quickly. In addition, I was planning to deliver a speech myself, which would require some research and writing, and I looked forward to the opportunity.

When Judge Walker arrived from the US, Garry and I carried his bags, escorted him around town, made sure he had meetings with all the proper officials, and attended to all his needs during the several days he was in town. He was a friendly, kind, and interesting man, and we got along well. I think he appreciated the efforts we made to ensure that his trip was comfortable and productive.

Garry and Dean present to the Georgian chief justice. Photo courtesy of the author.

The conference went off smoothly, and I was able to breathe a sigh of relief. Judge Walker and several other international experts were well received, and the conference was well attended by high-ranking members of the Georgian judiciary, including the chief justice and other members of the Supreme Court.

My speech concerned the significance of judicial independence from an American perspective, and addressed the Georgian public's perception of the judiciary, which, as noted above, was very low. I recommended that the Supreme Court conduct a public perception survey to determine precisely why the judiciary was held in such low regard, then develop an outreach campaign to address the public's concerns. Later, I learned that the Court had done exactly what I recommended, although without any attribution.

One day, Garry and I were having lunch with Judge Walker and Sean, the regional legal adviser for the United States Agency for International Development (USAID), at a nice Georgian restaurant when my cell phone rang. There was no caller ID, but I was expecting a call, so excused myself and answered the phone.

It was not the call I was expecting—to my surprise, if not shock, it was the Georgian ambassador to the US, calling from Washington. He explained that his wife had just had a baby and my daughter, who was a labor and delivery nurse at the time, had attended her delivery and provided excellent care. He was very appreciative and just wanted me to know. The call had come out of the blue, but I was very grateful for his reaching out to me, and very proud of my daughter.

During that lunch, Sean was able to arrange for Judge Walker to fly by helicopter with the Georgian president to a concert that evening in Batumi, a resort city on the Black Sea coast. Judge Walker was duly impressed. Sean went along for the ride, but there was not room enough for me and Garry. I didn't complain, because of a lifelong affliction of motion sickness.

After Judge Walker departed for home, I turned my attention to planning the trip to the US, referred to as a "study tour," for the group of Georgian judges who had been handpicked by the chief justice. The study tour would take us to Boston, Massachusetts, and Providence, Rhode Island, where we would observe the adversarial system up close, including—hopefully—a jury trial.

I had numerous connections within the legal profession and judiciary as a result of my role as the Vermont representative on a New England drug court commission. By early August I had an excellent itinerary lined up, and all arrangements were made for a departure in early September. But, as I will describe shortly, events intervened.

Chapter 9

Expat Life

That summer I became actively involved in the Hash House Harriers, which was referred to as a "running group with a drinking problem" or a "drinking group with a running problem," take your pick. There are Hash chapters all over the world.

Each Sunday the group would assemble in downtown Tbilisi, then set out casually on a course in the countryside, often several miles in length, that had been marked in advance by a couple of Hash scouts. It was not uncommon to miss a turn and get hopelessly lost. This was all part of the fun.

The Hash group was composed primarily of internationals working in Tbilisi, including folks from various embassies, NGOs, USAID, the World Bank, and other international organizations. Local people were also welcome. Often, there were as many as thirty or forty runners in attendance, and it was a great opportunity to socialize with other internationals as well as Georgians. We always ended up at a restaurant where the beer flowed in great quantities.

After you had shown your commitment to the group, you would become eligible for formal admission to the Hash. This would involve an induction ceremony at which you would be given your Hash moniker. My ceremony was presided over by a high-ranking American military officer, and held on a windswept hillside outside the city. I had to kneel down and repeat some silly oath of allegiance, and was then given the "nom de Hash" of "Early Release."

Shortly after joining the Hash, I participated in a regional event in Baku, Azerbaijan, an oil-rich former Soviet republic, an overnight train ride from

Tbilisi. There were runners from the three countries of the South Caucasus—Georgia, Armenia, and Azerbaijan. After running around the city during the day, which provided glimpses of the oil rigs in the harbor, we enjoyed a lavish outdoor meal with dancing and entertainment. As part of the festivities, one of the Hash runners, a woman, performed a Michael Jackson impersonation on stage which could easily have been mistaken for the real thing, moonwalk and all. I stuck with the Hash my whole time in Georgia.

I was taking lessons from a Georgian language tutor a couple of times a week, which was a nice ABA perk. The tutor came to the ABA office and we'd go to the quiet conference room, where she would instruct me in the Georgian language. The language is unique, nothing else like it in the world, its alphabet bearing no relationship to the Latin alphabet or any other. My starting point was learning to recognize each letter and the sound it makes, just like in kindergarten. I'm not particularly good at languages, so this was a struggle. As time passed, I was able to identify letters, which was particularly helpful at bus stops, but I never advanced very far and finally gave up. One time, I decided to try out my Georgian by requesting something simple in a vegetable market, and received a puzzled look from the clerk, as though I'd just landed from Mars.

I became friendly with the tutor, and in early August she invited Kristina, me, and Piper to accompany her and her husband to a resort town in the mountains a couple of hours from Tbilisi, where her brother owned a small hotel. Her husband drove and, after a hair-raising drive through the countryside, we arrived at the hotel in one piece. We pulled into the driveway where a group of small children was playing. As we were getting out of the car, the children noticed Piper in the back seat, about to jump out. They ran up to her, as children are inclined to do, and Piper acted instinctively and nipped one of the girls on the cheek. The nip broke the skin slightly and the child ran off screaming. The child's mother was apoplectic, assuming that Piper must have rabies, which was not an invalid assumption in Georgia.

Indeed, several months later I was bitten on the leg by a large street dog. I immediately went to the medical clinic that served expats. The doctor said it was the working assumption in his clinic that all street dogs were rabid, instructed me to roll up my sleeve, and administered the first of five shots that would be given to me at precise intervals over the next several weeks. The shots made me feel lousy, but at least I didn't contract rabies.

Anyway, the child's mother was very agitated throughout the whole weekend we were at the hotel, and insisted Piper be tested for rabies when we returned to Tbilisi. We knew Piper did not have the disease, but we understood the mother's concern and agreed to have her checked as soon as we got back. But, soon after our return to Tbilisi, and before we could do so, all hell broke loose.

Chapter 10

Evacuated to Armenia

On August 8, 2008, the call came at 6 a.m. from the headquarters of the American Bar Association Rule of Law Initiative in Washington, D.C. The three Americans in the ABA office in Tbilisi were ordered to evacuate the country immediately. Get out now!

Russian tanks and troops were invading Georgia through the Roki Tunnel, which separates the North Caucasus (Russia) from the South Caucasus (Georgia), and war had begun. Soon Russian tanks would be headed toward the capital and Russian jets would be strafing the military airport outside Tbilisi.

We were: Garry, Sveta, and their cat (ironically a Russian blue); Dan, his wife, and their cat; and me, Kristina, and Piper. We all strongly objected to leaving. We wanted to stay with our Georgian colleagues in the ABA office, and opposed the idea of fleeing at the first sign of trouble. Garry tried to make a case with the people back at headquarters for staying at least until the military situation became clearer, but to no avail. Our choice was stark: either leave at once and continue to have the support and resources of the ABA, or stay in Tbilisi and be on our own. We reluctantly chose the former.

In anticipation, we'd hired a van and driver the previous evening to take us to safety in neighboring Armenia, and we left with just a few clothes and our pets. We drove first to a local vet to make sure the pets had the necessary shots and papers to get across the Armenian border. In one of life's inexplicable coincidences, the Georgian vet, who spoke very little English, also had a dog whose name was Piper. I would not have believed this, except the dog's picture was on the wall with her name spelled out in English.

After leaving the vet, we took off south at breakneck speed for the

Armenian border. We got there quickly and negotiated passport control and customs without incident. All the animals got through easily. Then the fun began. We soon found ourselves in the Armenian mountains, with the driver going as fast as the van would allow. Despite my yelling from the back of the van to slow down, he refused to do so. We were screeching around corners, the backpacks and pets were thrown back and forth, and I was becoming motion sick. It was the ride from hell. The driver's interest was not so much in getting us to safety as quickly as possible, but in getting back to Tbilisi as quickly as possible for another van load of evacuees. This was a money-making proposition.

We reached the capital city Yerevan that evening, and were greeted by the Armenian ABA country director, an American, who'd booked us rooms at a local hotel. The hotel was not pet-friendly, but the two cats were smuggled in. Piper, on the other hand, had to stay at the local ABA office, where she was immediately adopted by the ABA staff and even by the night security guards.

We had been incommunicado for a while and our daughter and son-in-law back in the US were frantic, not knowing where we were or if we were safe. They managed to track us down through the US Embassy and we resumed contact, much to their relief. The mother of the child who had been nipped by Piper also tracked us down, and we again assured her through diplomatic channels that it was still our intention to have Piper examined by a vet. Justice Dooley also tried to find out where we were and if we were safe.

While the reasons for the Russian invasion and who was at fault are subject to debate, it appeared that Georgian President Saakashvili, who had an impetuous streak, allowed himself to be duped by a Russian provocation in the breakaway Georgian province of South Ossetia, where Russian influence was strong. He overreacted, mobilizing the army and causing the Russians, who seemed well prepared for this eventuality, to send tanks and troops through the Roki Tunnel into South Ossetia. Intense fighting broke out, and the Georgians were no match for the Russians. Much of the fighting took place around the city of Gori, Stalin's birthplace and the home of the Stalin Museum and statue, about forty kilometers from Tbilisi. Fortunately, the Russian tanks that were headed toward Tbilisi were ordered back by Russian commanders and never seriously threatened the capital, though the fighting continued at full force.

Georgia had been a republic within the Soviet Union before the USSR collapsed in the early 1990s, and this seemed a battle not only of tanks, guns, and planes, but a battle of wits between Saakashvili and Vladimir Putin, Russia's prime minister at the time, who strongly opposed Georgia's romance with the West, as did Russian President Dmitri Medvedev. Putin is alleged to have said he should hang Saakashvili by his balls, to which Saakashvili is reported to have said, "You don't have enough rope."

As the fighting raged on, we had no idea how long we would be in Armenia. Each day, we went to the local ABA office to try working from a distance and to check in with our local colleagues, all of whom remained safe since the Russians had called off their onslaught of Tbilisi. I became very concerned about the study tour to the US which was scheduled for September, just a few weeks hence; it looked like my weeks of planning for the trip would be for naught. And because the war was continuing with no end in sight, we were told by ABA headquarters to leave the hotel and find short-term apartments. Kristina and I found a garden apartment which was quite comfortable, with fruit trees in the front yard, not far from the ABA office.

As days passed, many more evacuees from Georgia spilled into Yerevan from various embassies and NGOs, many of whom we knew. We were told that the lines at the border had become very long, so in some sense we were lucky to be among the first to cross.

Yerevan was a very pretty city, at least in the downtown area, with many outdoor cafés and restaurants, and a picturesque Republic Square with an upscale Marriott hotel and outdoor patio, which we would come to frequent. It was summertime and everything was in bloom, and all the cafés were going full steam. Since it was now apparent that we would be in Yerevan for a while, we felt comfortable enough to take day trips around the Armenian countryside. One trip was to a monastery on the Armenian side of the border with Turkey. Mount Ararat, a volcanic mountain rising almost seventeen thousand feet, the purported location of Noah's Ark, loomed large on the Turkish side of the border, though Ararat is an iconic symbol in Armenian culture.

Kristina and I had an American friend who was active in the Armenian community in the US, who'd started the Armenian Tree Project, designed to reforest the country after it had been denuded for firewood in the early 1990s, as the USSR was imploding. She traveled to Armenia regularly, but was not there at the time we were. But her American cousin was, and she took us under her wing.

One evening soon after we arrived, she invited us to accompany her to a gala concert with one of Armenia's most famous conductors. We were still wearing the clothes we'd had on when we fled Georgia. After the concert, we went to a reception in honor of the conductor in a beautiful apartment overlooking the main pedestrian street. I recall chatting with the US chargé d'affaires out on the balcony. Down on the street I could see billboards showing posters of various protesters who were being detained, allegedly illegally, by the Armenian authorities.

At this time, a group of American donors from the Armenian diaspora was visiting, and were driven around the countryside in a bus to see the results of their largesse, typically a new or refurbished school or medical clinic. Our friend's cousin, who had connections with the visitors, asked Kristina and me to come along. When we arrived at the various school projects, the students would line up in their uniforms and clap and cheer as we arrived.

At one location, the refurbished school contained a new medical clinic which was being opened that day for the very first time to celebrate the arrival of the donors. There had not yet been any patients, but the medical staff was on site to welcome the guests. As I was entering the school I managed to brush up against some rough concrete in the doorway, causing a minor scrape on my left forearm which began to bleed. Someone noticed the bleeding and the medical team swung into action. I was rushed to the clinic where a battery of nurses and doctors hovered over me while the wound was cleaned and dressed, and a TV camera and reporter recorded the action. Once it became apparent that I would survive, the TV reporter stuck a microphone under my chin and quizzed me about the quality of my care at the new clinic, which I duly praised.

Our friend's cousin also took us to a nursery outside of Yerevan that produces the trees for the Armenian Tree Project, which had replanted Yerevan and great swaths of the countryside. As we were friends with the founder of the Project, we were greeted warmly and had a full tour of the site along with an informal lecture about the various species of trees, planting techniques, and the history of the project's successes, which were many. We then had an alfresco lunch in the pleasantly shaded courtyard of the nursery, complete with Armenian wine.

Another of our excursions took us to the Armenian Genocide Museum. As we toured the grounds and exhibits it was hard not to be convinced that the Armenians had in fact been the subject of genocide by the Turks back in the early years of the twentieth century, which of course was known to us anyway, despite Turkey's long-standing nonnegotiable position that genocide did not occur. Turkey is an outlier in this regard, as most of the civilized world accepts that it was genocide, including the US, where a congressional resolution was passed in 2019 acknowledging the genocide. Upon first arriving in Yerevan, I made the grievous mistake of ordering Turkish coffee and was quickly corrected by the waiter. "We don't serve Turkish coffee, only Armenian coffee."

After we had been in Yerevan for about three weeks, the hostilities in Georgia ended and we were given the green light to return. Once back in Tbilisi, it was immediately apparent that this proud little country had changed. A sense of defeat hung in the air. While all of our colleagues were fine, at least physically, many Georgians had been killed and Russia now occupied about a fifth of Georgian territory—the provinces of South Ossetia and Abkhazia. While South Ossetia did not appear to have any strategic or economic value, Abkhazia was located along the Black Sea coast and did have strategic and economic value. These two provinces continue to proclaim themselves independent countries, with Russia's support, but very few countries in the world recognize them as such. The US and other Western countries maintain that the two provinces remain part of Georgia.

The Georgians were routed, the war having exposed serious deficiencies in the Georgian army, which the US had trained and supported. The Russians claimed a complete victory and also made allegations of Georgian war crimes, which were eventually debunked. The Russians finally agreed to retreat, which they did very slowly, pursuant to a peace accord negotiated by the French president Sarkozy; their mission had been accomplished. This invasion would prove to be a prelude to the subsequent Russian invasions of Crimea in 2014 and Ukraine in 2022, as I discuss in the epilogue.

When we arrived back at our apartment, we discovered that all the food in the fridge had spoiled. The landlord had cut off the electricity, but hadn't bothered to check the fridge. This created a very unpleasant chore on our first night home.

A young Georgian man, Misha, whom Kristina tutored in English,

Holding hands during the national day of solidarity. Photo courtesy of author.

and who took care of Piper from time to time, had been called up on an emergency basis. He'd been ordered to the front, but when he got there, there were no weapons and no command structure. He had no idea what to do and no one to direct him, so he spent his time just trying to survive. He said he'd slept under a tank or other military vehicles each night.

Shortly after our return to Tbilisi, the Georgian government declared a national day of solidarity. At the appointed time, everybody in Georgia was supposed to leave their homes and jobs, and go out on the street to hold hands, forming a circle around the whole country. We joined our local colleagues out on the street and held hands as a huge parade marched up the main boulevard. Some marchers were holding posters of Putin looking like Hitler, and some of the posters read, in English, "Fuck Putin." It was a very somber and moving experience.

Soon after our return, we had Piper thoroughly checked by a vet; she was fine. We communicated this to the bitten child's mother, who was greatly relieved.

When we'd been back in Tbilisi for a couple of weeks, a delegation from one of our federal funding agencies, the same Bureau of International Narcotics and Law Enforcement of the US State Department, arrived to assess the damage and determine which activities in our work plan were still viable. We all sat around a table in the ABA office, and each of us in turn offered our opinions. For the most part, all our programs were intact and we were ready to carry on.

Because of where I was seated, I went last, immediately following Mamuka, one of the Georgian attorneys, who described the jury trial training program that he had worked on with Dan and Roger. (Dan had left the country by now, his one-year assignment having ended.) I then explained in no uncertain terms that I had been excluded from the program. The members of the delegation were surprised but had no real suggestions because, with Dan's departure, the program was now over.

Shortly thereafter, Garry sent an email to Donna in D.C., summarizing the meeting and expressing concern that INL might be displeased because of the judicial training snafu. I followed with my own explanation. This was the first time she had been made aware of the issue. To my surprise and relief, she responded by explaining that it was her clear understanding when she'd left Georgia that my involvement in the judicial training program had been worked out with Dan and Roger before my arrival, and that I was correct to have expected to be involved. I felt vindicated.

Not long after we returned to Tbilisi from Armenia, Kristina secured a job at the International School of Economics (ISET), a component of the Tbilisi State University system. ISET was designed to attract the best and brightest students of economics in the South Caucasus (Georgia, Armenia, and Azerbaijan), and those who qualified were given free tuition. Most of the professors were from Western Europe. The students had to write their theses in English, and Kristina's job was to teach them how to do so. As a native English speaker and teacher of English, she became a valued member of the faculty.

Chapter 11

Study Tour to the United States

Once things settled down, I turned my attention back to the study tour, which had been canceled because of the war. All of the arrangements had to be reworked from beginning to end, but I was able to piece together another good itinerary in Boston and Providence. I calculated that I'd sent out over two hundred emails in planning for the two trips.

In late October 2008, I escorted a group of about a dozen Georgian judges, none of whom had ever visited the US, or spoke English, to Boston and Providence for the study tour. Accompanying us were three Georgian attorneys, all of whom were fluent in English, who served as interpreters. The trip was an opportunity to introduce the Georgians to adversarial proceedings, and they were keenly interested in seeing an actual criminal jury trial. Being unsure about our dietary habits, and wanting to save money from their daily travel allowance, many of them stuffed their suitcases with food.

During our first three days in Boston, the judges observed various courtroom proceedings conducted by a judicial friend of mine, but were disappointed that there were no jury trials to watch. One had been scheduled, but it settled at the last minute, as is often the case. However, they were able to observe a busy arraignment session including the reading of charges, assignment of counsel, entry of pleas, and bail orders.

In Providence, as we were arriving at the Superior Courthouse, we were informed that a criminal jury trial was in progress and that we would be able to watch the case from the back of the courtroom following a recess. The presiding judge would meet with us shortly to explain the case before we took our seats. There was great anticipation among the group, as this was what they had been waiting for.

After a short wait in the hallway, the judge emerged from the courtroom and warmly greeted us. He patiently explained that the case involved an allegation of sexual assault of a child, a serious case. The incident had occurred a couple of years earlier, and the putative victim, a girl now about eleven years old, was about to testify. The alleged perpetrator was the girl's former stepfather, whom she had not seen since the incident.

We were ushered to seats among the many other spectators in a very large courtroom, close to the table where the defendant sat with his attorney. Soon the recess ended and the bailiff intoned, "All rise for the jury." Everyone stood as the twelve jurors strode to the jury box and took their seats. The Georgians were fascinated, since they had never seen a jury before.

The judge kindly informed the jury about the guests from Georgia, and the jurors all smiled and nodded in our direction. I was quite proud to be part of this experience; the Georgian judges and attorneys were getting their first view of one of the hallmarks of our democracy, and they were being treated very respectfully by the court.

The prosecutor then called the girl to the witness stand and questioned her about the incident. As the Georgians listened attentively through an interpreter, she testified that she had been sexually assaulted by her stepfather, known as Carlos, after school one day while her mother was at work. It was a sad and compelling story, and the child spoke with authority and credibility.

The prosecutor then followed standard procedure and asked the girl to look around the courtroom to see if she could identify the perpetrator. These trial mechanics, including the in-court identification of the defendant, were all new to the Georgians, and I was very pleased that my guests were actually getting to see the real guts of a criminal jury trial. They would certainly have a better appreciation of the adversarial system, and they would certainly have a story to tell when they returned home. Hopefully they would also become advocates for jury trials in Georgia. (Historically, like in Russia, trials were dominated by the prosecutor and the results were determined by compliant judges and rarely in doubt; a jury would be independent and not dominated by the prosecutor.)

The girl gazed around the room and came to focus on the defendant's table. She then pointed across the room in the direction of her former stepfather. The prosecutor asked her what he was wearing and she responded that he was wearing a suit, which he was. What color? Dark blue, she answered correctly. The prosecutor then perfunctorily requested that the record reflect that the witness had identified the defendant.

As the judge was about to grant the prosecutor's request, the defense attorney stood and addressed the court. She remarked that the witness stand in this large courtroom was some distance from the defense table, and she wanted to be sure whom the girl had identified. Would the court allow the girl to step down from the stand and approach the person she had pointed at? The judge immediately agreed, although this procedure was unusual since it would require the putative victim to come into close proximity to the alleged perpetrator, something that could have been highly stressful.

All eyes in the courtroom were glued to the girl as she nervously headed toward the defense table. She had verbally identified her stepfather from the witness stand and had pointed toward the defense table, but now she would stand directly in front of the perpetrator and leave no doubt about the person who had sexually assaulted her. Courtroom drama at its best! As she arrived in front of the defense table, the prosecutor, from the other side of the courtroom, spoke to her again. She turned in his direction as he asked her to point to the person who did this terrible thing to her. She then turned back toward the defendant, straightened out her arm, extended the index finger of her right hand, and slowly began to swing her arm directly toward the defendant as he sat motionless and tense.

But wait. Her arm kept swinging slowly, and her finger passed by the defendant. When her arm stopped moving, her finger pointed directly at one of the Georgian judges, who was seated just behind the defendant and who was also attired in a dark blue suit. "That's him," she said as she continued to point at the Georgian. "That man right there. He's the one who did this to me." The courtroom fell into an awkward silence. The Georgians were stunned. The judge was momentarily speechless. The jurors were obviously confused. Nobody seemed to know what to do. After what seemed like an eternity, but was probably only a matter of moments, the defense attorney gathered herself, rose to her feet, and said, "Your Honor, may the record reflect that the witness has *not* identified the defendant." The judge acceded and immediately called a recess.

The Georgians shuffled out of the courtroom and lingered in the hallway. Several of them laughed nervously, not really sure what had happened. The Georgian judge who had been identified as the perpetrator attempted what we would call a bad news/good news joke: "Although I've been identified as a sexual perpetrator, at least I'm not in Georgia where I would have been arrested on the spot."

We then departed the courthouse, so I was unaware how the case unfolded after we left, but I assumed that the faulty identification could be an important factor in the jury's decision-making, although not necessarily dispositive. I wondered how the judge would instruct the jury on this point. If it were me, I probably would have told the jury that this was one factor among many they could consider as part of the totality of the evidence. If the remaining evidence was sufficient to prove guilt beyond a reasonable doubt, then the jury should decide accordingly.

For example, let's say there was evidence the defendant had confided in a close friend that he had assaulted the girl, and that this friend testified credibly at trial against him. Or that the girl's testimony was airtight in all material respects, and there was evidence that the defendant's appearance had changed since the assault. Or perhaps her demeanor in that moment indicated that she had simply panicked at confronting her assailant face-to-face. In such situations, the faulty identification would be of lesser consequence. We learned later that the defendant had been acquitted of the charge, and I can only conclude that our presence influenced the result; my heart went out to the young girl who told a harrowing story of sexual assault.

Upon our return to Georgia, word of this event spread fast, and quickly became part of local folklore. The accused judge was jokingly referred to by members of the Georgian judiciary, including the chief justice, as Carlos. While at some level this was humorous, it was also disheartening in terms of the victim, since the alleged perpetrator went free.

Shortly after our return to Georgia, the judges threw a party for me and Kristina. They were appreciative of the opportunity to travel to the US, and felt like they had a much better understanding of the adversarial system and the judge's role in the system. Nevertheless, they remained puzzled by the in-court identification procedure. The delicious Georgian wine flowed copiously well into the night.

At a celebration such as this, referred to as a "supra," there is typically a toastmaster in control of the festivities, who offers various toasts as the event wears on. As alcohol consumption increases, the toasts get more and more emotional, often in honor of mothers or wives or children, and the toastmaster usually ends up with tears running down his cheeks.

Shortly thereafter, I was invited to sit in on a judicial proceeding. It was a Saturday morning soon after we'd gotten back, and the purpose of the hearing was to determine whether a person accused of assault the night before should be held in custody or released on bail or non-monetary conditions. One of the judges who had been to the US was presiding. This was an opportunity to see if anything from his observation of our adversarial system had been absorbed.

As mentioned, in Boston we'd sat in on a typical arraignment session where the judge had addressed a number of similar bail issues as he sped through his busy calendar. He'd set bail where it was warranted, such as when the defendant posed a risk of flight or danger, but declined to do so when there were minimal risk factors. In other words, the judge exercised discretion in each case and did not accede automatically to the wishes of the prosecutor. Such judicial independence was foreign to the Georgian judges, who always granted the prosecutors' requests, or more accurately, demands, as a holdover from the Soviet system which was dominated by the prosecutor.

I was pleased to see that the Georgian judge asked the prosecutor some tough questions about the need for bail, and when all was said and done, he denied the request, explaining that certain non-monetary conditions of release would be adequate. The prosecutor was stunned, as this rebuke was totally unprecedented, but the defendant's family was greatly relieved; they had been anticipating high bail, which they would not have been able to post, meaning the defendant would languish in jail awaiting trial. The judge made the same decision I would have made in that case, and I was quite proud that the judge had found the courage to stand up to the prosecutor.

Chapter 12

Jury Trials Again

As fall continued, it became time to review our work plan for the upcoming funding cycle. We agreed in-house that we would continue to include a two-part project related to jury trials—the first part being to train Georgian judges, as I had hoped to do all along, and the second part being to educate the Georgian public about the jury system. This project had the support of Sean, our contact person in USAID, so we felt relatively confident. The responsibility to carry it out would be mine.

I had some ideas about how to proceed with the judicial training component, which I would have used earlier on. I had brought with me to Georgia a videotape of an actual two-day criminal trial from Vermont. It involved a charge of attempted sexual assault on a female student at Middlebury College by a fellow student while the young woman was passed out, allegedly from something slipped into her drink. The tape included every aspect of the trial from beginning to end, starting with jury selection all the way to the announcement of the verdict.

My plan was to break down the trial into segments, such as jury selection, the judge's preliminary instructions to the jury (I was not the judge), opening statements by the lawyers, direct examination and cross-examination of witnesses, motions that arose during the trial, closing statements, the judge's final instructions to the jury, and the jury's verdict. Each segment would be translated into Georgian, and each would form the basis for a training session. I began editing the tape.

That fall, I also became involved with the rollout of the Judicial Reform Index (JRI), an ABA publication designed to assess the performance of the Georgian judiciary according to a series of generally accepted benchmarks.

The JRI was a highly anticipated and widely circulated publication, both locally and among the international community, like a periodic report card. An ABA expert, whom we never met or consulted with, had traveled to Georgia and conducted many interviews with key actors, then returned to the US to write his assessment. Unfortunately, the JRI proved to be a disaster.

When we received a draft of the report in Tbilisi, there were several factors that were trending downward. The draft was circulated to the Georgian Supreme Court and all other key persons and organizations for comment, which was standard procedure. The Supreme Court argued strongly that the report was simply wrong in important respects and that the performance of the judiciary had not deteriorated and, in fact, had improved.

Garry and I agreed with the Supreme Court based on our extensive experience on the ground. I wrote a critique of the draft, which was forwarded to ABA staff in D.C., outlining the reasons why we thought it should be rewritten. We then held several tense phone conversations with Washington to argue strenuously for our position. But they disagreed, dug in their heels, and refused to make any changes. We ended up losing the battle and the JRI was published as it was drafted. This proved to be a big mistake, not only because it presented an inaccurate picture, but because it adversely affected our long-standing positive relationship with the Georgian Supreme Court.

This outcome was an example of the sometimes-bureaucratic nature of international rule of law work: the staff in the field, with direct knowledge of what was going on in real life, getting overruled by the folks back at headquarters. But the box was checked back in D.C., and we moved on.

At the same time, late fall, I began work on the second part of the project to educate the public about jury trials. This was a critically important initiative since the public was generally unfamiliar with jury trials, except perhaps to the extent they may have seen dramatizations on American TV. They were more familiar with the extant system from the Soviet era, in which they had no confidence, where there were no juries and the process was dominated by the prosecutor, with guilty verdicts virtually assured.

In the US, jury trials are embedded in our DNA. They are a bedrock feature of our legal system and everyone understands as much. If a criminal defendant goes to trial, it is almost always a jury trial, and regular citizens are routinely called for jury duty. While a summons for jury duty may not be welcome news, most people are willing to accept the inconvenience as part of their civic responsibility, and many employers are willing to provide pay for the required time off.

In more than twenty-one years on the Vermont bench, I conducted well over one hundred jury trials, as I mentioned earlier, mostly criminal but civil cases as well, and found that jurors were almost always glad to have served, even if they were apprehensive and nervous when first called. Most jurors in criminal cases came away from the experience with a deep appreciation for some of our fundamental principles, like the presumption of innocence and proof beyond a reasonable doubt. I enjoyed working with the jurors, regular folks from the community who were performing their civic and constitutional duty, usually with a sense of pride—at least after the case was over.

In one of my jury trials, a serious sexual assault case involving a minor, which had been delayed too many times, I ran out of jurors before we could seat twelve in the jury box. I instructed the sheriff to go out on the street and collect an additional dozen prospective jurors, as was permitted by Vermont law. He returned shortly with the jurors, who were obviously stunned to find themselves in this predicament. I explained the situation and most of them understood; the ones who had pressing issues were excused. We then were able to impanel the jury and begin the trial, having to use only a couple of the substitutes, who served with good humor. But the situation did not go down well with the local paper. The *Caledonian Record* ran an editorial on December 9, 1986, "Jury Duty and Rule 20," which stated:

> Our state's judicial system offended the sensibilities of decent Vermonters last week when the Caledonia County Sheriff's office was ordered to summon people in public places in St. Johnsbury for immediate or next day jury duty. The concept of rounding up instant jurors sounds like a job best suited to the office of the Soviet Procurator General, not an American court in the Northeast Kingdom of Vermont. But yet this outrageous action is unfortunately legal under a court rule pertaining to

jurors.

We therefore urge the Vermont Supreme Court to strike a judicious blow for American liberty and the cause of justice by repealing rule 20.[39]

I was not mentioned in the editorial even though the sheriff acted on my order.

My experience with juries was not limited to my work as a judge. A week or so after I retired, I received a summons in the mail to report for jury duty at the local county courthouse a couple of weeks hence. After all, my name was on the lists of those registered to vote and those who hold a driver's license, from which jurors are selected, just like everyone else. In Vermont there was no prohibition for judges and lawyers to be jurors, although there had been in years past.

I arrived at the appointed time and assumed I would be immediately dismissed. Even though judges were allowed to serve, there was a general reluctance on the part of prosecutors and defense attorneys to pick judges for their juries. Judges simply knew too much of the "sausage making" of the criminal justice system. There was also a concern that judges would monopolize the discussions during jury deliberations, and would be looked to by other jurors for answers.

I told Kristina that I would probably be home for lunch, and we could go skiing in the afternoon. Not so fast. To my surprise, I was selected as a juror in a serious felony case which lasted for a couple of days, even though I knew the judge, the lawyers, and some of the witnesses.

During deliberations, the other jurors did not in any way default to me or expect me to lead the discussion and provide the answers. As feisty Vermonters, they had no problem speaking their own minds or disagreeing with me if they believed otherwise. We eventually came to a unanimous verdict of not guilty; the state's evidence simply did not measure up to proof beyond a reasonable doubt. It was a powerful experience, participating in the jury system from the other side of the bench.

The concept for the public education initiative in Georgia was to create a series of four thirty-minute television shows, each depicting a hypothetical case, with the public calling in to vote on guilt or innocence. The series, called

Filming my episode of Verdict. *Photo courtesy of the author.*

Verdict, became extremely popular with viewers. My particular task was to write the screenplay for the third episode. I constructed a murder case, doing everything I could to introduce reasonable doubt into the script, to see if the public would be willing to vote not guilty, as the evidence (or lack thereof) required.

I attended the filming of the episode, which involved professional actors speaking in Georgian. I offered to play the role of the murder victim, since this necessitated nothing more than falling to the ground and lying there dead, but the victim was younger and of Georgian ethnicity, so I did not fit the bill. My chance at stardom was thwarted, but I did come away from the experience as a notable screenwriter.

The night the episode aired, I waited anxiously for the verdict to be announced on TV following the public call-in. I was confidently expecting a verdict of not guilty, which would demonstrate some level of maturity among the Georgian public. The public saw the case otherwise, and by a substantial majority found the defendants guilty. My sense was that they assumed that if a person was in custody and on trial, he must certainly be guilty, since that was simply the way they had been conditioned to think. Obviously, more work needed to be done.

I began picking up vibes early in 2009 that one of our funding agencies, INL again, was no longer willing to let USAID and the ABA have control of the judicial training program, and had a completely different strategy in mind. Perhaps this was the result of the earlier fiasco. The new strategy called for a triumvirate of federal judges to travel to Georgia in the spring to prepare for a subsequent series of training sessions. I thought this was a joke. Apparently these judges had visited Georgia in the past, but this was all news to me, and upsetting news indeed.

In an attempt to protect my considerable investment in the matter, I wrote Garry a detailed memo in late January outlining my master plan for the training program. It called for a resident judge (me) to be in charge, but with input from traveling judges as we went along. I was also willing to extend my tour to see the project through, if needed.

As mentioned earlier, our work plan had been approved by USAID, including the training program, and Sean, our USAID representative, continued to support our position. But the situation was headed toward a turf battle between USAID in Georgia and INL back in D.C.

Very soon after my memo to Garry, I was informed that the training component was being removed from our work plan. When I confronted Sean over pizza and beer he was very honest and explained that he was a career employee and did not wish to fall on his sword over this issue. Thus, he had conceded to INL and the matter was closed. I respected his honesty, and I might have done the same thing in his shoes, but I was fuming.

With some time now on my hands, I'd been invited by the country director of another American NGO (DPK Consulting), which was active in Georgia in the area of court administration, to deliver the keynote address at a training session for Georgian judges and court administrators on time standards for processing cases in court. This was not an area of expertise for me, so preparing my presentation took a lot of time and effort, which was fine since I was no longer involved in the jury trial project.

The session was held in mid-February, with several dozen judges from throughout Georgia in attendance. I had prepared a slide show to accompany my remarks, and spent the first few minutes describing my legal and judicial background, showing slides of Burlington and Stowe, Vermont, to get the audience relaxed and interested.

I announced an upcoming photo of my house, which I said was typical in the States, then flashed a slide of a huge German castle sitting high on a mountaintop. There were gasps and looks of amazement from the audience. I let the photo sink in for a moment, then said, "Whoops, wrong slide," and showed a picture of my actual house—an 1823 Vermont farmhouse, hardly a castle. I think they appreciated the joke, as well as the substance of my presentation.

Since I was no longer involved in the jury trial project as the end of my tour approached, Kristina and I decided to do some traveling, as I'd accumulated quite a bit of leave. That spring we went to Dubai and Athens.

Dubai was a popular destination for Georgians, and there was a weekly flight from Tbilisi, down and back. The Georgians would load up on consumer items they could not get cheaply at home, if at all, such as car bumpers, huge flat-screen TVs, and the like. Their baggage carts would be overflowing as they lined up at the check-in counter.

We decided to treat ourselves in Dubai, and stayed at the plush Jumeirah Beach Hotel, right on the Persian Gulf with a view of the iconic and super expensive Burj Al Arab Hotel. We enjoyed plenty of body surfing, great meals, massages on the beach, and shopping.

Just before leaving for Athens, Kristina tripped on the sidewalk in Tbilisi and landed on her knee, which swelled up like a balloon. This only made matters worse, since her knees had been bothering her already. She was prescribed steroids and we decided to continue on to Athens. Our hotel had a magnificent view of the Acropolis. But, as it turned out, tourists had to walk up to the Parthenon, and Kristina was unable to do so. I went on my way, unfortunately having to leave Kristina behind. When I returned, I expected her to be quite dejected, but she wore a big smile. She had discovered a jewelry store nearby and decided that she needed a nice memento to cheer her up.

Several weeks later, the three federal judges arrived in Tbilisi. I was told to meet with them, provide information about the legal and judicial situation in Georgia, and to share my ideas about jury trials and training of the judges. This caused me a considerable amount of angst, if not resentment. I had been hired to train judges in jury trials; I had been in Georgia for nearly a year, was very familiar with the judicial system, and enjoyed good relations with the key players; further, I had a complete training program on the drawing board which had already been approved. Nevertheless, as a professional, I complied with my instructions even though I briefly considered leaving them to fend for themselves.

The evening of the judges' arrival in mid-April, we all attended a dinner at the residence of the deputy US ambassador, in their honor. I was suffering from a miserable cold, but it was a pleasant evening with no discussion of their program, if there in fact was one. We agreed to meet the following day at the Marriott Hotel in downtown Tbilisi for a substantive discussion.

I dragged myself out of bed that morning and went to the hotel, where we sat around a table, drank coffee, and had our discussion. I did the best I could to bring them up to speed, though I made it clear they were undercutting my efforts, which was news to them, just as their involvement had been news to me. In other words, it was duplication of effort with neither side being aware of the other. But the meeting ended cordially and we went our separate ways. I never learned whether they returned to present the training program or not, as it would have taken place after I left the country, and frankly I had lost interest.

Chapter 13

Our Departure

The day of our departure from Georgia, in late April 2009, was a day of mixed emotions. We were sad to leave, but anxious to get home. We booked a flight on Czech Airlines from Tbilisi to Prague, then on to the US. The first flight left around 4 a.m., as did most flights to Western Europe.

That evening we enjoyed a jovial going-away party at a downtown restaurant with our American and Georgian colleagues, then went back to our apartment to gather our luggage. Around midnight, the two ABA drivers appeared in front of our building to assist us and take us to the airport. They were local Georgian staff with whom I had developed a good relationship. We had thirteen pieces of luggage, and our dog and her paraphernalia, all of which had to be carried down three flights of stairs and loaded into the van.

As I struggled with the first load, it occurred to me that the two drivers were hanging around out on the street without making any effort to help with the bags. Making matters worse, Kristina's knees had become seriously impaired, and merely walking had become an ordeal. She was having great difficulty negotiating the stairs, especially while carrying a bag. When I got to the street, hot and sweaty, I said, "C'mon guys, give us a hand." Although they didn't speak much English, they got the meaning. One of them swung into action and helped with the luggage, while the other stood watch outside. After getting everything loaded, we headed to the airport.

Once there, we queued up with all our luggage at the check-in line. The airport was mobbed as usual at this ungodly hour. I knew I'd have to pay excess baggage fees, and when we got to the counter we were directed to another counter nearby to pay for the extra bags, nine in all. I went to the counter and presented my credit card to the young man behind the counter. No deal, cash only.

I was then directed to a bank kiosk beside the waiting area. We were able to obtain enough cash for the transaction, paid the fees, got our boarding passes, boarded the plane, and flew to Prague. During our layover, I finally checked the receipt and realized I'd been overcharged for the bags by about $250, which, remarkably, was refunded by Czech Airlines after we returned home.

Upon arriving at JFK in New York, Kristina's knees had gotten so bad, I had to wheel her through the airport in a wheelchair as well as handle all our luggage and the dog. Fortunately, we were able to breeze through customs. The officer was not the least bit interested in our luggage, even though we'd been away for a year. He only wanted to know if Piper had all her papers, which she did—finally, they came in handy. Welcome home.

My experience in Georgia had been largely positive, notwithstanding the Russian invasion and the jury training debacle, and I'm grateful to ABA ROLI for the opportunity. I very much enjoyed the work I did and the people I worked with, including the office staff, members of the legal profession, and the judiciary, especially the Supreme Court, and I believe I made some modest contributions to the rule of law.

The legislation amending the criminal procedure code, including the authorization of jury trials, was enacted by the Georgian Parliament on October 9, 2009, with an effective date of October 1, 2010. Initially, jury trials in Tbilisi were limited to premeditated murder cases, expanding to other types of cases and other jurisdictions as time passed. The first trial was held in Tbilisi in 2011, but it is my understanding from a colleague who worked for the ABA in Georgia for several years after I left that progress has been very slow because of the inordinate length of time it takes to select reluctant jurors.

Kosovo

Kosovo

0   20 Kilometers
0   20 Miles

Chapter 14

Hired by EULEX

Upon returning to Vermont in April 2009, after our year in Georgia, I applied for a position as an international criminal judge with the European Union Rule of Law Mission in Kosovo (EULEX). I was particularly interested in this position because I would actually be able to work as a judge hearing real criminal cases, as opposed to being a legal and judicial adviser as I had been in Russia, Kazakhstan, and Georgia.

EULEX was a security mission of the twenty-seven countries within the European Union, but it employed many persons who came from outside the EU—that is, from so-called third-party contributing states, including the United States, Canada, Norway, Switzerland, and Turkey. Surprisingly, English was the working language of EULEX in Kosovo, so I thought this might work to my benefit. I submitted my application in July 2009, through an organization called Civilian Police International (CPI), a contractor with the US State Department, located in northern Virginia. CPI was responsible for recruiting, vetting, and training all US judges, prosecutors, and police officers being deployed to Kosovo and working for EULEX.

Months passed and I heard nothing, so I eventually decided it was not to be. I was doing a lot of part-time work for the Vermont judiciary, and had plenty to keep me busy. We'd also bought a condo in Montreal, about two hours from our home in Vermont, and had booked a trip to Southeast Asia for three weeks, departing in November 2010. However, in September 2010, fourteen months after I'd applied, an email arrived from CPI: I had been shortlisted for an international judgeship. If I was still interested, I would be interviewed over the phone by a selection committee of three international judges working for EULEX in Kosovo.

Although my interest had waned a bit over the months, we'd bought the condo, and we'd already paid for the Asia trip, I decided to proceed with the interview, which was held in late September. I wanted to give it my best shot, so I did a lot of preparation in advance, trying to learn as much as I could about Kosovo and EULEX on short notice.

On the other end of the phone were three international judges, each from a different country, who fired a series of questions at me over the half-hour interview. The most difficult part was actually understanding the questions because of the different accents, pronunciation, and intonation. But at the end of the interview one of the judges complimented me on my responses, so I was feeling fairly confident. I was told that if I was recommended by the selection committee, my name would then be submitted up the chain of command to EULEX headquarters in Brussels for final approval. If approved by Brussels, I would also have to be approved by the US State Department.

Several more weeks passed and I heard nothing, so again assumed this was probably a dead end. Then another email informed me of my selection, and attached an employment offer. The offer was for one year, renewable, and included a generous compensation package, broken down into salary, housing allowance, and "danger pay." Danger pay? Maybe I should give this more thought. If I accepted, I would have to attend a ten-day training program at CPI headquarters in early December, then report to Kosovo in mid-January. After finding out that Kristina and our dog Piper could accompany me, and learning that the training schedule would not conflict with our planned trip to Southeast Asia, I accepted the offer. Then we went off to Singapore, Thailand, Cambodia, Laos, and Vietnam.

Upon my return, I reported for training at CPI headquarters. I was a member of a class of thirty trainees: one judge (me), one prosecutor, and twenty-eight police officers. The course consisted mostly of academic lectures and discussion groups focusing on the historical, political, economic, military, cultural, and security aspects of Kosovo. Several Americans who were already working in Kosovo had returned as instructors. While the sessions were very useful, there was virtually no instruction on the legal or judicial situation in Kosovo, so this would require on-the-job training when I got there.

The training also included a rigorous physical component. I earned my bona fides, at least in the eyes of the police officers, many of whom were a generation younger, when I successfully completed the difficult obstacle course while carrying two thirty-pound ammo cans and wearing a heavy flak jacket. I could have opted out of the physical requirements, given the nature of my work (sitting on the bench does not usually require carrying ammo cans), but I was in good shape and decided to plunge in. On the other hand, the prosecutor, a heavy man who was obviously not physically active, opted out.

Following completion of my training, CPI made arrangements to fly me to Pristina, Kosovo's capital, on January 14, 2011. The other twenty-nine participants deployed immediately upon completion of the training, but I had requested an additional month for Kristina and me to get our affairs in order—finding reliable house sitters, arranging our finances, figuring out what to do with our cars, packing, and a hundred other details. As it turned out, our house sitters would not be available until early March, so Kristina and Piper would have to stay behind for a few weeks.

During the month while we prepared, I was in contact with one of the other American judges in Kosovo (there were only two at the time), Charles Smith III, from Iowa, who had been there for over a year and had been promoted to second-in-command of all the international judges, vice president of the Assembly of EULEX Judges. He told me that I would most likely be assigned to the regional court in the southern city of Prizren, along the Albanian and Macedonian borders, where there was an urgent need for another criminal judge. I was also in contact by email with the presiding EULEX judge in Prizren, named Witold, from Poland, and we exchanged correspondence as I attempted to prepare myself for the assignment. He was friendly and helpful, and looked forward to my arrival in mid-January.

On January 13, I was able to zip up my suitcases and look forward to my final evening at home. Then the phone rang. A CPI employee on the other end said something like the following:

"Judge Pineles, you won't be leaving for Kosovo tomorrow, and I can't tell you when you will be leaving, or even if you will be leaving at all. There is a dispute between the US ambassador and the head of EULEX, a retired French general, about where you will be assigned. The ambassador wants you to be assigned to the regional court in Mitrovica, where the US spent lots of money rebuilding the courthouse after it was destroyed during the riots in 2008, and the general wants you to go to the regional court in Prizren. Not sure how this will turn out. It has nothing to do with you personally. We'll keep you posted."

The next two weeks were a roller coaster ride of uncertainty and anxiety. I had numerous phone conversations with CPI and my contact person in the US Embassy in Pristina, and some days it appeared the dispute would be resolved, other days not. The matter was finally resolved, and I was informed that I would be assigned to Prizren. The deal reached was that the next American judge would be assigned to Mitrovica. However, during my twenty-eight months in Kosovo, no other American judge was selected. Chalk one up for the French general.

At long last, the wheels touched down at the international airport in Pristina on February 5, 2011, after an overnight flight from JFK and a short flight from Vienna. I was finally reporting for duty as an international criminal judge with the Mission. My remit, as it turned out, would include war crimes, murders, judicial corruption, narcotics trafficking, human organ trafficking, and other serious cases.

Despite the extensive training I had undergone with CPI, I still wasn't quite sure what to expect when I hit the ground. I got an inkling immediately upon my arrival. The airport was named for Adem Jashari, a revered fighter for the Kosovo Liberation Army, or KLA. He and dozens of members of his extended family had been wiped out in a battle with Serbian paramilitaries very early in the war between Kosovo and Serbia in the late 1990s. I would become acutely aware that veterans of the KLA played outsized roles in Kosovo politics and society.

Chapter 15

Brief History of Kosovo

A brief primer on Kosovo's history will be useful in establishing the context for several of my criminal cases, particularly war crimes cases.

Kosovo is a small, mountainous, landlocked country located in the Western Balkans in southern Europe. It's about half the size of Vermont, and has a continental climate, warm in the summer and cold in the winter. It is surrounded, although not necessarily contiguously, by all of the countries of the former Yugoslavia: Serbia, North Macedonia, Montenegro, Croatia, Bosnia, and Slovenia, and also by Albania, which was not part of Yugoslavia.

Kosovo was part of the Muslim Ottoman Empire for hundreds of years, from the fifteenth century until early in the twentieth century, and is today a Muslim country, largely secular in the capital, Pristina, but more observant in the outlying areas. (Indeed, traveling throughout the countryside, we would see mosques that had sprung up like mushrooms, funded by Saudi Arabia or Turkey.)

In 1912, the Ottomans were defeated and Kosovo became part of southwest Serbia within greater Yugoslavia. Following World War II, Yugoslavia became a communist federation of the Balkan countries, and was ruled by the iron hand of Marshal Tito. Tito died in 1980 and Yugoslavia slowly unraveled into chaos and war.

But first, in 1984, Sarajevo, in Bosnia, hosted the winter Olympics, and Yugoslavia was touted as a shining example of ethnic harmony, even though serious tension bubbled just beneath the surface. Although Kosovo was part of Serbia, it was populated overwhelmingly by ethnic Albanians, at least three to one. They were predominately of the Muslim faith, spoke the Albanian language, and used the Latin alphabet. On the other hand, the minority Serbian population in Kosovo was of the Orthodox Christian faith, spoke the Serbian language, and used the Cyrillic alphabet just like their fellow countrymen in Serbia proper.

Kosovo has always been an important part of Serbia's psyche, and there are many important Serbian religious and historic sites in Kosovo. The Battle of Kosovo in 1389, over six hundred years ago, in which the Serbians lost to the Ottomans, remains a rallying cry for Serbian nationalism.

Slobodan Milosevic, the Serbian leader of Yugoslavia, was able to skillfully exploit the tensions between the majority Albanians and minority Serbians when he rose to power in the late 1980s. In 1989, he delivered his famous speech before tens of thousands of Serbs, commemorating the 600th anniversary of the Battle of Kosovo at the Field of Blackbirds outside Pristina, where the battle had been fought. He stoked the ethnic fires and implored the Serbs not to be bullied by the Albanians.

Up to this point, Kosovo had been accorded a certain degree of autonomy, but autonomy was rescinded and the Serbian minority then took complete control of Kosovo through intimidation and force. The Kosovar Albanians were forced out of their homes, jobs, professions, schools, and governmental institutions, and the 1990s was a decade of repression. Parallel structures were developed, particularly in education, with the creation of many home schools, so that Albanian children would not have to be educated in the Serbian language.

In response to Serbian repression, the Kosovo Liberation Army, or KLA, began to form clandestinely in the mid-'90s. This was an ethnic Albanian guerrilla and separatist group that smuggled weapons over the Albanian border and engaged in terrorist tactics against Serbian officials and police. In turn, Milosevic responded brutally, unleashing war and ethnic cleansing in Kosovo starting in 1998, killing approximately thirteen thousand and causing nearly a million Kosovar Albanian refugees to flee across the borders into Macedonia, Albania, and, with luck, Western Europe. The world watched in horror.

Peace talks were initiated in early 1999, at Château de Rambouillet in France, involving representatives of NATO, Yugoslavia, and the Albanian community in Kosovo. No agreement could be reached and the talks failed.

Then, on March 24, 1999, NATO commenced its bombing campaign to stop the humanitarian crisis. President Clinton and Secretary of State Madeleine Albright, along with British Prime Minister Tony Blair, were the moving forces behind this campaign. Russia, which was Serbia's ally, strongly opposed NATO's intervention.

Despite problems such as the mistaken bombing of the Chinese embassy in Belgrade, Serbia's capital, the NATO campaign eventually succeeded after seventy-eight days, and Milosevic capitulated. The Kosovo refugees flooded home, only to find widespread destruction and a total upheaval of society. Many Serbians fled to Serbia proper, leaving only a small minority remaining in Kosovo.

The KLA, formerly considered a terrorist organization by the West, had become NATO's ally on the ground, and was on the winning side. KLA soldiers were seen as freedom fighters and war heroes, and are still revered today in Kosovo. On the other hand, KLA soldiers are viewed as war criminals in Serbia. Indeed, some of them committed atrocities and war crimes, but objective observers say that the large majority of war crimes were committed by the Serbs. There was no equivalency despite Serbia's concocted narrative to the contrary.

Many Kosovar Albanians I knew had a gut-wrenching story to tell about

Photos of missing persons posted outside of parliament. Photo ©EULEX.

this period. Families were forced to flee, houses and crops were destroyed, villages looted, women raped, and friends and relatives—old and young— were murdered, often in cruel ways. Approximately sixteen hundred persons remain missing and unaccounted for (and presumed dead) to this day, and Kosovo honors the International Day of the Disappeared each August 30.

An article in *Balkan Insight*, dated November 29, 2021, titled "Kosovo's Forensic Investigators: 'We are the Voice of the Dead,'" describes the horror and revulsion experienced by those responsible for exhuming bodies of Serbian-massacred Kosovars, including those of children, from mass graves.[40]

After the war, and pursuant to United Nations Security Council Resolution 1244, adopted on June 10, 1999, the United Nations took control of all governmental and civic institutions in Kosovo, which were virtually nonexistent following the end of hostilities, including the judiciary. But the resolution did not determine the legal status of Kosovo vis-à-vis Serbia, and instead left this issue for future negotiations.

NATO also established a peacekeeping force in Kosovo, known as KFOR (Kosovo Force), including military units from many countries, including the US. KFOR still has an active presence today, and the US occupies the sprawling Camp Bondsteel in the southeast part of the country, not far from the border with North Macedonia. The camp is now used to house Afghan evacuees as they are vetted for security purposes, following our chaotic withdrawal from Afghanistan in 2021.

Forensics team exhumes the remains of a missing person. Photo ©EULEX.

Rebuilding the judiciary was an immediate priority. However, the ethnic Albanian judges, prosecutors, and lawyers had been marginalized for most of the 1990s, and were simply incapable of addressing the crimes that arose out of the war, not to mention their likely biases. So the UN devised a plan to recruit international investigators, prosecutors, and judges to come to Kosovo to handle war crimes and other serious cases arising during the war and the ensuing chaos, as well as serious cases arising after the war and during the UN mandate.

The UN also decided it would apply the law that had been in effect in the Socialist Republic of Yugoslavia in 1989. This body of law had applied throughout Yugoslavia before disintegration, included detailed provisions dealing with war crimes, and incorporated international treaties like the Geneva Convention. This international model for prosecuting war crimes and other serious offenses remained in place for the entirety of the UN mandate, which lasted until 2008. The UN did not distinguish between ethnic Albanian KLA fighters and Serbians, and all were subject to prosecution.

The war crimes cases could have been tried by the International Criminal Tribunal for the Former Yugoslavia, ICTY, which had been formed in The Hague in 1993 during the Bosnian war. However, the ICTY did not have adequate capacity for handling all of the cases arising out of the Kosovo conflict, so the chief prosecutor decided to focus only on the major perpetrators, such as Slobodan Milosevic, who died in 2006 before his trial had concluded. Further, the jurisdiction of the ICTY did not include cases which occurred after the war was over, or cases that occurred outside of territorial Yugoslavia (such as Albania), unlike the expansive jurisdiction of the UN.

As it turned out, however, several members of the Kosovo Liberation Army were prosecuted in The Hague. The two most prominent were Ramush Haradinaj, who has twice served as prime minister of Kosovo and is still involved in high-level politics, and Fatmir Limaj, a popular politician who has also served in high-level governmental positions and is likewise still active in politics. They were both acquitted in separate trials—Limaj in 2005, Haradinaj in 2008 and 2012—and each returned home to a hero's welcome.

Limaj was subsequently indicted on different war crimes charges back in Kosovo, and tried in 2011–2012. I was a member of the trial panel in that case. I was also in Pristina in late 2012, when Haradinaj returned from The

Hague after his second acquittal and the city was plastered with welcome home posters.

In March 2004, serious interethnic violence perpetrated by ethnic Albanians convulsed the country, and nineteen people were killed, both Serbs and Kosovars, and hundreds injured. Many Serbian religious and historical sites were damaged or destroyed, along with many UN vehicles. Urban legend has it that a gang of Serbians in the divided city of Mitrovica, in the north of the country, forced a group of Albanian children into the Ibar River, where they drowned, setting off days of wanton mayhem. The event is recalled as Remembrance Day in Serbia.

In late 2005, the process began to determine Kosovo's long-term legal status in relation to Serbia. Serbia insisted that Kosovo must remain part of Serbia, and Kosovo insisted on independence. Martti Ahtisaari, the former president of Finland, was appointed by the UN to lead the process. Ahtisaari subsequently developed a detailed proposal which was viewed as favorable to independence, including the right of Kosovo to become a member of international organizations. The proposal was then subject to unsuccessful negotiations between Serbia and Kosovo, each of which stuck to its long-standing positions. Ahtisaari then submitted his proposal to the UN Security Council. Despite intense negotiations, Russia and China refused to accept any proposal that was not acceptable to Serbia, and the proposal died in mid-2007.

Then, on February 17, 2008, a watershed event occurred: Kosovo unilaterally declared independence from Serbia. This bold stroke had the approval of the US and most other Western countries, but was strongly opposed by Serbia and its allies—Russia and China. President Putin predicted that the events in Kosovo would come back to haunt the West. And they did—in Georgia later in 2008, in Crimea in 2014, and in Ukraine in 2022

In March 2008, following the declaration of independence, there was rioting in the Serbian-controlled northern section of Mitrovica, and the courthouse was heavily damaged by protesters. The courthouse was restored with funding from the United States Agency for International Development (USAID), and reopened in 2011. Again, this is why the US ambassador wanted me assigned to Mitrovica rather than Prizren. Indeed, USAID had renovated many courthouses in Kosovo. At the entrance of each courthouse is a USAID plaque which reads "From the American People." This plaque would prove to be very useful to me in a debate over space allocation during my first assignment.

Also in 2008, after nine years of the UN mandate, the UN handed over much of its responsibility for many governmental functions, such as policing, customs, and the judiciary, to the European Union Rule of Law Mission, EULEX, although full implementation did not occur until April 2009. This transition made sense, after all, because Kosovo is part of southern Europe.

By this time, Kosovo's governmental institutions had been largely rebuilt and were operational. However, the handover of criminal cases from UN prosecutors to EULEX prosecutors was not particularly smooth, to say the least, which impeded the continued investigation and prosecution of certain difficult cases, including the *Medicus* organ trafficking case.

The UN retained some responsibility, primarily representing the interests of Kosovo in international organizations; presenting a periodic report to the UN Security Council, which is still the case; and, yes, sponsoring weekend bus tours throughout the Balkans for UN and EULEX personnel, a nice perk, which we availed ourselves of from time to time.

EULEX, like the UN, had broad criminal jurisdiction over war crimes and other serious crimes occurring during the war of 1998–99, as well as serious crimes occurring since the war, such as terrorism, organized crime, human organ trafficking, drug trafficking, corruption, and interethnic violence. EULEX carried forward the basic UN model of using international employees to investigate, prosecute, and adjudicate war crimes and other serious crimes, although for longer rotations as well as renewable contracts. Moreover, just like the UN, EULEX did not distinguish between Kosovar Albanians and Serbians in war crimes cases; there was no immunity for Albanians, even if they were perceived as war heroes.

According to the Humanitarian Law Center in Kosovo, in a detailed report published in October 2018 (*An Overview of War Crime Trials in Kosovo in the Period 1999–2018*), there were forty-four war crimes cases prosecuted by the UN and EULEX involving Kosovars and Serbians.[41] Twenty-five of these cases were against Serbians, with forty-four defendants in total, and nineteen of these cases were against Kosovars, with sixty-one defendants in total. Numerous other serious cases in addition to war crimes were also prosecuted during this time frame.

In 2010, the International Court of Justice, in a case brought by Serbia, upheld Kosovo's unilateral declaration of independence, finding that it was not contrary to international law, much to the dismay of Serbia and Russia. This was the state of play when I arrived in Kosovo in early February 2011.

In 2013, Kosovo and Serbia signed a historic normalization agreement (the first Brussels agreement). Both countries were and continue to be interested in joining the EU, but before they have any chance of being admitted they have to resolve their differences. Progress on the ground up to this day has been very slow because of deep-rooted mistrust, resentment, ethnic animosity, mutual recriminations, provocations, and fundamental disagreements about Kosovo's legal status. Kosovo insists on recognition by Serbia, while Serbia maintains that Kosovo is part of Serbia, and neither side has shown an inclination to budge.

There have been several rounds of talks over the years facilitated by both the EU and the US, including an initiative by the Trump administration in 2020, pursuant to which Kosovo and Serbia reached agreement on some economic issues, although implementation has been spotty. The agreement also provided that Kosovo would establish an embassy in Jerusalem with recognition by Israel, which has now occurred, even over the objection of the EU. The Biden administration, along with the EU, has encouraged the parties to continue negotiations with a view toward mutual recognition, but intransigence has been hard to overcome.

Indeed, two incidents in the fall of 2021 in the Serbian enclaves in the north of Kosovo further heightened tensions between the two countries. The first involved a change in Kosovo's policy regarding the type of Serbian license plates that would be permitted to freely cross the border, resulting in a thirteen-day blockade of two border crossings by Serbian protesters and overheated rhetoric from both countries. The dispute has not been resolved as of this writing.

The second was an organized crime sting in several locations in Kosovo, including in the north where organized crime is rampant, carried out by Kosovo police, in which homes and businesses were searched and several arrests were made, mostly of Albanians. The operation resulted in protests, road blockades, and violence, one Serbian man being shot and wounded, and news reporters being threatened and forced to flee. Serbian military forces mobilized on the Serbian side of the border, and again there was overheated rhetoric on both sides.

Kosovo is an independent, multiparty constitutional democracy, with a president, prime minister, and a unicameral parliament (Assembly). Kosovo is recognized by over one hundred countries, including the US, but not Serbia or Russia, or several other major countries, like China, Brazil, or India. Five of the twenty-seven countries which make up the European Union do not recognize Kosovo—Spain, Slovakia, Cyprus, Romania, and Greece—most likely because of their own internal situations, Catalonia being an example.

Kosovo's politics are rough-and-tumble, but the democratic process is generally respected. There was a parliamentary election in February 2021, and the transition of power from a legacy party to an opposition party proceeded fairly smoothly. Moreover, municipal elections in November also went relatively smoothly.

Kosovo has a young, well-educated population of about 1.8 million. Indeed, it is the youngest population in Europe. About 90 percent are ethnic Albanians. The rest are Serbians and other small ethnic groups.

Before the war, the Serbian population was as high as 25 percent, but was reduced drastically during and after the war when many Serbians fled to Serbia proper, leaving only about 7 percent in Serbian enclaves. The enclaves are most notable in the northern part of the country, particularly in the

Funeral procession for a slain customs officer. Photo ©EULEX.

divided city of Mitrovica and several surrounding cities and towns close to the Serbian border. Mitrovica is divided by the Ibar River, with Kosovar Albanians living south of the river and Serbs populating the north, where they constitute a majority.

There is a bridge over the river which has been a constant trouble spot. In years past, while I was there, it was not unusual for Serbs in the north to dump huge loads of dirt on the bridge to prevent travel from the south. During my tenure, a EULEX customs officer from Lithuania was murdered in 2013 in an ambush as he returned from his shift at a border crossing. The perpetrator has never been caught or identified, and the officer was memorialized by EULEX in 2021.

Serbs in the north developed parallel structures in education, health, policing, commerce, the courts, and governmental organizations, and have been financially supported by Belgrade. They do not wish to give up their way of life or their sense of identity. However, there is a "Serbian List" which functions as a political party and has representation in the Kosovo Assembly.

And Serbia and Russia continue to be allies. Despite being an EU candidate, Serbia has declined to impose sanctions on Russia for its unprovoked invasion of Ukraine, and on May 29, 2022, Serbia announced that it had secured a favorable natural gas deal with Russia, which can only be worrisome to the other countries in the Western Balkans.

Unfortunately, there was and continues to be a great deal of corruption throughout Kosovo which impedes Kosovo's development into a fully mature society. Many of the young, well-educated people despair about their future in a corrupt society with a weak economy, little industry, and few jobs, and many would like to leave.

While I was there in 2012, for example, the then-president of Kosovo appointed a high-level commission to study the problem of corruption and make recommendations for remediation. She appointed an Albanian prosecutor to serve as chair. He was working in EULEX's prosecution office, and was well regarded. Shortly after he was appointed, he himself was indicted for corruption for taking bribes to fix a case, and was ultimately convicted.

In its list of requirements for Kosovo to be a candidate for admission to the EU, reducing corruption is always near the top. In Transparency

International's "Corruption Perceptions Index," released in January 2022, Kosovo ranks 87 out of 180, well below other European countries, although not the lowest in the Balkans.[42] The local courts may not be helping. In an article published March 5, 2021, in *Balkan Insight*, "Kosovo's Courts Struggle to Hold Corrupt Officials to Account," it was reported:

> Corruption has blighted Kosovo's recovery from a 1998–99 war and hindered its economic and political development since the former Serbian province declared independence in 2008.
>
> Successive governments have adopted multi-year action plans to root out graft, with little to show for them when the next general election comes around, roughly every two years in Kosovo's recent history.[43]

KLA veterans have always been prominent in politics and government, and have included the president, prime minister, speaker of the parliament, and other high-ranking officials. They are still worshipped as war heroes and liberators among a significant segment of the population, even though, as noted, several were prosecuted at the ICTY, and more still in Kosovo during the UN and EULEX mandates. Several more were indicted for war crimes as recently as 2020 by the new war crimes court in The Hague, as I will discuss in the epilogue, including Hashim Thaçi, the former president, and Kadri Veseli, the former speaker of parliament.

But the political ground may be shifting. An article in the *New York Times*, dated March 6, 2021, "In a Land Dominated by Ex-Rebels, Kosovo Women Find Power at the Ballot Box," stated:

> The surge [in women elected to Parliament in the recent election in February 2021] reflects growing discontent with the endemic corruption and bullying ways of a postwar order dominated by swaggering male veterans of the Kosovo Liberation Army, the now disbanded guerrilla force that battled Serbia and paved the way for Kosovo's declaration of independence.[44]

Indeed, the current president of Kosovo is a woman, Vjosa Osmani, who took office on April 4, 2021.

But still, a clan mentality prevails in Kosovo. In my experience, a person's loyalty was often to his family, friends, and comrades rather than the justice system. Witnesses who appeared in trial were often reluctant to testify truthfully or to testify at all, and they regularly experienced amnesia or claimed duress or a bad translation in an attempt to avoid implicating other clan members. Witness intimidation is still an ongoing problem.

An article in *Balkan Insight*, dated November 24, 2021, "Fearful Witness in Kosovo Serb Politician's Murder Trial Changes Testimony," says it all: "The second witness in the trial for murder of Kosovo Serb politician Oliver Ivanovic said he wants to change the previous testimony he gave to prosecutors, explaining that he is afraid and should have remained silent."[45]

I am often asked about safety issues in Kosovo. My response is that we never felt unsafe personally, even walking around at night, although there were rare incidents of an international employee of EULEX being criminally victimized. You did have to be careful of street vagrants, who would roam through shops and restaurants to panhandle or grab whatever they could get away with.

I'm told that local Kosovar women are often harassed on the streets, though the incidents are rarely reported, and that domestic violence is a serious problem. Indeed, as reported by *RTK Live*, on November 30, 2021,

American flags celebrating 4th of July. Photo courtesy of the author.

"Head of the EU Office in Kosovo Tomas Szunyog said in his remarks at the launch of the online platform for legal aid by the Kosovo Law Institute that domestic and other violence against women are still a 'terrible' reality in Kosovo."[46]

Kosovar Albanians love Americans because of our support during the war and during their drive for independence. Hillary and Bill Clinton were wildly popular, and more recently, Donald Trump. There is a statue of Bill Clinton on Bill Clinton Boulevard, and many other streets have been named after Americans, such as Madeleine Albright and Wesley Clark, who led the NATO operation. President Biden also has a direct connection with Kosovo, as his deceased son Beau served in the military in Kosovo after the war. On many occasions I experienced the goodwill of Kosovars, such as being offered free taxi rides when the drivers learned I was American, which I always declined.

The currency in Kosovo is the European euro, and financial transactions are much the same as in the rest of Europe. There are ATMs everywhere, credit cards are accepted, and there is a reliable banking system.

Chapter 16

Getting Started in Prizren

After collecting my luggage and going through passport control at the Adem Jashari International Airport, I was met by two representatives of the Civilian Police International operation in Kosovo: Bill, the director; and Gene, the logistics officer. They whisked me into downtown Pristina, where CPI headquarters was located, about a twenty-minute drive.

The headquarters consisted of a very nice house in the trendy Peyton section of the city, which had numerous restaurants, cafés, nightclubs, a few embassies, and a residential section. The house had various administrative offices, a well-appointed living room with a big flat-screen TV and a large DVD library, an armory in the basement, and a pleasant terrace in the back. The amenities were for the use of the American contingent.

In the back was a separate residence where Gene lived, with a gym in the basement that included a basic selection of workout equipment. The compound was enclosed by a sturdy fence and secured 24-7 by rotating guards. Across the street was a private, secure parking lot for several CPI SUVs, and additional space for visitors. I later learned that the SUVs could be used for personal travel by Americans working for EULEX, and I signed one out from time to time for vacation trips.

Upon arrival, Bill took me to lunch at a restaurant across the street, and we became acquainted. He was in charge of all administrative matters for the American contingent in Kosovo, which numbered about sixty persons: three judges, including me; three prosecutors; and police officers. At one point the contingent had been several times larger, but would soon be reduced again to about thirty as the mission continued downsizing.

At the end of our lunch, Bill asked if I would like a macchiato. As an inveterate coffee drinker, I may have heard the term but was not real familiar with it. Nevertheless, I decided to try one. It consisted of a shot of espresso and steamed milk, nothing else—no caramel, pumpkin, mocha, whipped cream, or other additives.

There was a vibrant café society in Kosovo, with a café on just about every corner, where everyone consumed several macchiatos a day. Indeed, when internationals were interviewed by the local press, they were invariably asked about the number of macchiatos they consumed each day. I would soon develop the addiction.

Many of the cafés had a delivery service, and you could see waiters rushing through the streets carrying trays of steaming macchiatos. On warm days and nights, the cafés would be bursting with customers sitting shoulder to shoulder on the outdoor terraces drinking coffee, many of them unemployed young people. Alcoholic beverages were also popular. Although Kosovo is nominally a Muslim country, it is largely secular, and alcohol was readily available—no more restrictive than in the US.

After lunch, Bill directed me to the Royal Hotel a couple of blocks away, where I would stay until I was collected by a team from Prizren to start my assignment. It was a nice Western-style hotel, with a bar, restaurant, and free Wi-Fi. The nightly rate was eighty euros, about $110, at the time. Bill was a good guy, very friendly and helpful to me and the other Americans, and we liked each other.

I was supposed to stay in the Grand Hotel, but had been warned by an American prosecutor who said it had the reputation of being the worst hotel in Europe, and under no circumstances should I stay there. Indeed, there was an article about the hotel in the *New York Times*, dated March 1, 2018, "Not the Worst Hotel in the World, but 'the World is Very Big.'"[47]

It was the weekend, so I had some free time to wander around downtown Pristina. It was a city of about 200,000, not particularly attractive (to be charitable), with virtually no green space except for a nice park on the outskirts, lots of concrete, and helter-skelter buildings. The city was buzzing with thousands of people, mostly young, walking around and going in and out of cafés and shops. There was definitely a vibe to the place.

One particularly ugly and imposing building was a huge sports center, the Palace of Youth and Sports, which defined a section of the downtown area. It was built in the socialist era and was now dilapidated, but still used for various sports and cultural activities. Its gym was the home court for Pristina's professional basketball team, and the concert hall was in reasonably good repair.

Beneath the sports center, at ground level, was a shopping mall, and adjacent to the main entrance of the mall was the monument memorializing the birth of a new country. The monument was composed of the English capital letters N-E-W-B-O-R-N, with each letter standing about eight feet tall and painted bright colors. It was covered with patriotic graffiti and tourists' signatures. Nearby was Mother Teresa Street, a pedestrian-only street about ten blocks long, with many shops, kiosks, cafés, restaurants, and thousands of people walking about. This was the epicenter of the commercial section of the city. Mother Teresa, although born in Macedonia, was of Albanian ethnicity, like the vast majority of Kosovars.

There were also numerous government buildings in the downtown area, including the parliament at the far end of Mother Teresa Street. On a wall outside the parliament building were photos of many of the sixteen hundred missing persons from the war, which I walked by every day. Not far from there was the district court, which was the basic trial court. I would be reassigned to Pristina about eight months later, and would come to be very fond of the city, although not the courthouse.

NEWBORN, symbolizing a brand new country. Photo courtesy of the author.

One thing that struck me as I strolled about was the large number of EULEX vehicles driving around and displaying the distinctive EU logo of a circle of yellow stars on a blue background. They were all dark blue VW Golfs or Nissan Pathfinders. I was also impressed by the number of KFOR military vehicles plying the streets. There were still thousands of troops of various nationalities, whose mission was to maintain security and prevent Kosovo and Serbia from fighting each other again.

KFOR would be a constant presence during my time in Kosovo, and its main headquarters were located on the outskirts of the city in an area referred to as Film City, a former movie studio. Each of the national contingents in KFOR, such as Italy, France, Germany, or Austria, would have its own PX where we were allowed to shop as EULEX employees. The US also had a fairly extensive PX, with food, clothing, electronics, and other items, where I shopped occasionally.

Sunday afternoon arrived, and it was time to check out of the hotel and meet my escort team. I went to the bar to await the folks from Prizren, but they were already there—Witold, the Polish judge, and Edi, the court's administrative assistant. Witold was a tall man, around forty, with good English skills, an obvious sense of humor, and a twinkle in his eye. Edi was a Kosovar Albanian, about the same age, who spoke impeccable English and had an air about him as the go-to guy, or fixer—someone who knew everything and everybody, and knew how to get things done. These characteristics would become more and more apparent as time passed.

Off we went to Prizren with Edi behind the wheel in his BMW sedan. The trip was about forty-five miles and took about an hour and a half. For me it was another hair-raising panic ride up and over the mountains between Pristina and Prizren on a two-lane road with numerous switchbacks clogged with trucks spewing diesel smoke, crawling up and down the hills with very few places to pass. When such a place presented itself, there was a mad scramble to get by the trucks, often with near head-on collisions, only to come up behind another crawling truck.

The drive was not for the faint of heart, especially in winter with snow on the ground and darkness approaching, but Edi was an excellent driver and knew the road well, so we arrived safely. I attempted to maintain my calm from the back seat despite oncoming motion sickness, and was glad to arrive alive. I would soon drive this road many times myself, when business took me to Pristina, but I never felt comfortable. As a consolation, there were beautiful views of the 8,500-foot Sharr Mountains in the distance, which remained snow covered until midsummer. By fall 2012, a new divided highway opened between Prizren and Pristina, so it was no longer necessary to take this treacherous road.

It was dark when we arrived in Prizren, an ancient city close to the Albania and Macedonia borders, with a strong Ottoman influence, so I could not see much of it as we drove toward my hotel across the street from the courthouse. Witold and Edi dropped me off at the hotel. I checked in and went to my tiny room, up several flights of stairs. It had a single twin bed and barely enough room to open my suitcase, but was reasonably clean with a private bath and an internet connection. I had dinner in the hotel restaurant and went to bed early. The next day would be my first official day as an international judge with EULEX in Kosovo.

I checked out of the hotel the next morning, since Edi had arranged an apartment for me on a short-term basis, which we would visit later in the day. He met me in the hotel lobby and took me to the "log base," which was the quasi-military administrative headquarters for EULEX in the Prizren region, located about a mile from the courthouse. To gain entrance we had to go through a security checkpoint. The log base contained a motor pool, security office, medical clinic, a gym (which I would use frequently), and various administrative offices. It was surrounded by a high concrete wall with barbed wire, and an armed sentry stood guard in a guard tower.

I signed in, had several briefings, got my identification card, cell phone, gas mask, helmet, flak jacket, and a baseball cap with the EULEX insignia, and was assigned my vehicle, a dark blue VW Golf diesel. Technically, I was supposed to share the vehicle with another person, but he did not want to use the car, so I had it to myself while I was assigned to Prizren. We were allowed to use the car for personal use, with a daily mileage allowance and monthly reporting. But no one really seemed to care how many miles (or kilometers) you drove. In effect, the Golf became my personal vehicle, and I could fill it up at no cost at the log base. I parked it in the secure lot at the courthouse each night, as we were not allowed to park on the street for security reasons.

After processing, I made my first visit to the courthouse and the EULEX offices. The courthouse had been renovated by USAID as part of its model court program, and was reasonably well laid out, modern, and clean, with security and a metal detector at the main entrance. The EULEX judges and staff shared the building with the local judges and their staff. However, the EULEX suite of offices, up on the third floor, was woefully inadequate for all of us. This would soon become a serious issue.

Edi and Judge Witold introduced me to the other judges assigned to Prizren: Judge Tore from Norway, who had just arrived a week earlier; Judge Klaus from Germany, and Judge Vladimir from Bulgaria, both of whom had been there for a couple of years. We would all share a single, cramped office. Upon shaking hands with Vladimir (Vlado), he said, "If I could give you one word of advice it would be to lower your expectations." I would come to learn the wisdom of this statement. I was also introduced to the EULEX staff: two international legal officers (what we in the US would call law clerks), one from Finland and one from Bulgaria; and three local legal officers, all of whom spoke flawless English. I would henceforth be referred to as Judge Dean.

After introductions, Edi took me to the apartment he had arranged for me. It was in the ancient Sherdervan section of the city, about a mile from the courthouse, with an imposing mosque, warren of small streets, many small shops, and an iconic square with many restaurants and cafés surrounding

Prizren, showing Old Stone Bridge. Photo courtesy of Michael Cuniff.

a water fountain, all along the Lumbardhi River, which is crossed by the famous fourteenth century Stone Bridge. The apartment was a couple of blocks away from the river. Edi unlocked the iron security gate, then the inner door, and up we went to the second-floor apartment.

It was a one-bedroom unit with a combined kitchen-dining-living room, and a very cramped bath. It was modestly furnished, but looked clean and comfortable. There was a giant space heater, which had been turned off, and the apartment was bone-chillingly cold. It was early February, after all. Edi turned the heater on, showed me how it worked, and the apartment warmed up quickly. After a few minutes, we left my luggage, turned off the heater, and headed back to the courthouse.

At the end of the day, I decided to walk back to my apartment. Edi gave me detailed directions and off I went. The directions were easy to follow because the streets were well lighted. However, as I approached my street, the city suddenly went pitch-dark—a power outage. I would learn that power outages were virtually a daily occurrence. Soon I heard the noise of many generators kicking on, and sporadic lights appeared in the neighborhood, mostly down by the river where the restaurants were located. Apparently, the locals were well prepared for this eventuality.

My eyes adjusted to what little light there was on my street, and I made my way to the front door of my building, fumbled with my keys, finally got the two doors open, and walked slowly up the stairs in darkness to the second floor. I managed to unlock my apartment door and carefully entered. There was no interior light whatsoever, and none coming in through the windows along the street, and since we had turned off the space heater, the apartment was frigid again. I had a general recollection of the layout—the bathroom and bedroom were to the right, and the kitchen/living/dining room was to the left. I remembered that the bed was unmade and the bed clothes were in a closet adjacent to the bed. I couldn't remember where I had left my suitcase, but soon stumbled over it in the living room.

I assumed the power would come back on soon, so I left the apartment and headed down to the river to find a restaurant. This proved easy since there were many restaurants and they were all well lighted with generators and open for business. I chose one arbitrarily, went inside, and was shown to a vacant table. The other diners were eating as if nothing had happened. My waiter spoke broken English, and was very friendly and attentive after he learned I was an American. He helped me with the menu and I had a nice dinner and a glass or two of local wine, which tasted especially good under the circumstances.

The power was still off as I headed back to my apartment, which remained in complete cold and darkness. So much for my hope that the power would be back on soon. Now the task was to find the sheets and blankets and make the bed. I walked toward the bedroom with my hands on the wall until I came to the bedroom door. I remembered the approximate location of the closet, and felt around until I located what seemed to be sheets and blankets.

I took each item out of the closet one at a time, unfurled it in the general direction of the bed, and repeated the process multiple times until it seemed like I had enough covers to keep from freezing to death during the night. I then found my toilet articles in the suitcase, located a bottle of water I had seen in the fridge, stumbled into the tiny bathroom where I located the toilet and sink, and got ready for bed. Once in bed, I could feel the weight of all the covers, but at least I was warm. I soon dropped off to sleep.

The next thing I knew, I was startled awake by a deafening noise coming from outside my bedroom window. I thought perhaps we were being invaded. I jumped up and made my way to the window, where I saw in the early morning light a minaret equipped with a loudspeaker pointed in my direction, about fifty feet away. It was the early morning Muslim call to prayer, which would serve as my alarm clock for as long as I remained in the apartment. The call would be heard five times a day, every day, while I was in Prizren.

The power had come on during the night, so I turned on the lights and the space heater, found some instant coffee, took a cold shower, and got ready for the office. I stopped along the way at a pastry shop, where I had pastry and a macchiato. Once at the office I related my tale of woe, which struck the others as quite amusing. I was told that I'd get used to regular power outages, but should be prepared with at least a flashlight. I recalled Vlado's advice to lower my expectations.

I spent the day reviewing the case files assigned to me, which included a murder case, a war crimes case, and several others. They were all ready for trial and would be scheduled in court as soon as I had completed my preparation. So I had plenty to keep me busy and understood why the French general wanted me assigned to Prizren.

During my second day I was invited to a dinner party in celebration of the birth of the first child of one of the local legal officers. All the judges and staff and many friends and family would be attending, so I readily agreed. It would be a good chance to socialize with my new colleagues. We all left right after work and drove in several cars (I was a passenger) up into the mountains surrounding the city for about thirty minutes, until we came to a very nice restaurant where a huge table was waiting for us. It was a delightful evening with delicious local food, wine, and good company. We all toasted the family of the new baby.

Following the party, we drove back down the mountain to the city below. As we approached, I noticed the lights were out again. The driver soon pulled over and told me that this was where I should get out. I thought I knew where I was, so I disembarked with no further discussion. As I watched the taillights recede into the darkness, I realized that I really had no idea where I was, not even which side of the river I was on. Of course, I had neglected to purchase a flashlight during the day. Unlike the night before, it was late and the restaurants were closed, and the generators silent, so there was virtually no light except from the headlights of an occasional car. I had not yet put important numbers into my cell phone, so I couldn't call anyone for directions.

I wandered around for a while trying to find the river and determine which side of it I was on. Would I be sleeping out in the cold? Eventually I was able to locate the Stone Bridge and realized I was on the other side of the river from my apartment. From there it was easy. I crossed the bridge, found my street, found my cold and dark apartment, and soon crawled under the massive bed covers.

A couple of weeks after I arrived in Prizren, I received a call from my contact in the US Embassy, who said that he and several others from the embassy, as well as a state department official from Washington, would like to come to Prizren to see how I was doing. We met at a local restaurant overlooking the river. After lunch we went to the courthouse and I showed the group around, including our cramped suite, which surprised them with its inadequacy.

At the time, Judge Witold was about to begin the afternoon session of a murder trial in a courtroom down the hall. My guests were interested in seeing the proceedings, so we entered the crowded courtroom and took seats in the back. Witold and the two other judges (there was no jury) made their appearance and everyone stood until they were settled at the bench. As Witold was outlining the afternoon's proceedings, he noticed that my embassy contact was chewing gum. He stopped what he was saying, stared for a moment, and reprimanded him for showing disrespect for the court, all of which was spoken in English and translated into Albanian by the court translator. Everyone in the courtroom was startled, including me. The gum was quickly removed and stuck in a pocket, and an apology was issued. Nothing more was said about this embarrassing incident.

As I mentioned, we five EULEX judges shared one office. When all of us were present at the same time, the squeeze was unworkable—there were too many conversations, too many phone calls, not enough space for papers and files, and so forth. Something had to give. Judge Witold, who was the presiding judge, or "focal point," of our little band of judges, soon decided to take action. There was a large room adjoining our offices which was being used for storage of hundreds of archived, dusty files that had nothing to do with EULEX all spread out on the floor, and it seemed logical that we should be able to expand into that space.

Witold set up a meeting with the local presiding judge, who was in charge of the courthouse and responsible for space allocation, and we trudged to his office, which was large, light, airy, and nicely furnished, all paid for by USAID. Witold made his pitch for extra space through an interpreter. The local judge hemmed and hawed, and made various excuses as to why this space was unavailable—the storage space was necessary, the room might be used for a future courtroom, or might be needed for summer interns— and why he had to get approval from his superiors in Pristina. Nothing happened as several weeks passed.

In the meantime, our space situation was getting more and more desperate as Tore and I settled in, so Witold sent a formal letter to the local presiding judge imploring him to give us the space we needed and to do so immediately. This was followed by another meeting in the judge's spacious office, and we heard all the same excuses again. When all our logical arguments failed, I did something that I did only once in Kosovo, and reluctantly. I played the American card.

I said to him, "When you walk into this building each day, you pass by the USAID plaque on the wall which reads, 'From the American People.'

My country paid for the renovation of this building, including your large office and all your nice furniture. As an American I would appreciate if you would make the vacant space available to us immediately." This appeal seemed to resonate with the judge, and we received approval for the space later that day. All the dusty files were soon removed, and Judge Tore and I moved into our new quarters, where we were able to work comfortably and with minimal distractions.

Chapter 17

More About EULEX

Logo, European Union Rule of Law Mission in Kosovo.
Photo ©EULEX.

During my time in Kosovo, 2011–13, there were about twelve hundred international employees working for EULEX, and about one thousand local employees. The international employees were sometimes referred to as "misfits, mercenaries, and missionaries." I would fall into the missionary category, since I was in Kosovo to promote the rule of law. The vast majority worked in customs, policing, corrections, administration, and support services. There were also about thirty-five to forty international judges from all over Europe and the contributing countries, but only about a third of these were criminal trial judges, like me. The rest were appellate judges, civil judges, or judges who dealt with issues related to converting state-owned property to private property.

We had our own chain of command separate from the EULEX bureaucracy to protect our independence, and were organized into the Assembly of EULEX Judges headed by a president and vice president chosen by the judges. For much of my time in Kosovo, I was the only American judge, though I did overlap with two other American judges, one of whom was Vice President of the Assembly Charles Smith III, whom I mentioned earlier. The judges were all working on one-year, renewable contracts, like me, and most renewed their contracts, as I did, sometimes many times over. This was particularly true for judges from Eastern Europe who were paid multiples of their salaries at home and would stay as long as they could.

EULEX was a huge bureaucracy. Its headquarters in Pristina, called "Farmed" for reasons I never understood, were spacious, airy, and spotless, with convenient parking and a pleasant café for the enjoyment of the bureaucrats, who bustled about with self-importance. Many of my judicial colleagues and I would come to resent Farmed, since the folks there seemed to have little knowledge, concern, or appreciation for the difficult work we did in the field.

Within a couple of weeks of my arrival, I was invited to attend a ceremony at Farmed in honor of all the international employees who worked for EULEX. We would each be presented with a medal to recognize our valuable service. Because I had only been there a short time, I didn't believe I had earned a medal. Also, I had a scheduling conflict with a court case, so I couldn't attend. Subsequently, my medal was delivered to me. Out of curiosity, I asked my local Kosovar colleagues, all of whom were EULEX employees, if they had ever been recognized for their service. I received downcast looks and negative responses. I then presented a proposal up through the chain of command recommending that Farmed organize a similar ceremony for local staff. Even though the proposal had support from my immediate supervisors within the judiciary, the proposal went nowhere.

Several months later, when one of the Farmed bureaucrats, a French diplomat posted in Kosovo, was visiting the courthouse in Pristina where I had been reassigned, I raised the issue. His assistant who accompanied him was somehow aware of my proposal. She supported the idea but, in a nod to the hidebound EULEX bureaucracy, said it would have to be cleared in Brussels. Nothing ever happened—much too complicated.

At my goodbye party many months later, in May 2013, I decided to honor all of the local staff I had worked with, and present each of them with a certificate of appreciation. The event was well attended, with many friends and colleagues, whereupon Charlie Smith and I called each local employee to come forward and receive their certificate, along with a handshake and sincere "thank you." I think they appreciated the recognition.

EULEX was a favorite target among the local politicians, especially when something went wrong from their perspective, which it often did, like yet another war hero being indicted for war crimes, or a government official for corruption. For many years, despite frequent statements that it was time for EULEX to go, no one really wanted that to happen because of the stability that EULEX provided, not to mention the huge amounts of money it poured into local coffers.

I can't leave this subject without describing EULEX's leave policy. EULEX employees earned forty-eight days of leave per year, plus twelve holidays, for a total of sixty days, which equated to one work week per month. The stated purpose for this generous policy was to attract qualified candidates from throughout Europe to leave their homes, jobs, and families to come to Kosovo, which was perceived as a hardship post. We Americans, on the other hand, earned eighteen days of leave per year, plus twelve holidays, per state department policy, for a total of thirty, which was more than adequate. So Americans, like those in the police contingent, often covered for Europeans who were on leave. This generated a certain level of teasing— if not resentment—and in my situation as a judge, often created scheduling problems for my cases.

The airlines flying into and out of the international airport in Pristina caught on to this leave policy. Since most European capitals could be reached in two hours or less, the airlines developed routes that would leave Pristina on Friday afternoon and fly to such places as London, Berlin, Vienna, Prague, Budapest, and then return to Pristina on Sunday afternoon. Kristina and I took advantage of these schedules from time to time.

We usually took a cab to the airport, and on our return we would be quickly surrounded by many taxi drivers looking for a fare. As a former cab driver in Boston during law school, I was generally sympathetic, but negotiating a price was stressful. The proposed rate usually started around thirty-five euros, which was much too high and had to be negotiated down, and the process was annoying. Instead, I would simply take a twenty-euro bill out of my pocket, a fair price for a quick trip into the city, and display it as I was being approached. The first taker, which was almost immediate, got the job.

EULEX began downsizing several years ago, and virtually all of its former functions, including the judiciary, have been turned over to local authorities. No longer is there an international legal contingent of investigators, prosecutors, and judges responsible for serious cases like war crimes and human organ trafficking, and such cases are now handled by local officials with the exception of cases that fall under the jurisdiction of the new court in The Hague as I will discuss in the epilogue.

Chapter 18

Our New Apartment

About a month after my arrival, Kristina and our dog Piper joined me in Prizren. We soon outgrew the small apartment that Edi had found for me. Judge Witold suggested we move into his building, which was a modern seven-story apartment complex close to the courthouse. There was a unit available on the sixth floor that was owned by a Kosovar Albanian who worked in Sweden. I contacted the owner, who spoke good English, and we struck a deal, though there was no written agreement.

The apartment was actually quite nice, with lots of windows and a balcony that looked out over the valley with the snowcapped Sharr Mountains in the distance. In the evenings, we would stand on the balcony and listen to the call to prayer that emanated from the dozens of mosques in the surrounding area, Prizren being more observant than the secular capital Pristina. The sounds that filled the valley were often discordant because the various mosques were not necessarily in sync.

Unfortunately, there were still many power outages, usually around dinnertime. Word was that the power company was selling electricity to other Balkan countries rather than meeting the needs of the local population. Occasionally, the water would also be shut off.

Soon after we moved into the apartment, the graduation party season began for local high school kids. A restaurant right next to the apartment building hosted many of these parties late into the night. Our building was shaped somewhat like a horseshoe, with the open end facing the restaurant. The ear-piercing Albanian music would escape from the open front door of the restaurant and reverberate off the walls of our building, so it was impossible to sleep.

This happened several nights a week, and no one seemed to complain about the noise, as there was no culture of civic engagement. I would go to the restaurant, locate the person in charge, and politely request that they turn down the music, using a hand gesture. They were usually quite obliging and would shut the restaurant door, which provided a brief respite until someone opened it again. It was really a lost cause, but the party season eventually ended in a couple of weeks.

Piper became quite a favorite with the local kids in the building and surrounding neighborhood. She was well known and well loved. It was hard to make much progress when out for a walk with her because people wanted to stop and pat her. Further, the kids would follow us yelling "Piper, Piper," reminiscent of the Pied Piper of Hamlin.

From our balcony we could look down on the dumpster in the parking lot below. Every evening a couple of Roma kids would show up and climb into the dumpster to forage for anything that might have the slightest value. The Roma population was universally despised in Kosovo (and elsewhere in Europe); they were on the lowest rung of the ethnic and social hierarchy, and were generally perceived, rightly or wrongly, as professional thieves and vagrants.

Kristina expressed compassion for these kids and would leave food for them in the afternoon, near the dumpster. Once, she found a Michael Jordan jersey on the street near our building, which she ran through the washing machine and then hung up on the side of the dumpster. The next time she saw the kids, one of them was wearing the jersey as he climbed into the dumpster.

Unfortunately, the trash situation was a serious problem in Prizren, and Kosovo in general. Plastic bags and bottles and other trash were thrown everywhere as there didn't seem to be an ethic of outdoor cleanliness. One day as I was walking down the alley from our apartment building to the courthouse, I noticed a plastic bag filled with trash that had been placed up against the wall of a building. I didn't think much of it at the time.

Walking back that evening, I saw a large number of trash bags piled up at the same place. The next morning there was an enormous pile of trash bags that seemed to have grown exponentially during the night like some mythical monster. A couple of policemen were approaching, and I pointed out the pile. They just shrugged their shoulders and walked on. However, the next morning the trash heap had been cleaned up and the situation never repeated itself.

I used to walk Piper in a park nearby which had a stream running along one of its borders. The stream was littered with just about every conceivable item that could be discarded, such as appliances and old furniture. It was not a pleasant sight and marred the otherwise pretty and well-maintained park. Other public spaces and vacant lots were also often littered with plastic bottles and other trash, marring an otherwise beautiful country, suggesting again the lack of civic engagement in Kosovo.

Chapter 19

Kosovo's Legal System

As I settled in to work and prepared my cases for trial, I gradually familiarized myself with the legal system in Kosovo. As mentioned earlier, there had been no training about the legal system during my CPI days, so I had to learn on the job.

The courts were organized into regional trial courts, referred to as District Courts or First Instance Courts (later called Basic Courts), and a Supreme Court. There was also a separate Constitutional Court. (Just as I was leaving Kosovo, the Parliament created an intermediate Court of Appeals, which began operation in 2013, after I had returned to the US.)

Criminal law and procedure were governed by written codes adopted in 2004 and updated in 2012 and 2013, and were not unlike the codes used at home. However, the codes incorporated a very different judicial philosophy based on the European civil law system, going back to the days of Napoleon.

If something wasn't specifically authorized in the procedure code you couldn't do it. If something was stated in the code you had to do it, regardless of whether it made sense in a particular case. There was no such thing as the inherent power of the court, like the power of contempt, or procedural flexibility and innovation. It was either in the code or it wasn't, and failure to follow the code could have serious consequences on appeal, which I learned the hard way, as will be noted shortly.

Unlike in the US and other common law jurisdictions, such as the UK, there were no jury trials in Kosovo. Instead, three judges—typically two international judges and one local judge—heard and decided cases as the triers of fact. Having judges as the triers of fact was consistent with the typical continental European model and was comfortable for the European judges I worked with, although not for me.

In fact, many were quite skeptical of the jury system because they didn't understand how lay people could possibly make correct decisions, despite my efforts to persuade them otherwise. One German judge cited the O.J. Simpson case as an example. Coming from a common law tradition, I had to recalibrate my sights and learn a whole new system on the fly. Judge Witold told me nonchalantly not to worry about it, I'd pick it up quickly.

The international criminal judges like me were embedded in the Kosovo justice system. This meant that we followed Kosovo law and procedure, and we shared courtrooms and facilities with local judges. Serious cases which came within EULEX's jurisdiction, such as war crimes and corruption, were investigated and prosecuted by the Special Prosecution Office of the Republic of Kosovo (SPRK), staffed by international prosecutors, investigators, and legal officers, as well as by some local professionals.

When a prosecutor began an investigation, the court had to be formally notified and, unlike in the US, there were strict time limits for completing the investigation, although it could be extended for good reason. An indictment had to be filed within these time limits or the case was over, since the procedure had to be followed to the letter. Indictments in EULEX cases were almost always multi-count and multi-defendant.

A typical case could involve as many as ten or more defendants being tried at the same time, each represented by up to three attorneys. Indeed, one of the war crimes cases I will discuss (the *Limaj* case) involved ten different defendants, all of whom were former KLA soldiers and commanders. Cases could last for weeks or even months at a time, and could present a serious management problem because of the number of people involved.

The procedure code provided that judges would be assigned to several different roles: pretrial judge, confirmation judge, trial judge, or member of a three-judge appellate panel. (Certain changes were made in the revised code of 2013 defining these various roles.)

A pretrial judge would handle initial detention issues, search warrants, wiretaps, and the like while an investigation was underway. Defendants could be held in pretrial custody during the investigation, called "detention on remand," upon a finding by a pretrial judge of "grounded suspicion" that a crime had been committed, which is similar to our probable cause, and a finding that the defendant presented a risk of flight or risk to destroy evidence or intimidate witnesses. Prosecutors almost always asked for detention in serious cases, because defendants could easily flee over the porous border into Albania, and because witness tampering and destruction of evidence were a way of life in Kosovo. Such requests were routinely granted, but had to be reviewed every thirty days.

A confirmation judge would enter the case after an indictment had been filed, review the indictment for legal and factual sufficiency, and if satisfied would "confirm" the indictment. Otherwise the indictment would be dismissed or returned to the prosecutor for more evidence. In making the determination, the confirmation judge would rule on questions of admissibility of evidence, such as the legality of a search or wiretap.

If there was an appeal of a ruling made by a pretrial judge or a confirmation judge, a panel of three other judges could be formed to rule on the appeal. These panels could be created quickly so as not to delay the case, and were totally separate from the post-trial appellate process.

For example, if the pretrial judge refused to grant an application for detention, or the confirmation judge refused to confirm an indictment, the three-judge panel could affirm the decision or overrule it. This happened in the *Medicus* human organ trafficking case. The confirmation judge declined to confirm the indictment because he believed there had been an illegal search by the police, but the appellate panel reversed this decision and the case proceeded to trial.

Once an indictment was confirmed, the presiding judge of the main trial would be appointed, and would then be in control of the case throughout the trial. The presiding judge in EULEX cases was always an international. Two other judges would then be appointed to sit on the trial, another international judge and, as mentioned, a local Kosovo judge. International judges also constituted a majority in cases heard by the Supreme Court (and in the intermediate Court of Appeals, after it was created in 2013).

The idea behind participation by local judges in serious cases was that they would learn best European (or American) practices as well as have a stake in the outcome. This was part of the mentoring responsibilities of EULEX judges. My experience working with Kosovo judges was generally positive; they took their work seriously and were usually constructive in the decision-making process. Local judges also handled all the routine criminal cases, with no involvement by EULEX.

The procedure code prohibited either the pretrial judge or the confirmation judge to sit on the actual trial. This provision was designed to avoid the possibility of bias, since the judge may have come into contact with prejudicial information about the defendants during the pretrial or confirmation phases. Remember, the trial judges were the triers of fact without a jury, and the theory was that the trial judges should enter the trial without any preconceived notions. This provision would come to haunt us in the *Medicus* case.

The actual trial process was not unlike what Americans are familiar with in terms of presumption of innocence, burden of proof, examination and cross-examination of witnesses, objections to evidence, right against self-incrimination, and closing arguments, but there were some significant differences that were very strange to me.

Defendants themselves, in addition to their attorneys, could question and cross-examine witnesses, and could comment on the evidence throughout the trial, such as after each witness had testified or an exhibit was introduced, all of which could be tedious and unproductive. Defendants also had the right to present their own closing statements after their attorneys had done so. This provided the opportunity for political speeches and self-serving defenses that were not subject to cross-examination, especially if news reporters were present, which they almost always were.

In a significant difference, the procedure code also obligated the court to determine the truth, not just to preside neutrally over the trial. If there were gaps in the evidence we could call additional witnesses, order the production of documents, appoint experts, order a forensic evaluation, cross-examine witnesses, and so forth, which I took full advantage of regardless which side might benefit. This is very different from the American system where judges, at least theoretically, are neutral arbiters supposedly just calling balls and strikes.

At the end of the trial, the trial panel had a maximum of three days to deliberate and reach a decision, similar to jury deliberation but with a strict time limit. The decision, guilty or not guilty, would then be announced orally in court with everyone standing, including the judges.

The oral decision also had to include the sentence and an explanation of aggravating and mitigating factors, but there was no presentence report or separate sentencing hearing, as in the US. This meant the judges often knew little about the defendants, except what was learned during the trial. The oral decision had to be followed by an elaborate written decision according to a precise template, as specified in the procedure code. A decision could be reversed for failure to follow the template, even if it was substantively sound, as I learned to my detriment in the *Kabashi* war crimes case.

Another significant difference was the absence of precedent; the doctrine of *stare decisis* (precedent) did not apply. Each decision by the Supreme Court stood alone and was not binding on other cases. In practice, this meant that trial judges could rule however they wanted based on their own interpretation of the facts and law, even if a similar case had been decided otherwise by the Supreme Court.

Plea agreements were also rare in EULEX cases, even though allowed by the procedure code. Many European judges were quite skeptical of plea agreements, based on their understanding of the American system, which they believed was very coercive. On this point, they might be correct. The vast majority of criminal cases in the US, both state and federal, are resolved with a plea agreement and without a trial. In my time in Kosovo I was only able to achieve a plea agreement in one case, which involved an international drug trafficking ring, the *Fortuna* case, which I discuss further on.

Prosecutors had the right to appeal a trial court's verdict along with the defendants, something rarely permitted in US practice. Appellate courts could basically make their own decisions based on the record at trial because they had much more flexibility than our appellate courts. For example, the appellate court could "re-qualify" a charge, which meant finding the defendant guilty of a different charge, whether more serious or less serious, and adjusting the sentence accordingly. Or the court could find the defendant guilty, even though there had been an acquittal at trial. Or the court could find a procedural problem in the trial and order a retrial. This was all quite common, and worked to both my detriment and benefit while I was there. It sometimes seemed like the appellate courts felt obligated to find problems so they could upset the work of the trial courts.

Indigent defendants qualified for free legal services by local defense attorneys. The defense bar was reasonably competent and some had been trained in the West and were quite good. This was also true for EULEX's international prosecutors, who were generally very competent.

Chapter 20

Translation

A critical part of the international legal process was translating from one language to another—or several others—for documents or witness testimony in court. Thus, there was a whole translation procedure necessary to keep court cases moving.

As I mentioned earlier, the working language of EULEX was English, and all employees, international and local, had to be fluent. Of course, there was a spectrum of fluency—some were excellent and some struggled. I also found that written fluency was quite different from spoken fluency. Someone might talk with almost native fluency but not be as competent in putting words on paper with correct verb tenses, punctuation, and sentence structure. I was occasionally asked by judges who were not native English speakers to check their written work, which had to be clear and concise. Some judges were good, some not, and I was always willing to help.

The secondary languages were Albanian—the native language for the majority of the local population, and Serbian, which came into play in many cases. So all documents in a case had to be available in two if not three languages. For example, a statement given to the police in Albanian would have to be translated into English at a minimum, and possibly Serbian, or even other languages depending on the case.

Proceedings in court required the presence of a translator, who was busy going back and forth from one language to the other, seated next to the judges on the bench. If the case involved multiple languages, multiple translators would have to be available. The *Medicus* organ trafficking case is a prime example. There were multiple languages during the trial—Russian,

Hebrew, Polish, Turkish, and others—that all had to be translated into English and Albanian.

Even in straightforward two-language cases, the translation process was time-consuming and cumbersome. Let's say the EULEX prosecutor, speaking in English, was questioning a witness who spoke only Albanian. The question would have to be translated into Albanian and spoken aloud by the translator, then the answer would have to be translated back into English and spoken aloud. Nearly all of the defense attorneys were native Albanian speakers, as were most of the defendants, the others being Serbian speakers.

Sometimes there were disputes about the accuracy of the translation, usually by someone who spoke both languages. Getting it right was important. If the question was, "Did you see the defendant holding a gun?" and the answer was, "I did not see him holding a gun," the inclusion of the word "not" is critical. If the word "not" gets lost in translation, the whole meaning changes.

The translations were consecutive, not simultaneous. Every question, answer, observation, comment, argument, request, and ruling had to be completely stated and then translated, rather than translated in real time, like in the UN. This took more time, but I actually preferred consecutive translation because the extra time made it easier for everyone to follow the proceedings and for me to take my own notes.

Sitting on the bench during every court session, in addition to the translator, was the court recorder whose job it was to take the minutes of the proceeding, which constituted the official court record. While the translator was speaking the English version of what was happening, the recorder would be entering it manually into the computer. At the end of the proceeding, the recorder would produce the minutes for review by the presiding judge. This could be a tedious process, but had to be done properly, and the judge would have to make corrections to ensure that the minutes were accurate.

One time, at the end of a long, tiring court session, one of the defense attorneys, speaking in Albanian, made condescending remarks to the three of us on the bench, suggesting we were not clever enough to follow his argument. After hearing the translation, I said somewhat flippantly, "We didn't just fall off the turnip truck yesterday," then immediately concluded the proceeding. The translator was puzzled, as were the other judges, but I just let it go. It wasn't really important in the scheme of things.

The next day the court recorder, not a native English speaker, came to my office and said, "Judge Dean, I heard your remark and I've been through all my English-language resources, dictionaries, thesaurus, and guides to English word usage, and can't find any references to 'turnip truck.' I want to get it right, but I have no idea what it means." I explained that it was an idiomatic phrase meaning "not naïve." He scratched his head and left. When I reviewed the minutes, I saw he had interpreted it properly. Sometime later, I overheard a conversation in the hallway where he actually used the phrase correctly in speaking with one of his colleagues. I was impressed that he had picked up the somewhat obscure American expression.

Speaking of the occasional pitfalls of translations, during a quick weekend trip to Budapest, we checked into our hotel and were directed to a nearby restaurant and wine bar which was highly recommended. It was below ground, with brick walls and booths, and overall very attractive. Being a wine bar, there was a wine menu on each table, describing the many offerings in three languages, Hungarian, German, and English.

One wine was described in English as "The shell of the fruit dark blue, strongly velvety. His meat greenish-yellow, slightly succulent." Another was described as "Mainly among the ladies popular, pleasantly his spicy fragrance and sensuously because of the pleasant marzipan of a seducer's seed." Yet another was "The fruit the dry meat of his shell with medium thickness whitish yellow one, melting." A tough choice indeed, so we opted for the local beer.

Chapter 21

Clinton Boulevard Bombing Case

I was assigned as the pretrial judge charged with issuing a ruling on a prosecutor's application for detention on remand in a case that unfolded as follows:

On August 30, 2007, a police officer was shot dead on a downtown street in Pristina, allegedly by a hit man on orders of Enver Sekiraqa, who was believed to be a notorious organized crime figure in Kosovo, and who owned a café in the downtown area. Sekiraqa fled and was thought to be hiding in one of the Serbian enclaves in the northern part of the country, and later in Ireland. He was named in an international arrest warrant in connection with this murder, as well as organized crime and other offenses. His whereabouts remained unknown.

Then a bomb exploded in the early morning hours of September 24, 2007, in the commercial area where Sekiraqa's café was located. An article in the *Guardian*, "Kosovo Bomb Blast Kills Two," reported:

> Two people were killed and 10 injured after a bomb ripped through a shopping mall in the Kosovan capital, Pristina, today.
>
> Police and NATO-led peacekeeping troops sealed off the scene in the city center after the device exploded in the early hours of the morning.
>
> The explosion scattered glass and debris from at least a dozen shops on Pristina's Bill Clinton Boulevard, and caused a building to collapse.[48]

The bombing would come to be known as the infamous Clinton Boulevard

Bombing case. The motive was unknown but thought to involve organized crime or perhaps a revenge killing for the murder of the police officer. Two years later, in 2009, two police officers were tried and convicted for various offenses related to the bombing, and sentenced to twenty-five years in prison. One of the defendants was a man named Shpend Qerimi, a former member of an anti-drug unit.

Long after the trial, and while his appeal was pending before the Kosovo Supreme Court in 2012, he made statements to the police and prosecutor implicating four other police officers in the bombing. Qerimi claimed that he, along with these other officers, drove into downtown Pristina in two police vehicles on the night in question. They parked nearby and told the parking attendant to leave the area because they were involved in a police operation. They then detonated an explosive in the commercial area and immediately fled.

Based on these claims, the prosecutor initiated an investigation into the purported involvement of these other men. In addition to Qerimi's allegations, she obtained cell phone data which indicated the men had made phone contact with each other that night and early morning. The prosecutor then obtained arrest warrants, which were carried out on the morning of May 17, 2012, and the men were taken into custody. The crimes alleged were aggravated murder and organized crime.

She also filed with the court an application for detention on remand for each of the four suspects, requesting they be held in custody while the investigation continued. The application outlined her version of the facts and why detention was warranted.

I convened a hearing on the afternoon of May 17. The suspects appeared in court with their attorneys. The prosecutor argued vigorously that there was sufficient evidence to justify a detention order, while the defense attorneys, of course, argued otherwise. I agreed with the defense attorneys and issued an oral order from the bench denying the application and releasing all four men from custody. Given the gravity and notoriety of the case, it would have been easy for me to simply grant the application for detention and move on, which was typically what happened. But I believed my job was to carefully evaluate the evidence in light of the proper legal standard, regardless of the outcome.

The prosecutor was furious and complained to my boss, the Italian judge who was president of the EULEX judges at the time. He contacted me by phone and appeared to be siding with the prosecutor. I held my ground, reminded him of judicial independence, and told him I would not change my ruling. He instructed me to put my decision in writing so the prosecutor would have my legal reasoning set out in detail for the purposes of her appeal. I did so over the weekend, with assistance from my very capable legal officer from Liverpool. After summarizing the factual allegations contained in the prosecutor's application for a detention order, I outlined my legal reasoning as follows:

> There is no dispute as to the occurrence of this criminal offense. It is an established fact that a bombing took place which resulted in the death of two and serious injury to many. The issue to be decided is whether the factual situation outlined by the Special Prosecutor establishes a grounded suspicion that the four above-named suspects took part in that event.
>
> The concept of "grounded suspicion" presupposes the existence of facts or information which would satisfy an objective observer that the person may have committed the offense.
>
> The [primary] basis of the Prosecutor's assertion that grounded suspicion exists is the account of Shpend Qerimi. It is fair to say that Mr. Qerimi, whose case is currently in the appeal stage at the Supreme Court, has a great deal to gain and little to lose in cooperating with the prosecuting authorities.
>
> In the broad spectrum of evidence, however, the statements of someone who has been convicted of a serious crime and is serving a lengthy sentence is among the least trustworthy evidence that comes before the court. As such it must be treated with extraordinary caution, and requires the court to look for substantial corroborative evidence.
>
> Substantial corroborative evidence is simply lacking in this case. The cell phone evidence is by no means strong; it is, at best, suggestive of the locations of the suspects and their purported phone contact with each other well prior to the bombing. There is no cell evidence showing that the suspects were in Pristina or

anywhere near Pristina later that night. Nor is there any evidence of further phone contact between the suspects later that night, save for a purported ring that was not answered.

Other evidence which could support the account given by Qerimi is missing. For example, the prosecution has provided no eye witness evidence to support Qerimi's account, such as evidence from the parking lot attendant who was told to leave the scene (he presumably could have given evidence as to the presence of two police cars and the number of persons within them).

There are no statements by any other potential witnesses which would support Qerimi's version of events. Indeed, his version stands by itself. And there is no other forensic evidence to support his version, such as an examination of the door which was allegedly forced, or the type of explosive used, or where it might have been obtained . . .

There are no phone intercepts of actual conversations between the suspects during the investigation [of this case leading up to the arrests]. There is no evidence, such as financial records or spending habits, linking the suspects with any monetary proceeds from the reward which is mentioned by the prosecutor as one of the motives for the bombing.

There is no evidence from Qerimi's trial at first instance that would corroborate his story or implicate these suspects. Indeed, his present story shifts the blame from himself to the others whom he identifies, and he portrays himself largely as a bystander. This is hardly surprising, given the fact that he is facing the possibility of 25 years behind bars [if his appeal is denied].

In summary, it is this . . . judge's opinion that the cell phone evidence is insufficient to corroborate the long-after-the fact, self-serving story of Mr. Qerimi. Therefore, there is an absence of grounded suspicion that the suspects have committed the offenses for which they are being investigated.

It must be considered as remarkable that there is such a dearth of evidence against these suspects, given the notoriety of the crime, the number of people allegedly involved as perpetrators and the passage of almost five years, not to mention during the full main trial [of Qerimi].

It is so ordered.[49]

The prosecutor appealed to a three-judge panel, the appeal was granted, and the four suspects were ordered into detention. It's one of the occupational hazards of being a judge, whether at home or in Kosovo; sometimes you get it right, sometimes wrong, at least in the eyes of judges charged with reviewing your decisions.

At another detention hearing in a different case, I reached the opposite result. There were several defendants charged with a financial crime and the prosecutor asked that they be detained in custody. The defense attorneys again argued that the prosecutor did not have "grounded suspicion" that a crime had been committed. The prosecutor then asked for my permission to show a video tape, which I granted.

As the tape rolled, I could hardly believe my eyes. It had been taken surreptitiously, and showed a group of men, who just happened to be the defendants, sitting around a table counting out stacks of bills, each in the denomination of either one hundred or five hundred euros. At the time, a euro was worth about $1.35 US. When the counting was over, the total was about a quarter of a million euros. There was so much money, the stacks were falling off the table. It sure looked like grounded suspicion to me, as well as a flight risk, so I issued a detention order.

Chapter 22

Uttering Threats

I was the confirmation judge in a case that tested the limits of free speech and demonstrated the deep-seated animosity between Kosovo and Serbia. My responsibility was to determine whether the indictment established a grounded suspicion that the defendants had committed the criminal offense of uttering threats, in which event the case would be scheduled for trial.

I held a hearing on the matter with all of the defendants present. The indictment charged three defendants, Sami Lushtaku, Rizah Hajdari, and Qani Mehmedi, with making verbal and written statements that were so inflammatory and dangerous as to constitute a crime. The facts as alleged in the indictment were as follows:

A woman named Jeta Xharra was the host of *Life in Kosovo*, a popular weekly TV show on RTK, the public TV station. She had the reputation for being a feisty journalist, willing to examine controversial issues and confront prominent personalities.

In May 2008, her show was very critical of Sami Lushtaku, a former KLA commander and member of the leading political party, who was then the popular mayor of the town of Skenderaj, located in the Drenica region, birthplace of the KLA. Mr. Lushtaku was very embarrassed by the show, as were members of his family, and he vowed never to cooperate with Ms. Xharra.

Then, in September 2008, about a year after municipal elections in 2007, *Life in Kosovo* began interviewing many local mayors to see if they had fulfilled their campaign promises. Ms. Xharra decided to save Skenderaj for last. This would give Mayor Lushtaku an opportunity to see the other programs and perhaps agree to participate so as not to be the only one who refused to do so.

In March 2009, Jeta Abazi, a reporter for *Life in Kosovo*, and a camera crew were dispatched to Skenderaj. The reporter and crew followed the standard procedure used in other towns, conducting interviews of citizens, opposition figures, and local officials. Some of the commentary was complimentary to the mayor and the municipality, some critical. One of the interviewees, an opposition party member, spoke harshly of Skenderaj and Drenica, saying in effect that it was a dangerous place where no one dared to speak out. Other interviewees praised the mayor for following through with his promises.

However, despite having an arrangement to meet the spokesperson for the municipality at the municipal building, Jeta Abazi and the crew were thrown out of the building and told never to come back. Unfortunately, the trip ended badly, with Ms. Abazi and the crew being threatened by an unidentified man with a gun, who forced the camera to the ground. They requested a police escort to leave the town, as they feared for their lives.

RTK and Ms. Xharra waited for two months before airing Ms. Abazi's report, so it would coincide with World Freedom of Expression Day, and in hopes that Mayor Lushtaku would agree to give an interview, but this did not happen. On Thursday, May 28, Ms. Abazi's video report was broadcast on *Life in Kosovo* as one of three reports associated with freedom of expression.

Following the report, Ms. Xharra engaged in a discussion with the guests on that show. She was critical of the lack of cooperation and transparency from the mayor and the press spokesperson for refusing to talk, and opined that this attitude created an atmosphere ripe for a physical assault, which in fact had occurred. The guests were generally supportive of the mayor's right to refuse to be interviewed, and complimentary of Skenderaj, which was described as one of the safest communities in Kosovo. They stated that the report was not sufficiently balanced. Immediately following the show, significant criticism was directed toward Ms. Xharra and her show. The primary source of this criticism was *Infopress*, a newspaper considered to be linked to Lushtaku's political party.

The criticism began on Saturday, May 30—the first possible day for publication after the RTK TV show on May 28. *Infopress*'s front page carried the headline, "RTK Terrorizes Drenica," followed by ten bullet points critical of RTK, such as "Should Kosovo citizens continue to pay for a TV station such as RTK that serves Serb-Slav circles?" and "Is it worth paying for RTK to watch shows that attack the KLA, Drenica, and the national dignity?"[50]

In the same edition, there appeared an article, "A Broadcast that Terrorized Drenica," by Qani Mehmedi, one of the three defendants, a journalist with many years of experience both in Kosovo and abroad. The primary thrust of the article was to find fault with the show's criticism of Drenica. Included within the piece were several references to Serbia, including:

> . . . two messages for which fascist Serb propaganda would have paid good amounts of money;

> . . . journalists who get their questions from various kitchens in Belgrade; and

> . . . broadcasts that Radio Television of Serbia used to make during the hardest years for Kosovo when there was a fascist campaign against anything that was Albanian . . .

The *Life in Kosovo* reporter, Jeta Abazi, was likened to "those Serb reporters who used to come to Kosovo in the guise of journalism." The article also said that Jeta Xharra and her show deserved a "professional bomb." Additionally, in the May 30 edition, readers were offered two opinion pieces: one which was highly critical of the TV station for its perceived attacks on the values of the KLA, Drenica, the mayor of Skenderaj, and the citizens of the area; and the other, which focused on the perceived misdeeds of Ms. Xharra for insulting Drenica and Mayor Lushtaku and for spreading untruths "like the ones which were realized about this region by Serbian television during the war." More negative commentary appeared on June 1.

A reporter for *Infopress* was then dispatched to interview Sami Lushtaku. One question asked by the reporter was "Bearing in mind that Drenica is the birthplace of the KLA, birthplace of Adem Jashari, the legendary commander, do you think that this show's aim was to strike at KLA's values?" The mayor replied with references to Serbia, including, "Jeta Xharra serves the interests of the secret Serb police, and she is the one I least want to deal with." On June 2, the interview with Lushtaku was published in *Infopress*, on page 4, while the headline on the front page stated, "Lushtaku: Jeta Xharra Serves the Serb Secret Police."

Further, in the June 4 edition of *Infopress* there was an opinion piece by Rizah Hajdari, one of the defendants, titled "Jeta's Four Betrayals." The betrayals were: betrayal of herself, betrayal of her profession, betrayal of the citizens, and betrayal of democracy. Jeta Xharra was described as "treacherous," a "traitor," and as a "sneaky person who obviously is ready to destroy just to fill her ego." The article concluded with "Jeta chose to have a short life."

On June 5 there was an editorial in *Infopress* critical of RTK for its criticism of Drenica, Skenderaj, its citizens, and their values. The editorial asserted that, at an earlier time such propaganda was served up from Belgrade kitchens.

Other newspapers were beginning to take notice of the inflammatory rhetoric. On June 5, two other papers came to the defense of *Life in Kosovo* in their editorials. One also published an open letter entitled "Organizations and citizens concerned about freedom of speech in Kosovo," which was signed by nine organizations and fifty-nine individuals.[51]

On June 6, *Infopress* published a clarification regarding the opinion piece by defendant Hajdari, saying that such pieces did not represent the views of the newspaper and that by publishing them the paper promoted free speech. It then proffered an explanation of the phrase, "Jeta chose to have a short life," stating it had been taken out of context and that the author was probably trying to imply that the show, *Life in Kosovo*, not its host, Jeta Xharra, was going to lose its reputation and credibility.

On June 8, defendant Qani Mehmedi offered a lengthy opinion piece in *Infopress*, in which, with reference to his earlier article, he attempted to clarify his statements by drawing a distinction between actually referring to Jeta Xharra and Jeta Abazi as spies serving Serbia, which he denied, and merely asserting that their actions looked like the actions of Serbian detectives from the past. The piece itself was published in the interior of the paper, but Mr. Mehmedi's picture and quotes from the piece were printed on the front page. By now, the *Life in Kosovo* website had begun to receive email comments threatening the life or well-being of Jeta Xharra. Some of these were graphic and vile in nature:

> "If we catch you in Skenderaj again we are going to fuck you up, did you hear me?"

"You are the biggest shits on earth, these dirty things you are doing serve no one. You are nothing, you are shit. Trust me, when I heard that fucking 'journalist' who was pretending to ask questions, she reminded me of the Serbs. Be careful because I will cut your vaginas, you Jeta and that little pussy girl. I have warned you once. Be careful!"

"We deserve to fuck your mothers. In particular those Jetas from your staff."

"I will fuck your families, your sisters. Now you are criticizing Sami Lushtaku, he was the first man in the KLA and you are now criticizing him. Where have you been at the time of war, you spies. Fucking Jeta Xharra."

"You, Jeta Xharra, must apologize for insults against heroic Drenica, against the center of Albanians . . . or otherwise I will be the one who will manage the attempted murder against you."

"I am going to kill you Jeta Xharra on 29 June 2009 at 1:00hrs. mid-day."[52]

The international community by now had begun to mobilize. Starting on approximately June 8, numerous letters were written and circulated by organizations and individuals, such as the Council of the Independent Media Commission, Organization for the Security and Cooperation in Europe, Human Rights Watch, Freedom House, Reporters Without Borders, Amnesty International, and others, all of which were critical of the *Infopress* coverage.

On June 11, Jeta Xharra met with Kosovo police. She believed she was being seriously threatened and stated that the headlines and content of the *Infopress* articles were also being repeated on evening news programs. She also informed police that Jeta Abazi had been seriously threatened on the streets, which had caused her (Abazi) to resign from her work as a journalist.

On June 17, a letter was written to then–Kosovo Prime Minister Hashim Thaçi over the signature of Joel Simon, executive director of the Committee to Protect Journalists, which cited the *Infopress* articles, editorials, and commentary, and referenced the death threats against Ms. Xharra and her team. The letter urged the prime minister to condemn and investigate the matter. Attached to the letter was a list of many prominent international individuals and organizations which supported Mr. Simon's plea.

On June 23, the Press Council of Kosovo issued an adjudication against *Infopress*, finding that it had breached Articles of the Press Code of Kosovo for publishing the inflammatory articles.

As for the Lushtaku interview, the Press Council determined that it contained unsubstantiated accusations such as could pose a direct physical threat to Jeta Xharra and members of her team. Also, the sentence "Jeta chose to live a short life," from Rizah Hajdari's June 4 piece, and "Jeta's four betrayals" amounted to incitement and hate speech in contravention of the Press Code. *Infopress* was assessed the maximum fine of one thousand euros and ordered to publish the adjudication.

The criminal statute in question provided that "Whoever seriously threatens to harm another person in order to frighten or cause anxiety to such person shall be punished by a fine or imprisonment of up to six months."[53] In arguing that the indictment should be confirmed, the prosecution stated that the factual background outlined above must be considered in light of recent historical events related to violence against journalists in Kosovo. The prosecution cited four cases of journalists who had been murdered for being critical of the KLA. The defendants, on the other hand, argued that their words were entitled to free speech protection; if the TV shows were protected by freedom of speech, then certainly their responses were likewise protected.

In issuing my ruling, I noted that freedom of speech and freedom of the press are enshrined in Kosovo's constitution, as in any democracy. These rights should not be infringed unless absolutely necessary to protect other important rights, such as the right to personal safety; an appropriate balance must be struck. I also noted that freedom of speech and freedom of the press are intended to protect speech which may be offensive, harsh, and unpleasant, not merely innocuous speech. Accordingly, it was necessary to interpret any law which could be used to circumscribe speech and press very strictly.

I also pointed out that the role of the confirmation judge was not to decide whether an offense was proven beyond reasonable doubt—that is the role of the trial panel after full examination of all the evidence presented at the main trial. Rather, the confirmation judge must decide only whether there is sufficient evidence to support a well-grounded suspicion that a defendant had committed the criminal offense alleged in an indictment, in which event the case would be moved to the trial phase.

I agreed that the spoken and written words at issue had to be evaluated within the political and historical context of Kosovo, a post-conflict area, as argued by the prosecutor. In such a context, references and comparisons to Serbian spies, traitors, betrayal, punishment, professional "bombs," and the like could only be interpreted as threatening to those who were the subject of such comments. Indeed, each of the defendants was aware of this context. Sami Lushtaku, Rizah Hajdari, and Qani Mehmedi all admitted knowing about the murders of the journalists identified by the prosecutor. They also obviously knew of the inflammatory nature of their remarks, as it appeared that many of the inflammatory comments were carefully chosen to provide maximum effect.

On balance, I concluded that there was a well-grounded suspicion that each of the three defendants had committed the offense of uttering threats. Therefore, I confirmed the indictment and advanced the case to trial on the merits. The trial panel subsequently found the defendants not guilty after hearing all the evidence, to the utter shock and amazement of Jeta Xharra and, frankly, me as well.

I was assigned as the confirmation judge in another case where the two defendants, officers in an insurance company, were charged with bleeding the company dry in the amount of several hundred thousand euros. I convened a hearing and learned that the local Kosovar prosecutor who had filed the indictment had himself been charged with taking bribes in another of his cases. A substitute prosecutor was filling in for him at the hearing.

I informed the parties that I would not proceed with the case until I was assured this case had not also become tainted by the prosecutor. I instructed the substitute prosecutor to report back to me after the case had been carefully reviewed. The prosecutor complained to his boss who in turn complained to my boss, the Italian judge, who again contacted me about my ruling. We had another discussion about judicial independence and I held my ground. Several weeks later, I was informed that the case had been carefully reviewed by the Special Prosecutor's Office and that there was no evidence of any inappropriate behavior by the original prosecutor in this case, so I convened another hearing at which I confirmed the indictment.

I butted heads with this Italian judge on several occasions, though we were friendly on a personal level. He was responsible for writing my performance evaluation and I assumed he would not be kind.

Then, one evening, at a going away party for one of our legal officers, he sat beside me and began exchanging pleasantries. After a while he shifted the subject to my work as a EULEX judge. I expected the worst. Instead, he said that he really respected my hard work, my independence, and my ability to articulate my reasoning and stick with my position, even if he disagreed. When he left the mission, he gave me a very strong evaluation.

Chapter 23

Murder Case of Cene Daka

The first case of mine that actually went to trial in Prizren was a murder case. It also ended in a way I could not have anticipated.

On a hot summer night in August 2010, around 11:30 p.m., during the Muslim holy month of Ramadan, a notorious loan shark in Prizren, Sejdi Hoti, was found dead in his office, killed by a single gunshot wound to the head. The body was discovered by Hoti's girlfriend, who frantically called the police.

A squad of officers, along with the local prosecutor, were called to the scene. After several hours of preliminary investigation, they focused their attention on a man named Cene Daka, who was thought to owe Hoti a substantial sum of money.

The prosecutor ordered police to search the residence of Cene Daka, on the outskirts of town. The search team consisted of police investigators, forensic officers, and eleven members of the Regional Operational Special Unit (ROSU)—fifteen officers in total, all in uniform, with the ROSU officers carrying rifles.

Daka lived at the end of a dead-end road. The search team arrived in the neighborhood around 3 a.m. Unsure which house was his, they knocked on the door of another house and received directions. The team then headed to Daka's residence and took up positions outside the six-foot wall surrounding the property.

An officer knocked on the outer door and shouted "Police!" After several minutes Daka appeared in the courtyard and opened the door. He was dressed in his underwear, as if he'd been sleeping. An officer explained they were there to search his house on the prosecutor's order because of a murder in Prizren. Daka, in his mid-sixties, expressed great concern repeatedly throughout his interaction with the officers, because his son was also a police officer and he was worried something had happened to him.

Daka did not appear to pose any risk, so most of the officers remained outside the wall while several others walked with Daka across the courtyard and through the open door into the residence, although the officers never asked Daka for his consent to enter nor did he offer it. It was a small house, with a central corridor and a room to either side. Once inside, Daka was asked if he had anything illegal in his possession; he said he had a gun under the pillow of his bed, pointing to one of the rooms. One of the officers went into the room, lifted the pillow, and recovered a pistol. Daka was unable to see the gun being retrieved because he was not allowed in the room. Upon searching the other room, the officers discovered several documents that appeared to connect Daka to the murdered loan shark.

After confiscation of the weapon and documents, Daka signed a form acknowledging that the items had been recovered during the search, but he was never shown the gun, because it had already been placed in an evidence bag. Daka was then arrested and held in custody on suspicion of murder.

At no time did either the prosecutor or the police obtain a written search warrant from a judge, or even contact a judge for a verbal search order, as required by Kosovo law. Nor did the officers attempt to arrange for two disinterested witnesses to observe the search, as required by Kosovo law. The neighbor who had been asked for directions was not asked to be a witness, and while it was the middle of the night, there would have been people out on the commercial road a couple of hundred yards away, because of Ramadan.

Ballistics tests showed that the gun was in fact the murder weapon. Further investigation showed that Daka did owe Hoti a large sum of money and that Hoti had been demanding payment. Daka was then indicted for murder by the local prosecutor, and continued in detention. During further investigation, Daka's son was interviewed. At the time, the son was a police officer working in Pristina. The son said that he had visited his father in jail and demanded to know if he had committed the murder. If so, the son would have to seek reconciliation with the victim's family according to the ancient Albanian Code of the Kanun, which authorizes blood revenge unless there is reconciliation.

Daka adamantly denied involvement. Instead, he insisted that Hoti's girlfriend was the real murderer, and that the police were trying to protect her, an attractive young woman, and frame him by switching her gun for his when he was not able to see what was happening during the search. In fact, the investigation revealed that Hoti and his girlfriend had argued all that day, providing her with a motive too.

Daka was fortunate to have a competent defense attorney with some training in the US. He filed a motion to suppress evidence, and argued that the murder weapon should be declared inadmissible as evidence because of the absence of a search warrant issued by a judge. Normally, such a fairly routine case would not have been a EULEX case, and would have been handled by local authorities, but it was transferred to EULEX because the actions of the local prosecutor and police were under scrutiny for their failure to obtain a search warrant. The case was taken over by a competent EULEX prosecutor from Poland. I was appointed as the presiding judge of the three-judge trial panel. Also serving on the panel were a judge from the UK and a local Kosovar judge.

We subpoenaed the police and prosecutor to testify about the search, and they were outraged that their actions were being called into question, especially in a public proceeding presided over by a foreigner. Several police officers and prosecutors took the witness stand, and each attempted to justify their actions, but none of them had a valid explanation for the absence of a warrant, since there had been plenty of time to obtain one.

The local prosecutor who had ordered the search without a warrant angrily marched to the witness stand as if he were in charge of the courtroom. He haughtily answered our questions and criticized us for challenging his authority, but was finally forced to acknowledge that he could not point to any provision of the procedure code that authorized him to order a search without a warrant.

The police also attempted to persuade us that an exception applied to the two-witness requirement, stating that because of the late hour there were no other people around. This struck us as hollow since, as mentioned above, there was a commercial street nearby and it was Ramadan, and there would have been people up and about as dawn approached on that summer morning, not to mention Daka's neighbor.

During our proceedings, which extended over four sessions, we noticed two young men with a thuggish appearance seated in the front row. They scowled at those of us on the bench as we asked the police witnesses some inconvenient questions. We learned later that these were the two sons of the loan shark who had been murdered.

Following arguments by the prosecutor and defense attorney on the facts and law surrounding this issue, the defendant himself asked to make a statement. He broke into sobs as he spoke, and with tears dripping down his face, denied having anything to do with the murder.

After hearing the evidence and arguments, the three of us on the trial panel agreed unanimously that the search was illegal. There was no written search warrant or verbal order, nor did any of the exceptions outlined in the procedure code apply, such as explicit consent or urgent circumstances. We also determined that the exception to the two-person rule did not apply.

We then declared the murder weapon inadmissible, and the prosecutor's case collapsed. Without the gun he simply could not prove the case. We then released Daka from jail. Subsequently, I wrote a decision outlining our findings of fact and legal conclusions. The EULEX prosecutor indicated that he intended to appeal our ruling.

Needless to say, this ruling created a huge stir within the local law enforcement community, where traditionally the prosecutor and police were given free rein to do whatever they wanted, regardless of the legal requirements. This was a hard lesson for them.

On a Sunday morning a few weeks after Daka was released, while the prosecutor's appeal was still pending, I received an urgent message from Edi, my administrative assistant, which went something like this:

> Judge Dean, Cene Daka was gunned down this morning in a drive-by shooting with 17 rounds from a Kalashnikov. The shooter has probably escaped over the Albanian border. The code of blood revenge has prevailed.

To my knowledge, no one was ever charged with this murder, though one might speculate that the loan shark's two sons were somehow involved. An article in the *New York Times*, dated July 10, 2008, titled, "In Albanian Feuds, Isolation Engulfs Families," the code was described this way: "Under the Kanun, an Albanian code of behavior that has been passed on for more than 500 years, 'blood must be paid with blood,' with a victim's family authorized to avenge a slaying by killing any of the killer's male relatives."[54] Under this revenge scenario, Daka's son, the police officer, would have been vulnerable, too, but to my knowledge he was not targeted.

Regardless of this unfortunate outcome, I think we made the right legal decision. Indeed, the EULEX prosecutor, who was not happy with our ruling, nevertheless began a series of training sessions for the local police and prosecutors, so they would understand the importance of following proper legal procedures and not make this mistake again.

Another of my cases in Prizren involved a juvenile who was tried as an adult for destruction of UN property during the riots of 2004. There had been a conviction, but there was an appeal and the Kosovo Supreme Court had reversed the conviction and remanded the case to be tried a second time.

I read the Supreme Court's decision carefully, and the issue seemed to be that the defense attorney had challenged the mental competency of one of the prosecution's key witnesses. In doing so, the attorney had waved around a document purporting to be a note from a psychiatrist about the witness's mental state, but the document was never offered into evidence, nor did the court on its own order that it be admitted. Nevertheless, the Supreme Court faulted the trial court for not affirmatively admitting the document into evidence, since it might have been significant in terms of the witness's credibility. This was an example of the obligation of the trial court to actively seek the truth rather than be just a neutral arbiter.

I was able to locate the document in question, which would become part of the record during the retrial, possibly affecting the outcome. However, in researching the applicable law, I discovered that the defendant had by now aged out. He'd been fifteen when the crime was committed, but was then over twenty-one. Under the code, he could not be retried, regardless of whether there was a strong case or not. So the case had to be dismissed.

Soon after reaching this conclusion, I convened a hearing notifying the prosecutor and defense attorney of my decision, and both agreed this was the correct outcome. At the time, the young man was in jail on an unrelated matter. I later learned that he died of a drug overdose shortly after his release. I never met him. Perhaps if he had appeared personally in court before I dismissed his case, I could have learned more about him and helped him reenter society more productively. It was a sad outcome for one of my first judicial decisions in Kosovo.

Chapter 24

Edi Finds Kristina a Job

Speaking of Edi, our administrative assistant, he proved to be a great resource during my time in Prizren. His family had been prominent in the old Yugoslav days, and he knew everyone and everything, including the best restaurants in the area. If things were slow on a particular day, we would all head off to a nice restaurant for lunch. My favorite, about a twenty-minute drive from the courthouse, near the Albanian border, specialized in fish dishes, with the fish swimming in a moat surrounding the restaurant.

Edi also acted as gatekeeper for the judges. No one got to meet or talk with us without going through Edi. He relished this role, though there were certain judges who had worked in Prizren before my arrival who did not appreciate Edi's interference. Edi was also instrumental in helping Kristina get a job at the fledgling University of Prizren.

The rector of the university was an experienced administrator from Germany. He had been hired to get the university off the ground but he did not speak Albanian; he did speak English, but not fluently. Kristina is fluent in German, and was hired to translate various documents from German to English, including his speeches to students and faculty. She also taught several English courses to the students.

The university buildings were totally inadequate, with overflowing toilets and the like, but there was a German military base on the outskirts of Prizren and the German government had decided to give the site and all its buildings, including a hospital, to the university once the military contingent downsized. There was a ceremony to honor this event, and Kristina translated the rector's speech, which was delivered in English to the university community as well as to a number of visiting dignitaries from Germany.

However, the plan soon went sour. Many faculty members had other jobs, which probably paid them more, so they often would not show up for class. The students would arrive on time, wait a few minutes, and leave. One of the rector's assistants, another German, had the responsibility of taking class attendance—not for the students, but the teachers.

Finally, enough was enough, and the rector fired certain no-show faculty members, including prominent professors who'd complained to the higher-ups within the educational bureaucracy. The rector then began receiving threats against his personal safety. It became so bad, he felt the need to hire a security guard for self-protection. When word of this situation made its way back to Germany, the German government rescinded its offer of the military base.

At the end of the spring term, Kristina prepared a final exam to give her English students. On the day of the exam, she arrived at the appointed place to find a large number of students who had never attended class, and whom she had never seen. They said they had enrolled in the class, but admitted they had never shown up. Nevertheless, they all expected to take the exam. Kristina quickly understood what was going on and monitored the students carefully. She suspected that the newcomers intended to cheat their way through the exam, and that's what they tried to do. When she caught someone cheating, she made a display of grabbing the exam paper and ripping it up. Soon, most of them left.

Chapter 25

War Crimes Case of Ejup Kabashi

While I was assigned to Prizren, I had my first exposure to a war crimes case involving a member of the Kosovo Liberation Army, who was considered a local war hero.

In July 1998, as Serbian paramilitary troops ran rampant throughout Kosovo, murdering civilians and creating general mayhem, the Kosovo Liberation Army (KLA) was also engaged in its own war crimes. In the village of Opterusha, warnings went out that the KLA was planning to take action against the Serbian population of the village. About fifteen Serbians decided to seek shelter in the home of a Serbian family in the village.

As darkness approached on the seventeenth of July, KLA troops appeared in the yard. There was a knock on the door, then a man's voice yelling threateningly, "Don't leave the house tonight." One of the Serbian men in the house recognized the voice of Ejub Kabashi, or Jupa as he was known, who was one of the village residents of Albanian ethnicity. The man immediately told his wife he had just heard Jupa's voice outside the house, and what he had said.

Immediately thereafter, shooting began, and the house was under siege off and on throughout the night. Some of the men inside the house were armed, and returned fire. Remarkably, no one inside was killed or injured. When early morning arrived the shooting stopped and the occupants of the house were ordered outside. At the time, there were many KLA troops in the yard. Two of the Serbian women recognized Kabashi carrying a rifle and wearing a black KLA uniform among the large contingent of soldiers. They also saw another KLA soldier whom they recognized, Haxhi Mazreku.

All of the Serbian occupants of the house were loaded onto a tractor-driven wagon and transported out of the village. Later, the women and children were separated from the men and taken to a nearby Serbian monastery where they were given refuge. The men were never seen alive again. In 2005, about six decomposed bodies were discovered in a cave far downriver from the village. DNA evidence proved that these were some of the Serbian men from Opterusha.

Several years later, the two Serbian women who had recognized Kabashi and Mazreku and were then living in Belgrade, Serbia, were located by EULEX investigators. They provided statements to the investigators and agreed to come to Kosovo and testify. Both of their husbands were among those who had been killed.

On March 30, 2011, based on evidence provided by the two women, Kabashi was indicted for committing a war crime under the Geneva Convention and under applicable Yugoslav law in effect at the time of the offense, specifically for terrorizing the Serbians, all of whom had been noncombatant civilians. But he was not charged with the murder of the Serbian men, since the prosecutor did not have enough evidence to support such a charge. Haxhi Mazreku was also charged with the same war crime. Five other Kosovar Albanians were indicted, charged with giving false statements to investigators for the purpose of covering up Kabashi's involvement, so-called alibi witnesses.

The case went to trial in Prizren for several weeks off and on from June to August 2011. I was a member of the three-judge panel along with Judge Tore from Norway, who was the presiding judge, and a local judge of Bosnian ethnicity. The local judge was clearly very nervous about participating in a war crimes case involving the KLA. She was visibly anxious on the bench and shrank as low as she could in her chair, never saying a word.

Kabashi was viewed as a war hero by the local Albanian citizenry, and the courtroom was packed each day with his supporters. Many men from surrounding villages showed up each day wearing a distinctive cone-shaped white woolen hat called a *plis*, which was common among Albanian villagers. They would all laugh and joke and pat Kabashi on the back before the proceedings began. The courtroom was guarded by several uniformed police officers carrying automatic rifles.

The weather was hot and humid under the Balkan sun during the trial, and the small air conditioners could not keep up. The courtroom would become like a sauna as the day progressed, especially for those of us on the bench wearing black robes. One day, a couple of the defense attorneys sauntered into the courtroom about half an hour late while we sat on the bench waiting and fuming. Judge Tore interpreted this as an intentional act of disrespect and let them know clearly that this was never to happen again. They offered some lame excuse, but thereafter were always on time, if not early.

It is hard to overstate the drama when each of the two Serbian women was ushered into the courtroom to testify. They displayed great courage in this very hostile atmosphere, though they were clearly terrified. Indeed, one of the women vomited in the ladies' room before coming in to court. Everyone in the courtroom was riveted during their testimony, and the women told their stories methodically, clearly implicating Kabashi and Mazreku.

While fuzzy on some of the details of what had happened so many years earlier, they were clear and consistent on the essential facts. The women knew Kabashi as one of the villagers; the husband of one of them had recognized Kabashi's voice that evening; Kabashi had issued a warning not to leave the house just before the shooting began; the women saw him in the yard the following morning; and he was dressed in a KLA uniform and carrying a rifle. They also saw Mazreku that morning, in uniform and holding a rifle.

Kabashi's defense case was based on a purported alibi. While he admitted he was a member of the KLA, and was very proud of his service, he testified that he had been wounded while attempting to flee from Serb paramilitaries in early July, two weeks before the Opterusha incident, and was in a field hospital at the time. He also claimed that he had never heard of this incident, even at the time of the trial, which was clearly nonsense.

His attorney presented several alibi witnesses, including the doctor from the field hospital, as well as those individuals who had been indicted for giving false statements. The testimony of the doctor was evasive and inconclusive during the trial, but his field notes indicated that Kabashi was indeed treated for a wound in the hospital—but in August, after the Opterusha attack, not in early July, before the attack.

The other witnesses, those many years later, all claimed to recall the exact date or nearly the exact date when Kabashi was wounded, and it was in July, before the attack. For example, one witness claimed to remember the exact day because it was the same day he plowed a particular field on his farm.

Another, because it had been the same day he paid an electric bill. Another, because it was his birthday on July 11. These stories were preposterous and obviously fabricated. Kabashi's lawyer also argued that, even if the women's testimony was to be believed, it was not enough to convict Kabashi since there was no direct evidence that he himself had done anything wrong; he had simply been present at the scene.

Haxhi Mazreku's defense took a different tack. His evidence showed that he was a KLA soldier; that he was aware the attack was going to take place; that he opposed the attack; and that he'd warned the Serbians in advance, so they could protect themselves. Yes, he was present in the yard the morning he was observed by the two women, in uniform and with a rifle, but had only been there a short time. He'd refused to participate, left a short time later, and was subsequently reprimanded by one of his commanders for not participating.

As for Kabashi, we unanimously determined that the two Serbian women were credible, and that Kabashi and his alibi witnesses were not. We concluded the evidence was sufficient to prove beyond a reasonable doubt that Kabashi had participated in the siege of the Serbian household. Although there was no direct evidence as to any specific acts committed by Kabashi, he was criminally liable under the theory of being part of a joint criminal enterprise (known as JCE). This was a theory developed in case law at the International Criminal Tribunal for the Former Yugoslavia, which was applicable in Kosovo. It allows the prosecution of members of the group for actions of the group. Thus, we found him guilty of a war crime.

There was a hush over the courtroom as Judge Tore announced the verdict and imposed a sentence of five years in prison. This was a light sentence in my view, but resulted from a negotiated compromise among the three of us.

As for Mazreku, two of us believed his defense was credible and we found him not guilty. Since we constituted a majority, our determination prevailed. The third member, Judge Tore, believed that the theory of JCE should also apply to Mazreku, even if we accepted all of his defense evidence.

As to the five alibi witnesses, we found all of them guilty of providing false statements for the purpose of protecting Kabashi. We sentenced each of them to six months in prison but suspended the sentence for a period of one year, on good behavior.

Following the trial, Judge Tore wrote our decision and judgment order, to which I contributed, outlining in excruciating detail our findings of fact and legal conclusions, including a thorough analysis of the theory of joint criminal enterprise. Kabashi then appealed our verdict to the Kosovo Supreme Court.

To our shock, a three-judge panel, including two international judges, reversed our verdict on two grounds: that there was no evidence of any specific acts by Kabashi, and that we had committed a procedural error by not following the precise template for judgment orders, a hyper-technicality that had nothing to do with Kabashi's guilt or innocence. The Court then ordered a retrial.

I was furious at this outcome on both grounds, as was Judge Tore. We felt strongly that there was more than sufficient evidence against Kabashi under the joint criminal enterprise theory, and that our failure to follow the precise template had nothing to do with guilt or innocence. At this time, the EULEX criminal judges were scheduled to have a training session, and one of the agenda items was the proper template for decisions and judgment orders under the criminal procedure code. I drafted a memo which I intended to circulate to the other judges at the training session, outlining the absurdity of the Supreme Court's decision on this point.

I argued that, even if we hadn't followed the exact template, it was at most a harmless error and should not be one of the reasons for a reversal in a war crimes case. I also discussed the cost of this decision—the monetary cost of a retrial, the human cost of putting the Serbian woman through the ordeal again, not to mention the ongoing uncertainty for the defendants. Judge Tore and I discussed the issue at length in preparation for the training session, but at the last minute the session was canceled and we never had another opportunity for a general discussion on this point.

The case was far from over. It was retried before a different three-judge trial panel presided over by a EULEX judge from Poland, which heard all the same evidence we had heard in the first trial. However, this panel determined that the evidence was insufficient to support a conviction and acquitted Kabashi and his alibi witnesses. When I heard this verdict, I was dumbfounded. I recall discussing the verdict with the presiding judge and opining that a guilty war criminal had gone free.

The prosecutor then appealed to the recently established Court of Appeals, and the three-judge panel with two international judges, in January 2014, reversed the acquittal and found Kabashi guilty of a war crime against the civilian population. The decision made it clear that the evidence presented in both our trial and the retrial was sufficient for a guilty verdict under the theory of joint criminal enterprise, and imposed the same five-year sentence. The alibi witnesses were also found guilty and given six-month sentences, suspended for one year. I was back in the US by then, but when I learned of the decision I felt a high degree of gratification.

Chapter 26

Corruption, Jails, and Prisons

There was a jail directly behind the courthouse in Prizren. Adjacent to the main entrance to the jail was a coffee shop with tables out on the sidewalk. I walked along this sidewalk every day because it led from the courthouse to our high-rise apartment. I couldn't help but notice that quite often there were several attractive young women sitting outside enjoying themselves.

I got to recognize them, and we would smile and greet each other as I walked by. This tableau struck me as odd because I rarely saw any other customers at the café. I asked the local staff about this, and was told that the women were prostitutes who would go into the jail at night. I was never able to verify if this explanation was accurate, but it seemed a plausible explanation.

The main prison in Kosovo, named Dubrava, had been the scene of a horrific massacre during the war. Serbian forces reportedly slaughtered more than one hundred Albanian prisoners in May of 1999, as NATO bombing was underway. The perpetrators have never been identified. After being reassigned to Pristina, I, along with several other EULEX judges, was given a tour of Dubrava, since that was where defendants who were found guilty and sentenced to prison in our cases would end up, at least theoretically. It was a drab and depressing facility.

Word had it that defendants were able to buy their way out of prison if they could afford the payment. Supposedly, they would process into prison on the first day of their sentence, make their payment, then be released until the last day of their sentence, when they would process out. This may be an urban legend, but it enjoyed some currency among my peers.

Another scam, which I knew to be true, involved high-profile defendants held in custody while their cases were pending, who would feign illnesses. Cooperative doctors, along with prison officials, would approve a transfer to the relative comfort and lack of security at the Pristina hospital, rather than requiring them to remain in jail. One of my colleagues and I caught on to the scam, and required such defendants to be examined by an independent doctor before being released to the hospital.

A shocking example of this hospital scheme occurred about a year after I left Kosovo, as described in an online Reuters article dated May 20, 2014: "High-Profile War Crimes Suspects Escape Kosovo Hospital."[55] It reported:

> Police in Kosovo launched a manhunt on Tuesday for three high-profile war crimes suspects who appeared to have fled a hospital where they were each being treated under guard while standing trial.
>
> All three had been due in court on Thursday. Local media reports said the men, veterans of the 1998–99 Kosovo Albanian guerrilla insurgency against Serbian forces, had been resisting plans to transfer them to a detention center in the northern part of Kosovo populated mainly by ethnic Serbs.

The trio was captured three days later. But the most well-known of the three, Sami Lushtaku (the same Sami as in the case of uttering threats), was at it again after his conviction for war crimes as a member of the notorious Drenica group of KLA fighters. He attempted to escape from the Pristina Detention Center in August 2015, but was captured within hours—then, again unsuccessfully, from the hospital in Pristina in September 2015.

The extent of corruption involved in these escapades was described in an article in *Balkan Insight*, dated November 17, 2017: "24 Charged over Kosovo Ex-Guerrilla's Prison Breaks."[56] The subtitle read, "Twenty-four people have been charged with involvement in plots to help former KLA commander Sami Lushtaku escape from custody three times while he was on trial for war crimes." The twenty-four mentioned included officials from the ministry of justice, prison officials, doctors, the director of the Dubrava prison, and others.

Chapter 27

Assignment in Pristina

After about seven months in Prizren, in August 2011, I requested a transfer to the trial court in Pristina, Kosovo's capital. Although I was very fond of my colleagues in Prizren, and enjoyed my work there, the caseload was now under control and I was anxious for a faster pace and more significant cases, which I was assured would be the situation in the much larger court in Pristina. Also, I had been contacted by the other American judge in Pristina, who asked if I would be interested in participating in a major case involving human organ trafficking which was scheduled to begin in the fall.

That judge was leaving the mission soon and would not be able to sit on the case. In order to entice me, she said that I would lend some "gravitas" to the proceeding. I believe she meant that an American judge would be held in high esteem by prosecutors and defense attorneys, which did appear to be the case, whether justified or not. For example, it was not unusual for local defense attorneys to try to ingratiate themselves by saying something like this to me: "I am confident that you, as an American judge, will make the right decision and find my client not guilty."

My transfer was approved, effective at the end of September, and I was assigned to the organ trafficking case. The case, which came to be known as the *Medicus* case, gained worldwide attention. It would occupy a good deal of my time for the next year and a half.

Our landlord in Prizren was furious that we would be vacating the apartment, despite six weeks' advance notice. Even though we had no written contract and had never discussed how the lease could be terminated, he claimed to be entitled to six months' notice, and that I would have to pay him the difference, but there was no such legal requirement. I politely explained that this was not going to happen, but he kept calling from Sweden to press his point.

In anticipation of our move, Kristina and I began searching for an apartment in Pristina. On the recommendation of one of my colleagues, we contacted a real estate agent who happened to be of Serbian ethnicity. We traveled from Prizren to Pristina on weekends and he showed us a number of apartments around the city, one of which was on a hillside overlooking the valley below.

The owner of this apartment happened to be present when we arrived. It must have been obvious to her, a person of Albanian ethnicity, that our agent was Serbian because she began describing how the Serbian army had been located across the valley during the war and how she feared they would come and destroy her apartment. This was not a pleasant recollection for her, which was clear from her description and demeanor. Our agent, not to be upstaged, reached in his pocket, pulled out a pack of cigarettes, lit one, and blew a big cloud of smoke across the living room while the landlady scowled. The apartment was too large for us anyway, so we departed.

On the drive back to Prizren after one of these expeditions, my cell phone rang. I was behind the wheel so Kristina took the call. It was our landlord calling again from Sweden to demand more money. At that moment we were driving along a winding mountainous section of road with no shoulder and heavy traffic. He demanded that we pull over immediately and continue with the call. Kristina explained that there was no place to pull over, and hung up. This was our last contact with him.

Despite seeing many apartments, we did not find one that we were enthusiastic about. They were too big, too small, too expensive, too far from the courthouse, and so forth. As the date approached for my reassignment, we became concerned; we needed a place to live, and we needed it soon.

As it turned out, I had to go to Pristina on a weekday for administrative business, and planned to stay overnight. As I was wandering around the Peyton neighborhood near my hotel late that evening, I noticed a "For Rent" sign on a fence that surrounded a nice-looking house right around the corner from CPI headquarters. As I was peering over the fence, a man approached and asked me in good English if he could help. He was the owner of the house and said he was just about to complete renovating of the upper floor into an apartment; it would be ready in about a week. Would I like to take a look?

We went around to the back of the house and up the exterior stairs to the apartment. It was just what we were looking for—a clean, quiet, well-lighted, two-bedroom, one-bath unit with a pleasant backyard. And Piper would be welcome. The apartment was located directly above the living quarters of the landlord (Besim was his name) and his family, consisting of his wife, their three young daughters, and his elderly parents. I took photos of the apartment to show Kristina when I got back to Prizren. She liked what she saw, so I negotiated an oral rental agreement, and in late September we moved in. I did not quibble over the rent, which was cheap by American standards but high on the local market, since this was just what we were looking for and I wanted a happy landlord this time rather than a disgruntled one.

The day we moved in was a shocker. There was yellow police tape blocking off a couple of streets in the neighborhood, and we learned that an education official had been murdered in his office by an angry teacher, who had been denied a promotion. We wondered if such violence was a common occurrence, but a violent situation never occurred while we lived there.

Taking the apartment turned out to be an excellent choice. It was in an upscale neighborhood—at least by local standards—relatively quiet, convenient to the commercial area downtown, near several foreign embassies, close to several decent restaurants, and within a twenty-minute walk of the courthouse (or a five-minute drive). We got along well with Besim and his family and neighbors. I could also walk quickly to the CPI house around the corner to conduct business, socialize, pick up a video, or use the gym. As an added convenience, I was able to park my car in the secure CPI lot.

Our apartment was also close to the sprawling campus of the University of Pristina, which was a good place to walk Piper. There were always students crossing the campus on their way to class, or milling about on the green providing positive energy to the neighborhood. However, the National Library, located on campus, had the dubious distinction of being nominated as one of the ugliest buildings on the planet. Also on the campus was an unfinished, graffiti-covered Christian Orthodox Church, an unwelcome reminder of the Milosevic days. The future of the church is disputed to this day.

We were located just around the corner from the statue of Bill Clinton,

Dean and Kristina's apartment, top floor. Photo courtesy of the author.

on Bill Clinton Boulevard. Diagonally across the street from our apartment was a medical and dental clinic, where it was possible to just walk in and see a doctor or dentist. On one occasion, I had a bad cold and went to the clinic. I was immediately ushered in to see the doctor, who spoke limited English. She checked me out, determined that I had bronchitis, and prescribed medication. I left the clinic and walked back across the street, where I met one of our landlord's cousins on the sidewalk. She said, "I just heard you have bronchitis. I hope you feel better soon. The medication should help." So much for medical privacy.

After we'd been living in the apartment for a while, a café opened across the street. We learned that they offered delivery service to our door, so we had a standing order for two macchiatos and pastry every workday morning at 7:30. The pastries were fresh and the coffee arrived steaming hot. Unfortunately, the café eventually went out of business.

Kristina was able to land a job on the faculty of the American University in Pristina, which was under the auspices of the Rochester Institute of Technology. This was an elite, competitive university by local standards. The faculty was highly qualified and the students were hardworking and smart, a far cry from the University of Prizren.

National Library. Photo ©EULEX.

If there was a downside to our situation it was that the house and apartment were heated with lignite, a dirty brown form of coal. This was common throughout Pristina. Besim had a truckload of lignite delivered to the front of his house at the beginning of each heating season, which was then carted to the side of the house and shoveled into the basement through a hatch. The burner spewed tiny particles of lignite into the atmosphere which settled on everything nearby, such as cars and sidewalks. The ambient air throughout the city was polluted all winter, and it could be very unpleasant to venture outside, not to mention that this smog may have been the source of common respiratory illnesses.

Besim's father had been a high-ranking police officer before the war, but was now retired and living with no source of income. He and Besim's mother were completely dependent on their son. Besim's dad would often complain in Albanian, which Besim would translate, about how the Serbian government had stolen all of Kosovo's pension funds, thereby depriving him and his colleagues of a source of income during retirement. He and Besim would talk at length about the lost decade of the 1990s, when Serbia took complete control of Kosovo's institutions, causing the Albanian community, out of necessity, to develop parallel structures in order to preserve themselves, their languages, and their culture.

On my first workday in Pristina I had to pick up my dark blue VW Golf

from the motor pool, a few miles outside of the city center, having turned the
other car in before leaving Prizren. I arranged a ride to the motor pool with
the Supreme Court's driver. He dropped me off and left. However, my car
was not ready; it was filthy and the battery was dead. One of the motor pool
guys got the car running with jumper cables, and I headed off to a nearby
car wash. I pulled into one of the bays, turned off the engine, and waited
while the attendants washed the car. I then turned the key—and nothing
happened, the battery had died. Just then, another EULEX car pulled in to
the car wash, and the driver had cables, so we got my car running again.

Before returning to downtown Pristina, I had to stop at UN headquarters
on the outskirts of the city to do some paperwork. I pulled into the secure
parking lot, this time leaving the engine running. I was gone about twenty
minutes, and the car was still running upon my return. I headed back toward
the center of the city, confident that the battery was sufficiently charged.
But, as I approached a major intersection in the steep left-hand turn lane,
I managed to slip the clutch and the car jolted to a stop. The battery had
gone dead again. I was completely blocking the turn lane, and cars started
honking. I got out in my suit and tie, raised the hood, and threw up my
hands. A Good Samaritan stopped to help, but we couldn't get it started. The
horns continued to blare. In desperation I called the Supreme Court driver,
who arrived about fifteen minutes later, while angry drivers tried to negotiate
their way around me. He was able to start the car, and I thankfully drove off
to get a new battery. Welcome to Pristina.

Pristina, as noted earlier, was a gritty city of about 200,000, crawling with
internationals, swarming with EULEX vehicles, and full of contrasts. While
there were many modern amenities you would expect in any European city,
such as good restaurants, internet service, and an international airport, Pristina
could also be gray and dirty, with poor sanitation and undrinkable water,
poverty, unregulated urban sprawl, power and water outages, little downtown
green space, polluted air, and congested traffic. Nevertheless, I became quite
fond of Pristina after learning my way around, and we frequently dined out.
The waitstaff, if they knew we were Americans, were always happy to serve
us because we were better tippers than the Europeans, who merely "rounded
up."

Chapter 28

Pristina Courthouse

The courthouse was a large, old, dilapidated structure not yet renovated by USAID, even though it was the largest courthouse in the country and located in the capital. The EULEX judges, about six of us, and our legal officers, clerks, and staff, occupied a suite of drab offices on the third floor. The rest of the building was occupied by the local judges and their support personnel, and several courtrooms which we all shared.

During my first weeks in Pristina I shared a small, cramped office with one of the EULEX legal officers before moving to a larger office with another judge—a whip-smart young lawyer from Riga, Latvia, whom I would come to rely on heavily for both her legal research and her deep knowledge of Kosovo law and procedure.

When I first arrived at the courthouse, there were no Western toilets in the building, only "Turkish toilets," or squatter toilets—basically a hole in the floor—in unlocked restrooms. These were used by judges, court staff, litigants, and members of the public. As the day progressed, the toilets would become foul, creating a very unpleasant experience, not to mention a health hazard.

I mentioned this to my boss, the same Italian judge, who chuckled and said that when he'd worked in East Timor, he'd had to leave the courthouse and dash into the woods when nature called. He said he'd give me the keys to his nearby apartment when I needed to use the facilities. Another colleague said she timed her intake of liquids so she could make it until lunchtime, then rush to her apartment. In any event, I was advised of Rule Number One—always have my own supply of toilet tissue at the ready. I recalled the advice from my colleague in Prizren, to lower my expectations.

During the afternoon of my second day at the courthouse, nature called. I went to the restroom with the Turkish toilet, but it was filthy and I just couldn't bring myself to use it. I then remembered the coffee shop directly across the street from the courthouse. Maybe there was a restroom there with a Western toilet.

I dashed outside, crossed the street, and entered the establishment. There was a table of young local men toward the back, and I could sense their eyes upon me. I sauntered up to the bar and, attempting to appear casual, ordered a coffee. I then asked in English if there was a "toilet," a word everyone understood. The man pointed to the back of the place, just beyond the table where the young men were seated. I nodded to them as I passed. They returned the gesture. By now, the situation was beginning to get serious.

I opened the door and quickly looked around, noticing there was no toilet paper or any other suitable material for that purpose. Oh God, I'd forgotten Rule Number One (or was it really Rule Number Two?). I turned and walked quickly by the table where the young men now seemed to sense what was going on, passed the bar where my coffee was now waiting, indicated I'd be right back, and dashed to my office in the courthouse where I grabbed a handful of toilet paper. I then ran back across the street to the coffee shop, and went immediately into the restroom. The men were now chuckling as I passed.

Well, I made it. But wait—there was no seat on the toilet. So I suffered the minor indignity of sitting on the cold, uncomfortable rim. When I had completed the task, I pressed down on the flusher, but nothing happened. I tried several more times with the same result. I opened the door, and with a rising sense of embarrassment, called the barman over, and shrugged my shoulders meekly as he peered into the bowl. He curtly pointed to the sink, then grabbed a small bucket under the sink and gestured for me to fill the bucket and pour it into the toilet. I did so repeatedly as the young men nearby could no longer contain their laughter. Finally, the toilet functioned, and I was overcome with a great sense of relief in more ways than one. I then paid for my coffee and left the place.

Over the next few weeks, as a result of constant cajoling, I was finally able to get a locked restroom with a Western-style toilet installed on our floor of the courthouse, much to the delight and appreciation of my EULEX colleagues. This may be my lasting legacy in Kosovo: "Yes, I remember Judge Dean. Wasn't he the American who got the toilet installed?"

While smoking in public buildings was officially prohibited, no one in the courthouse paid the slightest attention to this rule. Members of the public would wander up and down the long hallways with cigarettes in hand, and it was not unusual to see local judges smoking outside their chambers while standing under a "No Smoking" sign.

Security was minimal in this courthouse. While there was a metal detector at the front entrance, members of the public could move freely about the building and go directly to a judge's office. The local judges conducted much of their business in their offices, and there was often a small crowd of litigants and lawyers in the hallways, awaiting their turn.

The security problem was not as acute in the EULEX suite of offices on the third floor, since it was somewhat removed from the beaten path. Nevertheless, prosecutors, defense attorneys, and an occasional litigant could show up in your office unannounced, wanting to talk about a case, often on an ex parte basis, which didn't seem to bother the other EULEX judges. (There was no code of ethics for EULEX judges despite my recommendation at a judges' meeting shortly after my arrival.) I tried to get a locked door installed in our corridor, but was not able to generate sufficient enthusiasm among my European colleagues.

During trials, which often involved prominent personalities with many supporters packed into the courtroom, we judges would have to enter the courtroom through the public entrance, then walk to the bench through the gathered masses on either side of a narrow aisle. There was no entrance or exit behind the bench. While there were usually heavily armed police officers in the courtroom, I was never quite sure whose side they would be on if all hell broke loose in a case involving a popular politician or war hero.

When entering and leaving the building, we would also have to use the public entrance, walking the gauntlet through throngs of people out on the street, and banks of TV cameras filming us and the defendants. Sometimes, after a tense courtroom session, we would not leave the building immediately, but would peer out a window and wait until the crowds and cameras dispersed before exiting.

Chapter 29

War Crimes Case of Fatmir Limaj

This was another war crimes case, with a surprising and shocking trajectory from beginning to end.

Soon after my arrival in Pristina, I was poking around in the court clerk's office in the EULEX suite when the president of the Assembly of Judges, the same Italian judge, entered the room and informed the clerk that one of the judges he had assigned to the war crimes case of Fatmir Limaj had decided to leave the mission and return to his home country. The case was scheduled to begin soon and he needed to find a replacement immediately. I piped up and said that I was available, since I didn't have a full caseload yet, and he agreed.

Fatmir Limaj was a charismatic leader in the KLA, having earned the nom de guerre "Commander Steel," and was now a very popular war hero. After the war he became a powerful politician and achieved several high governmental positions, including minister of transportation. He was prosecuted and acquitted in The Hague in 2005, but was subsequently indicted in Kosovo for similar but unrelated war crimes. The case unfolded as follows:

During the war in 1998–99, there was a detention facility in the village of Klecka which was operated by the KLA and allegedly under Limaj's command. The facility housed Serbian prisoners and suspected Kosovar Albanian collaborators. One of the KLA guards at the detention center was a man named Agim Zogaj, who kept a secret diary recording the comings and goings of all the prisoners and what happened to them.

For years after the war, Zogaj did not disclose this diary to anyone. However, in the mid-2000s, Zogaj came to believe that Limaj and his associates had somehow learned about the diary, which contained incriminating evidence, and Zogaj feared for his safety, which had been threatened on several occasions. He finally went to the Kosovo police in 2009, where he told his story in great detail and disclosed his diary. Subsequently, he told his story to the EULEX war crimes prosecutor, a flamboyant Italian who always dressed in bright pastel sport jackets.

Zogaj claimed that a number of Serbian prisoners and Kosovar Albanian collaborators from the detention center had been marched to a nearby field where they were summarily executed by KLA soldiers under Limaj's command, then buried. He said that one of the prisoners had been

Infamous diary of Agim Zogaj. Photo courtesy of BIRN.

killed with a blow to the neck from a scythe. Zogaj then led a EULEX forensics team to the scene, where they discovered the bodies, just as Zogaj said they would. One of the bodies displayed a wound to the neck consistent with a blow from a scythe, just as had Zogaj claimed. In addition, the scythe itself was recovered from the grave.

Limaj and nine other former KLA soldiers were then indicted for war crimes against civilians and prisoners of war, as prohibited by the Geneva Convention and Yugoslav law in effect at the time of the offenses. This caused a huge furor within Kosovo society because Limaj and the others were considered freedom fighters and war heroes. Zogaj was placed in the EULEX witness protection program and was thereafter known as "witness X."

As the case made its way toward trial, the EULEX prosecutor arranged for the defense attorneys representing Limaj and the other defendants to question Zogaj under oath, similar to a deposition. At the time of the questioning, the defense attorneys had in their possession all the statements Zogaj had previously given to the police and prosecutor.

The questioning took place over four days in July 2011. The attorneys questioned Zogaj for nineteen hours, asking him over one thousand questions. Limaj was represented by a prestigious British barrister (Queen's Counsel) from London, who asked a disproportionate share of the questions. Zogaj stuck to his story, his answers remaining consistent with the story he'd told the police and prosecutor.

It was curious how Limaj was able to afford a British barrister. Rumor had it that, as minister of transportation, he was able to shake down owners of various gas stations that were regulated by the ministry, but I was never able to confirm this rumor.

Shortly after the intense questioning sessions, the prosecutor filed an indictment against Limaj and the nine others for war crimes related to the conditions and treatment of prisoners at the Klecka detention center. (The case would be referred to as both the *Limaj* case and the *Klecka* case.) The indictment was then confirmed by a EULEX judge.

The trial was scheduled to begin in Pristina in early November 2011. The other international judge was from the UK, Jonathan Welford-Carroll, known as Judge Jonty, and was the presiding judge. He had considerable experience as a judge in Kosovo, including war crimes cases, and maintained excellent control in the courtroom. He also happened to be my office mate, and we were on friendly terms. The third member of the panel was a local Kosovo judge, who would have given anything not to be on a panel adjudicating war heroes.

Then, in late September 2011, just weeks before the trial was to begin, we received an urgent message from the witness protection program. Agim Zogaj, witness X, was found dead, hanging from a tree in a park in Duisberg, Germany, where he had gone to visit his brother. The German authorities had ruled the death a suicide.

Zogaj and his family had been under enormous pressure, not only because of the threatening reach of Limaj and his associates, but also because the prosecutor was depending on him to build the case against popular war heroes. Apparently, Zogaj decided that suicide was the only way to end the misery for himself and his family. Zogaj's widow was obviously distraught, and she and the rest of his family blamed the prosecutor and EULEX for his death.

His death was a human tragedy, but also represented a significant failure of the witness protection program. One might logically ask how the key prosecution witness in the most important case being tried at the time could have been allowed to travel to Germany unaccompanied and with no security plan while there. It remains a mystery to me, but it had a clear effect on the international community's view of EULEX's ability to protect sensitive witnesses.

This also presented a serious legal dilemma. We had to decide whether evidence from a dead man was admissible at trial or not. This is how the dilemma was described in the October 6, 2011, edition of the *New York Times*, under the headline, "Death of War Crimes Witness Casts Cloud on Kosovo":

> The death of a key witness in Germany in the war crimes trial of one of Kosovo's most powerful politicians has cast doubt on the effective prosecution of the case and threatens to derail local and international efforts to establish the rule of law here. Intimidation, fear, clan loyalties and a culture of silence have long impeded the development of a functioning justice system in Kosovo, analysts say, and the death is seen as a major setback.[57]

Under Kosovo and European law, the admissibility of Zogaj's evidence depended on whether the defense attorneys had had an "adequate and proper" opportunity to question him before he died. If Zogaj's statements and diary were admissible, then the trial would go forward. If not, Limaj and the others would have to be declared not guilty because the prosecutor could not prove the case without this evidence. Zogaj was the only person who could actually name names about what had happened in the field that fateful day, and who gave the orders.

We conducted lengthy hearings on this legal issue. The courtroom was packed with the defendants' supporters and heavily armed security officers, and the street outside was swarming with police officers wearing riot gear and carrying automatic rifles. Because of the high tension surrounding this case, which was palpable, and because our faces had been shown on TV and in newspapers, Judge Jonty and I were required to travel back and forth to the courthouse in an armored vehicle. I also had to have a bulletproof and bombproof door installed in our apartment, as well as metal security bars across the windows. So as not to bring unwanted attention to Besim and his family, I had the armored vehicle pick me up and drop me off each day around the corner, rather than right in front of the apartment.

The numerous defense attorneys raised many procedural arguments, all challenging the admissibility of witness X's evidence, but the essence of their position was that the questioning had been inadequate. Since the questioning had occurred before the trial, they claimed to have been denied the opportunity to develop additional lines of questioning that might arise as the trial unfolded. Their bottom line was that all the evidence provided by witness X must be ruled inadmissible.

After the hearings, the three of us on the trial panel discussed the matter in chambers, and Jonty and I discussed the matter ad nauseam when we were alone together in our office. He believed strongly that there were serious procedural violations and that the questioning had been inadequate, while I was not yet persuaded. His main position was that, even though witness X had been extensively questioned, he would never be put through the actual trial process where he could be cross-examined in light of the specific allegations in the indictment and the evidence admitted during the trial. He basically adopted the core of the defendants' argument. The local judge agreed with Jonty, likely an easy decision since she was extremely uncomfortable participating in the case.

This was the most significant case in Kosovo at the time, and it had garnered international attention, so I tried hard to agree with my colleagues. Obviously, a unanimous decision would be preferable to a split decision in a case of this magnitude. Indeed, I actually drafted a memo to myself in which I attempted to justify the inadmissibility of Zogaj's evidence, but I remained unconvinced.

I also conferred with Judge Tore, who had been transferred from Prizren to Pristina months earlier and had an office just down the hall. He was not comfortable discussing the substance of the matter, since he occasionally sat on the Supreme Court and might become involved in the case at some time in the future, but he was clearly aware that I was contemplating a dissenting opinion. His knowledge about my intentions would prove to be important, for reasons that I could not have anticipated at the time.

Ultimately, after much analysis and discussion, I concluded that Zogaj had been adequately questioned, that the other procedural arguments were unavailing, and that the trial should go forward. I then wrote a twenty-three-page dissenting opinion addressing every issue and outlining my reasoning in detail, signed on March 26, 2012.

My position was not that Limaj and the nine others were guilty, simply that Zogaj's evidence was admissible and that the case should proceed to trial, where all the evidence could be evaluated. I became quite confident that my position was correct, as it was amply supported by cases from the European Court of Human Rights that my talented legal officer from Slovenia had uncovered in her research.

Judge Jonty was not pleased with my position. Indeed, he did not believe that the criminal procedure code even authorized a dissenting opinion at the trial court level, but on this point I disagreed because of the relevant article of the criminal procedure code which referred specifically to "separate opinions." The code then provided that the record of decision-making and voting, which would include separate opinions, must be placed in a sealed envelope and examined only by a higher court during an appeal. Regardless of our disagreement on this issue, it really made no difference as to the ruling on admissibility, since I was outvoted 2–1 and Zogaj's evidence would not be admitted at trial.

After the announcement in open court that all of Zogaj's evidence would be inadmissible, the prosecutor decided there was no point in offering any other evidence since, without Zogaj's evidence, there could be no conviction.

The ten defendants were then acquitted in two separate court proceedings: six defendants on March 30, 2012; and four defendants, including Fatmir Limaj, on May 2, 2012. The proceedings were bifurcated because the six defendants were not alleged to have had command responsibility, whereas the other four were alleged to have had command responsibility, and the legal elements differed. In each proceeding, the courtroom was filled to the rafters with the defendants' supporters, while Judge Jonty read the verdicts of not guilty.

At no time did he mention my dissenting opinion, nor did I, having in mind the requirement that the decision-making and voting of the judges must be kept confidential except for a higher court. Indeed, in another high-profile case a local judge had been severely chastised after disclosing that he had dissented in a guilty verdict in a war crimes case. He made this public disclosure after receiving threats because of his presumed participation in the guilty verdict.

It's fair to say that several of the hearings became quite tense because the stakes were high. On one occasion, Limaj's attorney, the British QC, made an argument that I thought was demeaning to the court as he approached the bench from the back of the courtroom. I momentarily lost my judicial composure and angrily wagged my finger at him, a gesture I regret. (The QC is now the chief prosecutor at the International Criminal Court, and is actively gathering evidence of Russian war crimes in Ukraine.)

After the verdicts in each set of cases were announced orally in court, the defendants were jubilant, and were mobbed outside the courthouse by throngs of well-wishers and TV cameras. The prosecutor, on the other hand, was livid, and stated his intent to file an appeal with the Kosovo Supreme Court in both sets. Our legal officer was then tasked with drafting the detailed written decision and judgment order conforming to the oral verdicts issued in the courtroom, which had found all the defendants not guilty. This document then provided the basis for the prosecutor's appeals.

Limaj surrounded by jubilant supporters.
Photo courtesy of BIRN.

Shortly after the trial proceedings concluded, I was visiting CPI headquarters around the corner from my apartment when I ran into an American police officer who had been one of the investigators in these cases. He was angry about the acquittals and assumed I had participated in the verdict. I confided in him that I had issued a dissenting opinion. I also sent a copy of my opinion confidentially to the US Embassy. For the most part, I had nothing to do with the Embassy. This was intentional, since I did not want anyone to think I was somehow being influenced by high-level American officials who played an important role in Kosovo politics at the time. But in this case, given its notoriety, I wanted the Embassy to be aware of my opinion.

Several months later, I ran into Judge Tore in the hallway of our suite. He asked if I knew that the appeal was going to be heard by the Supreme Court in a few days. I did not. He also said the legal officer working on the case was not aware of my dissenting opinion; apparently it was not contained in the court's file, contrary to the requirements of the code. I contacted the legal officer and offered to email him a copy, which I did. I can only speculate as to why my opinion was not in the official court file. Was it lost, was it clerical error, or was it perhaps something more nefarious?

The Supreme Court issued its decision in the case involving Limaj and three others on November 20, 2012. The court overturned the acquittals, and in so doing adopted virtually all the arguments I had made in my dissenting opinion, even incorporating some of my reasoning verbatim. The Court then determined that all the evidence of witness X was admissible, and ordered a retrial before a different trial panel.

As described in EUbusiness, in an article dated November 21, 2012, "Kosovo Court Orders Retrial of Ex-Rebel for War Crimes,"

> (Pristina) – Kosovo's Supreme Court on Tuesday ordered a retrial against a top ethnic Albanian guerrilla commander–turned–politician, cleared in May of committing war crimes against Serb and Albanian civilians and war prisoners during the 1998-1999 conflict....
>
> The date for the retrial in the so-called "Klecka case," seen as one of the highest-profile war crimes cases in Kosovo, has yet to be set.[58]

This decision was not well received by Judge Jonty. He fired off some angry emails in which he opined that this was one of the worst decisions ever. But the Supreme Court likewise overturned the acquittals of the other six defendants in a separate decision, in December 2012, and also ordered a retrial.

The cases were then retried after I returned to the US, with another EULEX judge from the UK presiding. The verdicts were not guilty of all charges, issued in 2013. The panel determined there were serious credibility issues with Zogaj and his evidence, sufficient to create more than a reasonable doubt. The prosecutor appealed again, but the acquittals were ultimately affirmed in 2016.

Fatmir Limaj was again prosecuted in another war crimes case, and acquitted again by the trial court in 2018. He was also acquitted of corruption charges in a case arising out of his tenure as minister of transportation, in 2017. Mr. Limaj has spent a decade or more as a defendant in a series of high-profile criminal cases, but has not yet been convicted. Whether he ever will remains to be seen. All the while, he has remained active in politics, though his popularity has gradually decreased.

As I mentioned, Judge Jonty and I were required to take serious security precautions in this case, but this was not the only time I had to do so. At one point, I was assigned to a case in the divided city of Mitrovica, with Albanians living on the south side of the Ibar River and Serbians on the north side. The courthouse serving the city and region was located in the north and, as I described earlier, had been destroyed in the riots following Kosovo's declaration of independence in 2008. It was rebuilt with American funding and reopened in 2011.

That case lasted only a week or so, and was not particularly serious or notorious, but the security precautions were serious. I drove from Pristina to Mitrovica each day, about forty miles each way, to meet two other international judges and the court staff at the log base on the south side of the river. (Only international judges sat on trials in this court. Local judges in the north were of Serbian ethnicity and worked under a parallel legal structure; there was no agreement that Serbians could participate in EULEX trials.)

Upon arrival at the log base we would gather for a quick macchiato, then load ourselves and our gear—gas masks, helmets, bulletproof vests—into our armored van and make our way circuitously over the river and through winding back streets to the courthouse, hoping not to draw attention. At the courthouse we were met by several security officers and ushered inside with our gear. Except for our presence, and that of the lawyers and defendants, we were the only ones in the building, which was otherwise deserted and eerie. At the end of the court day, we would reverse the process and return to the log base. Fortunately, during this trial there were no security incidents.

The court administrator, a Serbian woman, said she felt like a stranger in Mitrovica, the city where she had grown up and where Albanians and Serbians had coexisted peacefully. It remains divided to this day, with ongoing ethnic hostility and occasional violent flare-ups, as I described earlier, but I'm led to believe there is considerable cross-river commercial activity.

Chapter 30

Wedding Crashers

Our landlord Besim was employed by EULEX as a warehouse worker. He was a university graduate and obviously underemployed, but EULEX paid well and there was nothing else available for him. We became quite friendly with his family, as well as with their relatives and friends, and were often invited to join them for backyard feasts including copious amounts of the local moonshine, *raki*, which from previous experience I knew to consume in only small quantities.

On one occasion, Kristina and I were invited to the wedding of Besim's nephew. This was a gala affair with over a hundred guests, and the men and women were all dressed in their finery. The women in particular were resplendent, with flowing gowns and elegant hairstyles. Weddings were major events in Kosovo society, and we were honored to be invited, as the only non-Kosovars in attendance.

Shortly after we arrived at the venue, the band started playing Albanian music at a typical ear-splitting level, which reminded us of the graduation parties in Prizren. Many of the guests immediately headed for the dance floor where they formed a large circle, holding hands with the persons on their right and left, and doing a basic two- or three-step routine as the circle went round and round. The dance was called *kolo*, which means "wheel."

The circle got larger as more and more people joined, and kept going round and round. Soon, someone motioned for Kristina and me to join the circle. I was a bit reluctant, but by this time I'd had a glass of wine or two and Kristina was game, so we joined in. The dance was fairly simple, and we caught on quickly. Around and around we went. Many of the local guests were impressed that the Americans had the courage to join the circle, and we were applauded for our efforts. It was great fun. The circle continued to rotate throughout the evening, as people went in and out.

We had one other wedding experience while living in Pristina. One Sunday we drove to the Serbian enclave of Gracanica, a few miles outside of Pristina, to visit the beautiful walled Orthodox monastery, where people went not only to see the monastery, but to buy pork products or eat at a restaurant that served pork, since pork was not readily available in Pristina because of Muslim food restrictions.

We passed through the main entrance into the lovely green courtyard where the church was located, and where a large crowd was gathering. It was a Serbian wedding party, and the bride and groom were greeting well-wishers before everyone entered the church for the ceremony. Waiters were circulating among the guests, handing out glasses of sparkling wine. Although we were not guests, we were moved by the spirit of the moment, and had no hesitation in joining the other celebrants and partaking of the wine. The 2005 movie *Wedding Crashers* came to mind.

Chapter 31

Insurance Scam

Before the war in 1998–99, Kole Puka worked as a lawyer in the town of Klina. He represented many people involved in car accidents who'd been injured or killed, and who had a claim against a particular Kosovo insurance company, either individually or through a surrogate. Many of these cases had been filed in court, but were unresolved at the time the war broke out. Because of the total upheaval in Kosovo society caused by the war, many accident victims or their survivors believed their claims were no longer valid, and they made no attempt to pursue them, or even to contact Puka.

After the war, Puka was appointed as a municipal judge in Klina. This gave him access to the court files of many of his former clients who had been injured or killed. He then concocted a very creative scheme of insurance fraud.

He created an official-looking dossier for each case, including the official stamp of the court, then submitted a claim to the insurance company, but without informing his former clients that he was doing so. There was a high-ranking employee in the insurance company, named Hilmi Hana, who was in cahoots with Puka. It was Hana's job to review all claims for compensation on behalf of the company, and approve or disapprove each one. He approved every claim that Puka submitted.

Years before, a co-defendant in the case, Zef Marleku, had opened a bank account, giving Puka access. The insurance company paid the awards into this account, supposedly in trust for the injured parties. Puka withdrew the money in cash and split it with Hana. The accident victims had no knowledge whatsoever of these compensation awards. The prosecutor claimed that Marleku was also in cahoots with Puka.

Over the course of several years, in the mid-2000s, the company paid out over 1.2 million euros in phony claims (about $1.6 million) on behalf of twenty-four accident victims or their families, an average of the equivalent of over $66,000 per claim, but completely without the victims' knowledge. Puka then laundered the money into expensive real estate, including a waterfront villa in neighboring Montenegro.

The case began to unravel when Hilmi Hana died and insurance inspectors became suspicious of all these transactions. A criminal investigation began in 2009, and the house of cards began to crumble. It was only during the investigation that the accident victims or their survivors learned of the compensation awards paid to Puka, and they were stunned, to say the least.

I was appointed as the presiding judge, along with a judge from Portugal, Judge Vitor, and a local judge. Because of the large number of victims and the financial complexity of the case, the trial was very time-consuming and taxing. We held twenty-seven court sessions, heard dozens of witnesses, and reviewed scores of financial documents; it was really twenty-four separate cases rolled into one. The evidence clearly showed that Puka had engaged in a massive insurance scam. He really had no defense, apart from a general denial. We found him guilty of fraud, money laundering, and other lesser charges, and imposed a lengthy prison sentence.

Marleku, on the other hand, put up a vigorous defense. Even though the bank account was in his name, he claimed he had absolutely no knowledge of Puka's use of the account or the large amounts of money going in and out. While his claim of ignorance seemed absurd on its face (who would believe that?), he presented a considerable amount of evidence, such as bank records and testimony from bank personnel, to support his defense. In effect, the account had lapsed for him; while it existed, he never used it or even inquired about it. The evidence also showed that he had no ongoing relationship with Puka, and did not benefit in any way from Puka's scam. His evidence was sufficient to establish a reasonable doubt, and we found him not guilty.

I announced the verdict in open court, then followed up with a lengthy written decision which analyzed each of the twenty-four cases. We referred the matter to civil court to unravel the money trail and provide restitution for the victims to the extent possible, as required by the procedure code. As it turned out, Puka had other criminal cases in progress. It is my understanding that the sentences in those cases were ultimately consolidated with our sentence, and to the best of my knowledge our case was never appealed.

Years later, in May 2018, Kristina and I took a vacation to Spain and Portugal. I had long since fallen out of contact with Judge Vitor, the Portuguese judge with whom I had been very friendly. Through a mutual American friend I was put in touch with another Portuguese judge, Jose Manuel, who had worked in Kosovo after I left. He and I exchanged emails and agreed to meet at our hotel in Lisbon.

At the appointed time, Kristina and I were in the hotel lobby awaiting his arrival. The door swung open, and in he walked. Trailing behind him was none other than my old friend Vitor. As it turned out, Jose Manuel knew Vitor, and knew we'd been friends in Kosovo, so he surreptitiously arranged the rendezvous. Indeed, this was a complete surprise and we greeted each other warmly. Vitor then presented me with a bottle of Portuguese wine, labeled "Bom Juiz, vino tinto Reserva 1999." *Bom juiz* is Portuguese for "good judge." The four of us had an enjoyable lunch at a local restaurant, then a tour of Lisbon and the spectacular Atlantic coast. Kristina and I drank the wine after carrying it back to the US, but I still have the bottle with its catchy label and fond memories.

Chapter 32

Plea Agreement in an International Drug Trafficking Case

This case, known as the *Fortuna* case, is the only one during my tenure in Kosovo where I was able to resolve the case with a plea agreement and pleas of guilty. The case had been tried earlier, and the defendants found guilty by a different EULEX panel, but the Supreme Court reversed the convictions and sent the case back for retrial. At the retrial, I was the presiding judge along with a German judge and a local Kosovar judge.

At the time of the retrial, the defendants had already served nearly three years in prison as a result of their original convictions for international drug trafficking. The sentences in the first trial had been unusually harsh by European standards, mid-teens if I recall correctly, and called for many more years of incarceration. I had learned from experience that sentences in Kosovo and Europe in general were considerably less than in the US, and the sentences in this case were definitely outliers.

The defendants and their lawyers were anxious to avoid another full-blown trial, with all its uncertainty, fearing they might receive equally harsh sentences if convicted again. The defendants were willing to enter guilty pleas in return for reduced sentences, and the prosecutor was also amenable to a plea deal, agreeing that the original sentences had been unduly severe.

I was willing to consider a plea agreement with the prosecution and defense, but my two colleagues had to be convinced. Although the criminal procedure code permitted plea agreements, the concept was novel to my colleagues, who were familiar only with a full trial, which was the norm in Kosovo and most of Europe.

I had to painstakingly walk them through the process, explaining that an agreement could resolve the case much more efficiently and serve the interest of justice as well. The three of us on the panel held several conferences with the prosecutor and defense attorneys to hash out the details. We ultimately reached an agreement that was acceptable to the prosecutor, the defendants, their attorneys, and to us on the court. The defendants would plead guilty to the trafficking charges in return for reduced sentences based on the following factual scenario to which the defendants admitted.

The investigation in this case began in 2008, and focused on Adbyl Kukaj and Xhemë Thaqi, who were believed to be involved in an international drug ring transporting heroin from Albania through Kosovo and onward to Western Europe. The evidence against them consisted primarily of lawful police intercepts of phone calls and text messages over time, between the two defendants themselves and with their criminal associates.

On September 1, 2009, Thaqi spoke by phone from Kosovo to one of the co-conspirators in Albania about a planned shipment of heroin from Albania to Kosovo, and discussed remuneration to be paid to a courier who would actually move the drugs into Kosovo. From these conversations, it was apparent that the final destination of the narcotics was Switzerland.

On September 2, Thaqi traveled to Albania to work out the details of the shipment. While there, he instructed Kukaj, who remained in Kosovo, to prepare to receive the shipment in the following days and to make arrangements to immediately forward the shipment onward from Kosovo by a second courier. Kukaj then hired the second courier, as instructed.

On the evening of September 4, Thaqi met the first courier, who had been successful in transporting the drugs from Albania into Kosovo, using a van with Albanian plates. It was agreed that the actual delivery of the drugs to the second courier would be made the following morning.

The next morning, September 5, the first courier arrived at the agreed location and handed over the van to the second courier arranged by Kukaj. The police were aware of this arrangement through their intercepts, and were prepared to intervene. As the second courier was driving away, followed by a police surveillance team which was trailing the van at a safe distance, the courier stopped by the side of the road on a sweeping curve.

Because of the curve and the height of the corn in the adjacent field, the surveillance team could not immediately see the van coming to a stop.

The van was met by a Golf vehicle, and the Albanian license plate on the van was quickly changed to a German plate. The surveillance team came around the bend and observed what was happening. They drove by the van and Golf, in order not to disclose their activity, and stopped several hundred yards down the road, out of sight. They were unable to record the German plate, except for the first two letters.

By this time, the courier had become suspicious and threw the drugs away, into the cornfield, which was not seen by the surveillance team. The van and the Golf then sped away in separate directions. The police subsequently caught the van and conducted a search, but to their surprise they found no drugs.

Within minutes of this situation, Thaqi, who was on his way to Macedonia with his girlfriend, spoke to his Albanian contact by phone. The content of their coded conversation indicated that the surveillance operation had been discovered and that the drugs had been thrown into the cornfield. Thaqi was then involved in coordinating the successful recovery of the drugs from the cornfield, as confirmed by several conversations intercepted later that day. Through other intercepted conversations in the following days, it was established that the narcotics were successfully transported to Switzerland.

Based on this agreed-upon factual scenario, the defendants then entered their pleas of guilty to drug trafficking on March 18, 2013. Thaqi, who bore more criminal responsibility than Kukaj, who'd only arranged for a courier, was then sentenced to five years in prison, with credit for time served since May 27, 2010. He would remain incarcerated for nearly two more years. Kukaj was sentenced to three years, with credit for time served since May 27, 2010. He was released from incarceration in about two months. The parties and the court were satisfied with this outcome.

Chapter 33

Small World Story

Every so often, Kristina and I felt the need to leave the chaos and stress of Pristina and Kosovo and escape to some other venue. As I mentioned, the international airport had flights to various locations in Western Europe on Friday afternoons, with return flights on Sunday afternoons. This enabled us (and many others) to get away for a short change of scenery, or for the Europeans to go home, without using any annual leave. So, over the course of two years, we took several weekend trips to European cities like Vienna, Munich, Prague, Zurich, and Budapest. We had an excellent sitter for our dog Piper when we were out of town.

We also took occasional weekend trips in one of CPI's SUVs to various places in the Balkans and surrounding areas which could be reached in several hours' driving time, like Macedonia, Montenegro, Croatia, Bulgaria, and northern Greece. We were particularly fond of Macedonia, and we could reach the capital, Skopje, within about two hours.

At the time, Greece and Macedonia were in a dispute about Macedonia's use of the name "Macedonia," which Greece claimed exclusively for itself. This dispute was keeping Macedonia from becoming a member of NATO. The Macedonians did not take the dispute lying down. At the jaw-dropping main square in Skopje were many unusual statues, including a huge statue of Alexander the Great. Both countries claimed Alexander as their own, with Macedonia exhibiting the statue as a striking symbol of their defiance. The countries eventually settled the dispute, with Macedonia's agreement to rename itself North Macedonia.

The story I am about to tell occurred during a week-long leave we took to Jordan. We booked the trip, which included a guide named Samir, through a travel agency. He would meet us at the airport in Amman and show us around the country from top to bottom, then leave us for three days of R & R at a hotel in Aqaba, at the tip of the Gulf of Aqaba, where Jordan, Israel, and Egypt meet.

Our itinerary called for a flight from Pristina to Istanbul (where we'd been a couple of times before, so were just passing through), then a flight to Amman on Royal Jordanian Airlines. We arrived in Istanbul on time after an uneventful flight, and checked our bags. We had time to kill, so we enjoyed some Turkish coffee and wandered around the many shops in the airport.

According to my watch we still had time before heading to the gate. I then happened to glance at a clock on the wall and, to my horror, the time was one hour ahead—our plane was scheduled to depart in a matter of minutes. I had forgotten that there was a time change between Pristina and Istanbul.

I darted ahead toward the gate as fast I could, with Kristina following. As I approached the gate, the door to the passageway onto to the plane was slowly closing. I pleaded with the ticket taker to please see if she could arrange for us to board the plane, but she said once the door was closed that was it, no exceptions, captain's orders. Well, now what? We returned to the check-in counter and were able to rebook the flight for several hours hence, but were unable to contact the travel company to notify Samir of our delay. When we finally landed in Amman, Samir was there, and had been waiting for hours.

From there, everything went smoothly. Over the next few days we saw all the spectacular sights of Jordan, including Wadi Rum desert and the mind-boggling stone carvings of Petra, where I rode a donkey named Suzy up a treacherously steep and narrow path to the monastery, thousands of feet above ground level. If Suzy had missed a step, we would have cascaded to the floor below with no way to stop. I gained great respect for donkeys.

After our R & R in Aqaba, we were picked up by Samir for our drive back to Amman for our flight to Istanbul. After loading our bags and getting in the car, he asked if we would mind giving a ride to one of his wife's relatives, who was also going to the airport. Samir's wife was Palestinian, as was her relative. We said we'd be delighted to have him come along, and we picked him up a short time later.

We peppered him with questions. He was living in Israel and working on a development project in Gaza. He was fluent in English and we had a fascinating conversation. He asked the type of questions you would expect, starting with where were we from? We said we were from America, which was obvious to him, and from Vermont, a very small state he'd probably never heard of. He paused for a moment, then said, "Oh, I've heard of Vermont." He went on to say that he'd actually worked with someone from Vermont several years earlier, in his project in Gaza. We said that was pretty remarkable, and pressed him for details.

Do you remember his name? we asked. He did not immediately recall, but after thinking for a few moments said, "Yes, I think I can remember his name. It was Ron Crisman, who was working in some sort of financial capacity." At this point, I thought Kristina was about to go into shock.

When we first moved to Vermont in 1973, Kristina was unable to get a job right off as a teacher—her profession—so she began searching for temporary work. The state budget department, headed by Crisman, was looking for people to conduct a survey of other state departments to determine their needs for computerization. Kristina was interviewed for the job by Ron, and hired, even though she had absolutely no expertise in this field. He was her boss, and they eventually became friendly. Until hearing his name in the car in Jordan, she had not thought about him for years. A small world, indeed!

Chapter 34

Human Organ Trafficking

In July 1999, shortly after NATO's intervention brought an end to the war, and while chaos and lawlessness engulfed Kosovo, an American investigative journalist named Michael Montgomery, who was a Balkans correspondent for London's *Daily Telegraph*, returned to Kosovo to produce a radio documentary about a purported Serbian massacre of Kosovo civilians in the town of Cuska.

Montgomery had heard from various sources that the Kosovo Liberation Army had also engaged in atrocities, as he explained at a conference in Belgrade on September 4, 2015. A subsequent article in *Balkan Insight*, with the headline "Kosovo Organ Trafficking: How the Claims Were Exposed," quoted Montgomery as follows:

> At that time [1999] we heard that there were people – Serbs, Roma, some Kosovo Albanians – killed by the Kosovo Liberation Army, and they simply vanished and it was very strange and we started looking into that. . . .
>
> And because of our work in Cuska, we got very good sources on the Kosovo Albanian side and we started talking with low levels of the KLA and they started telling us these stories of captured civilians being moved across the border to Albania.
>
> We had multiple sources but not everything lined up. We had people who heard that people have been taken away for their kidneys. There were a couple of houses we were able to locate where these things allegedly happened, but we decided

we didn't have enough information to publish and that at the
time our evidence didn't support the allegations.[59]

Then, in 2004, Montgomery traveled to Albania, this time with a team of
investigators from both UNMIK (United Nations Mission in Kosovo) and
the ICTY, to investigate claims of organ extractions. They went to what has
become known infamously as the "yellow house," where they discovered
various medical paraphernalia in an outside trash heap—pieces of gauze, a
used syringe, and empty intravenous drip bags—and splatters of blood on
the floor of the house that could not be credibly explained by the owner.

While the evidence recovered could have been related to organ extractions,
it was deemed insufficient to warrant criminal charges. The investigation
was dropped and, inexplicably, the evidence was later destroyed at the
ICTY.

Several years later, in 2008, a book was published in Italian by Carla
Del Ponte, who had been the chief prosecutor at the ICTY from 1999
to 2007. The English version of the book (2009) was titled, *Madame
Prosecutor: Confrontations with Humanity's Worst Criminals and the Culture
of Impunity*.[60] Del Ponte made explosive allegations based on numerous
reports of horrific crimes committed by the Kosovo Liberation Army:
abductions, torture, murder, and the disappearance of hundreds of
Serbian soldiers, collaborators, and various ethnic minorities during and
immediately after the war, from 1998 to 2000.

She also referred to credible reports that between one hundred and three
hundred abducted persons had been trucked across the Kosovo border
into northern Albania where, at a yellow house, they'd had their organs
extracted for shipment into the illegal international market.

It is reasonable to ask why Del Ponte did not prosecute these cases
during her tenure as chief prosecutor at the ICTY. According to her, there
were insurmountable problems obtaining hard evidence and witnesses
willing to testify. There was also difficulty pinpointing precise dates, which
was critical since, as noted earlier, the ICTY did not have jurisdiction over
cases that occurred after the war ended on June 11, 1999, nor did it have
jurisdiction over countries that were not part of the former Yugoslavia,
such as Albania.

In any event, Del Ponte's shocking allegations, particularly those concerning organ trafficking, received worldwide publicity and condemnation. The *Guardian* ran an article in its online edition on April 8, 2008, with this headline: "Former War Crimes Prosecutor Alleges Kosovan Army Harvested Organs from Serb Prisoners."[61] Radio Free Europe ran a story on April 23, 2008, entitled, "Balkans: Allegations of Organ Trafficking in Del Ponte Memoir Spark Scandal."[62]

At the conference in Belgrade in 2015, Montgomery offered his opinion regarding Del Ponte's motives: "I think she put information in the book because she wanted to spark an investigation, and it did."[63] Indeed, Del Ponte's allegations, though widely derided in Kosovo, led the Parliamentary Assembly of the Council of Europe to commission one of its members, Senator Dick Marty from Switzerland, to conduct a thorough investigation into Del Ponte's claims. Marty and his team conducted the investigation and produced a dense twenty-seven-page report in December 2010, titled, "Inhuman Treatment of People and Illicit Trafficking in Human Organs in Kosovo."[64] If Del Ponte's allegations were explosive, Marty's claims were more so, because of the level of detail and the naming of names of high-level KLA veterans.

Marty claimed that he'd found evidence corroborating Del Ponte's allegations of murder, torture, organized crime, and forced disappearances of hundreds of Serbs and Albanian collaborators, and also of trafficking in human organs, all perpetrated primarily by what was known as the Drenica Group of KLA guerrillas, with then–Prime Minister Hashim Thaçi identified as the ring leader (Drenica being the birthplace of the KLA). Specifically with regard to organ trafficking, he said in paragraph 156:

> The last and most conspicuous subset of captives in the post-conflict period, not least because its fate has been greatly sensationalized and widely misunderstood, comprises the captives we regard as having been the "victims of organized crime." Among this subset are a handful of persons whom we found were taken into central Albania to be murdered immediately before having their kidneys removed in a makeshift operating clinic.[65]

During the same period of time, 2008–10, an investigation was underway in Kosovo by EULEX of claims that illegal kidney transplants were taking place at a medical facility named the Medicus Clinic, just outside the capital, Pristina, in 2008. Initially, there was no discernible connection between this case and the organ trafficking which purportedly had occurred years earlier, during war time and shortly thereafter.

However, Marty made this startling claim in paragraph 168:

> . . . we found a number of credible, convergent indications that the organ trafficking . . . described in our report is closely related to the contemporary case of the Medicus Clinic . . . However, out of respect for the ongoing investigations and judicial proceedings being led by EULEX . . ., we feel obligated at this moment to refrain from publishing our findings in this regard. Suffice to say, we encourage all countries . . . to do their utmost to halt this shameful activity and assist in bringing its [perpetrators] and co-conspirators to justice."[66]

Marty's report, because of its specificity, its discussion of organ trafficking, and the purported connection to the Medicus Clinic, as well as its identification of prominent perpetrators by name, sent shock waves throughout Kosovo and around the world, and was covered extensively by international media. The *Guardian,* on December 4, 2010, ran a story, "Kosovo PM is Head of Human Organ and Arms Ring, Council of Europe Reports," with a subhead stating that a "two-year inquiry accuses Albanian 'mafia-like' crime network of killing Serb prisoners for their kidneys."[67]

The report, like Del Ponte's allegations, was widely denounced in Kosovo as false and biased against the KLA liberators. Despite the strong denials in Kosovo, Marty's report was officially adopted in a formal resolution by the Council of Europe (CoE) in January 2011.

The resolution, which summarizes the findings of Sen. Marty in three and a half pages, mentions organ trafficking no fewer than eight times. And it implores EULEX to undertake a full-scale criminal investigation into all of the horrific criminal behavior detailed in the report, including organ trafficking.

EULEX responded, and in September 2011 commissioned a full-scale criminal investigation, to be headed by an American, Clint Williamson, who was appointed that October. He was an experienced war crimes prosecutor and the former US War Crimes Ambassador at Large. This investigation was headquartered in Brussels and formally named the Special Investigative Task Force, or SITF. Its mandate was as follows:

> [T]o investigate and, if warranted, prosecute individuals for crimes alleged in the CoE report. In addition to the much-publicized allegations of organ harvesting, the SITF will examine possible unlawful detention, deportation, inhumane acts, torture and killings, as well as any other crimes, related to the allegations contained in the report.[68]

I met with Williamson at the CPI facility in Pristina as both the SITF investigation and the *Medicus* trial were getting underway. We'd agreed to share information to the extent ethically permitted, but the occasion never arose. The SITF report would not be issued until nearly three years later, in July 2014, well after the conclusion of the *Medicus* trial.

Chapter 35

Medicus Case

B
eginning at roughly the same time as the allegations by Del Ponte were first disclosed, the case involving the Medicus Clinic unfolded in Kosovo.

Medicus clinic. Photo courtesy of BIRN.

On November 4, 2008, a young Turkish man named Yilmaz Altun collapsed at the Pristina Airport in Kosovo prior to boarding a flight to Istanbul. He was with another man, later identified as Moshe Harel, an Israeli national. Altun was examined by a doctor who observed a fresh wound on his abdomen. Altun said through an interpreter that he'd had a kidney removed at a medical clinic called Medicus, just outside of Pristina, and that the recipient of the kidney might still be at the clinic.

This incident set in motion a series of events leading to one of the longest running and most notorious criminal cases in the history of Kosovo. Little did I know, when I arrived in Kosovo in February 2011, that I would become deeply immersed in this case and in the netherworld of illegal organ trafficking for a substantial part of my time in Pristina.

It turned out that customs officials at the airport had been suspicious for some time because of the number of people coming into the country on their way to the Medicus Clinic. The police were notified of the incident at the airport and went immediately to the clinic to investigate the possibility of illegal kidney trafficking. In Kosovo, kidney transplants were only allowed between relatives, and this did not appear to be such a case.

At the clinic, they discovered an elderly Israeli man still recovering from a kidney transplant. He was obviously not a relative of the young Turkish man. The police then conducted a thorough search of the clinic over several days, seizing medications, voluminous medical documents, and other evidence for review by forensic experts. They did not obtain a warrant prior to the search. Accompanying the police as they conducted their search were representatives of the health inspectorate, who had authority to inspect health facilities.

Based on a lengthy follow-up investigation involving many foreign countries, the experienced and dogged EULEX prosecutor from Canada, Jonathan Ratel, filed an indictment in late 2010, long after the incident at the airport, against seven individuals, alleging

EULEX prosecutor Jonathan Ratel.
Photo courtesy of BIRN.

trafficking in human organs, organized crime, and other serious offenses.

Some of the delay can be attributed to the sloppy handover of cases to EULEX by UNMIK. Indeed, Sen. Marty said in his report, paragraph 12:

> The EULEX mission, operational since the end of 2008, thus inherited an extremely difficult situation. Numerous files on war crimes, notably those in which KLA combatants were listed as

suspects, were turned over by UNMIK in deplorable condition (mislaid evidence and witness statements, long time lapses in following up on incomplete investigative steps), that EULEX officials stated their fears . . . that many files would simply have to be abandoned.[69]

In any event, the indictment alleged that dozens of illegal kidney transplants had occurred at the clinic during 2008. The defendants included Lutfi Dervishi, a prominent urologist who worked at Pristina Hospital and owned the Medicus Clinic, and his son Arban Dervishi, a university graduate who managed the clinic. Also indicted were chief anesthesiologist Sokol Hajdini, and two of his assistants at the clinic, as well as two high-ranking government officials.

Defendant Lutfi Dervishi.
Photo courtesy of BIRN.

In early 2011, a EULEX judge was appointed as the confirmation judge and tasked with reviewing the indictment for factual and legal sufficiency. He determined that the search of the clinic by police had been illegal in the absence of a proper warrant, and that the evidence from the search was inadmissible at trial. His decision was reversed by a three-judge appellate panel and the case scheduled for trial later in 2011. The case, known as the *Medicus* case, gained international attention.

The actual trial began in October 2011. I was appointed as a member of the three-judge panel along with Judge Arek, an experienced and competent Polish judge who was presiding, and a local Kosovo judge. The trial extended off and on for nineteen months, with many delays, and included over seventy witnesses and thousands of pages of documents. What unfolded was an extraordinary tale of a well-organized, well-funded international conspiracy to traffic in human kidneys for profit.

The trial got off to a rocky start. One of the defense attorneys got into a heated argument with Judge Arek in open court on some minor procedural issue during our first session. He was shouting at the top of his lungs, creating an undignified courtroom scene. At the beginning of our next session, I made a statement for the record to the effect that this sort of outburst was an affront to the dignity of the court and should never happen again, and it did not.

As our first order of business, we had to address a motion filed by one of the defense attorneys to disqualify the presiding judge, not because of the outburst but because he had served for a brief period, months before, as a pretrial judge in this same case, and had issued a routine order extending the investigation. Under the procedure code, as discussed earlier, a pretrial judge was not supposed to serve on the trial panel in the same case.

The code required that this motion be referred to the president of the Assembly of EULEX Judges, who was also an *ex officio* member of the Supreme Court, for a ruling. The president was unavailable, so the motion was then referred to the vice president, who also sat on the Supreme Court. At the time, this position was occupied by the only other American judge in Kosovo, Charles Smith, whom I referred to earlier. He ruled that Judge Arek had in fact acted for a brief period as a pretrial judge in this case, but that his action was perfunctory and did not constitute any evidence of bias. He declined to disqualify the judge, and the trial continued. I agreed completely with this ruling, but it would come back to haunt us.

As the trial resumed, we then had to address a motion filed on behalf of Lutfi Dervishi, the lead defendant, to declare the search of the Medicus Clinic illegal because the police and the prosecutor at the scene did not obtain a search warrant from a judge, either in writing or verbally. If the search was illegal, then all of the evidence obtained during the search could be inadmissible at trial, and if so the case would probably have to be dismissed.

Dervishi was represented by the only American lawyer actually admitted to practice law in Kosovo. This motion was a reprise of the issue addressed months earlier by the confirmation judge and appellate panel, but the procedure code allowed the issue to be raised again at the trial. We heard many witnesses on this subject, both from the police and from the health inspectorate. We determined that there was no excuse by the police and prosecutor for not getting a warrant, since they had ample time to do so and no valid reason not to do so. Therefore, the police search was illegal.

We also carefully scrutinized the testimony of the health inspectors and their statutory authority, and determined that they had an independent legal basis to search health facilities without a search warrant. They'd accompanied the police every step of the way, and participated in the collection of all of the medical evidence.

Based on this separate, independent authority, we upheld the validity of the inspectors' search and determined that all of the evidence was admissible in the trial. I must say, however, that the three of us on the trial panel were never completely satisfied with our own decision on this point, since the health inspectors, even though they had broad authority, served a health function and not a law enforcement function. In any event, after issuing our ruling on this issue, we turned our attention to substantive allegations of organ trafficking.

The excellent prosecutor, Ratel, who devoted an enormous amount of time to preparing the case for trial, had been and continued to be in contact with many foreign governments through diplomatic channels in search of evidence and witnesses. This included Turkey, Israel, Germany, Poland, Switzerland, Belarus, Russia, Moldova, Ukraine, Kazakhstan, Canada, Israel, Serbia, and the US. Some countries cooperated quickly; some cooperated slowly and needed prompting; some, including Russia and Moldova, did not cooperate at all. We did hear testimony from witnesses from several of these cooperating countries, either in person or by video link, all of which had to be translated from the witnesses' mother tongue—whether Turkish, Hebrew, Polish, Russian, or some other language—into English and Albanian. The courtroom was poorly equipped to accommodate our need for sophisticated technology, and much time was wasted trying to get the video equipment to function properly.

The trial panel was also in formal diplomatic contact with the Council of Europe in an effort to arrange for Dick Marty to testify in the trial, since supposedly he had important information about the *Medicus* case, as he'd stated in his report. Our intent to call Marty became internationally newsworthy.

As reported online in EUbusiness, in an undated article titled, "European Envoy to Testify in Kosovo Organ Case":

> Judges in a landmark trial of alleged organ trafficking in a Pristina clinic will call Council of Europe envoy Dick Marty as a witness, they said Wednesday.
>
> In his report on wartime abuses Marty alleged that senior

commanders of the ethnic Albanian guerrilla Kosovo Liberation Army (KLA), including current prime minister Hashim Thaçi, had been involved in organized crime and organ trafficking during and after the war.[70]

We assumed, of course, that Marty would eagerly testify in the case. To our shock and anger, the Council refused to permit him to do so, saying that he was legally immune from testifying. His home country, Switzerland, agreed. Here's how I expressed our opinion on this issue in our final written judgment:

> There is an obvious and significant discrepancy between the declarations in Mr. Marty's report and the ensuing resolution by the Parliamentary Assembly, both of which made lofty statements about truth, accountability, cooperation and the shameful nature of illicit organ trafficking . . . and the formalistic position now taken by the Council. When given the opportunity to assist in the truth seeking function in a real life, ongoing trial alleging such trafficking, Mr. Marty and the Council of Europe quickly retreated behind the cloak of immunity.[71]

Perhaps the Council of Europe did not want to jeopardize Marty's sources of information in the *Medicus* trial while the SITF investigation was underway. Perhaps he feared for his safety in Kosovo. Or perhaps, as many people in Kosovo believed, his evidence was simply weak or nonexistent.

Regardless, here's how the conspiracy worked: Advertisements were placed in Russian-language newspapers and on the internet in countries such as Ukraine, Kazakhstan, Belarus, and Israel, soliciting financially vulnerable people to donate their kidneys for money. Those who responded to a local contact in their home country generally had heartbreaking stories of financial misery, such as insufficient funds to feed their families or for necessary medical treatment. They were told that a kidney extraction was a simple, low-risk procedure, and were promised payment usually in the equivalent of $10,000 to $20,000.

Those who expressed interest were given a medical exam locally to determine their suitability for donating a kidney. If medically acceptable, they were then flown to Istanbul, where they met with Moshe Harel, the Israeli national, who was alleged to be the chief facilitator, or fixer, for the conspiracy. After further medical tests, acceptable donors then flew on to Kosovo for transplant surgery at the Medicus Clinic, which was well-equipped for organ transplants. They were given a letter of introduction from the clinic saying that they were traveling to Kosovo for cardiology treatment, which would facilitate their entry into the country.

At the same time, potential kidney recipients were being recruited in the US, Canada, Poland, Israel, and elsewhere. These people were suffering from serious kidney failure, and were willing to pay upwards of $100,000 for a kidney. They were also flown to Istanbul for medical tests on their way to Kosovo. This was obviously a very lucrative enterprise. We tried to follow the money trail, which ultimately took us to Switzerland, but the Swiss authorities refused to cooperate and we were never able to locate the proceeds, which amounted to hundreds of thousands of euros.

A key player in the conspiracy was a skillful Turkish transplant surgeon named Yusef Sonmez, known in the Turkish press as Dr. Frankenstein. He had conducted over two thousand kidney transplants around the world, many of which were allegedly illegal. He had formed a partnership with the Kosovo urologist Lutfi Dervishi to perform transplant surgeries at the Medicus Clinic, and was the lead surgeon for such operations. They had met at a transplant conference in Istanbul a couple of years earlier.

Both Moshe Harel and Yusef Sonmez were also indicted in Kosovo, but unfortunately could not be extradited for trial. Moshe Harel was present in Kosovo when the events first unfolded, but then fled the country. He was arrested in Cyprus in December 2017, on a Russian arrest warrant, and held in custody until March 2019, when he was released following the Cyprus court's denial of the extradition request. The present whereabouts of Sonmez and Harel are unknown, at least to me.

The evidence at trial showed that approximately twenty-three illegal kidney transplants were conducted at the clinic during an eight-month period in 2008, involving forty-six individuals, half donors and half recipients. Seven of these transplants were proven by direct testimony from the donors and recipients during the trial; the others were proven by circumstantial evidence such as flight manifests, countries of origin, and medical documents, even though the donors and recipients did not testify at the trial.

The kidney donors had been exploited in many different ways, and "exploitation" was an essential element of the crime of trafficking. They were taken advantage of because they were financially vulnerable; didn't speak Albanian, English, or Turkish; were all alone in Kosovo, far from their home countries; were never properly informed about the risks of kidney surgery; had never provided informed consent; had been led to believe that kidney transplants were legal in Kosovo; and had no one to protect their best interests.

Upon arrival at the clinic, donors were required to quickly sign bogus documents stating that they had appeared before a phony, nonexistent ethics committee, and that they were donating their kidney to a relative for humanitarian purposes, which was blatantly false in all cases. Some donors had severe second thoughts at the clinic but were given no chance to back out; they were promptly wheeled into surgery and their kidneys were removed. After surgery, some donors received less money than they had been promised, and in several cases, no money at all. Moreover, some suffered recurring health problems once back in their home countries.

The donors were all victims of this conspiracy, and considered themselves as such. Several of the recipients, on the other hand, viewed the donors as life-saving humanitarians without whom they would now be dead. This may be true, but the recipients were able to receive new kidneys only because of their wealth, and had no regard for the fact that the donors were being exploited.

The defendants presented several defenses. First, they argued that the clinic was legally authorized to perform transplant surgeries. This argument was based on a letter dated May 12, 2008, from Ilir Rrecaj, the head of the ministry of health and one of the defendants, and addressed to the Medicus Clinic in response to an inquiry from the clinic about the possibility of conducting transplants. The letter, which received a great deal of attention during the trial, was couched in hypothetical terms: If at some point in the future the law is changed to authorize transplants, then the clinic is adequately equipped to do so.

We concluded that the letter could not be read as a current authorization, either grammatically or substantively, and rejected this argument. Moreover, even if the letter could reasonably be construed to authorize current transplants, it would not be a defense to trafficking, which was based on exploiting the donors. In other words, whether the clinic was legally authorized to perform kidney transplants was irrelevant to the charge of trafficking, because a facility could be so-authorized but still be guilty of exploiting vulnerable donors. The prosecutor charged Rrecaj as being part of the conspiracy based on this letter, and argued that he was attempting to provide legal cover for the other defendants. But, based on our interpretation, we determined Rrecaj was not guilty of any crime.

It was also argued that the doctors were just doing their jobs as medical professionals and didn't know anything about exploitation or an international conspiracy, thereby shifting blame to the Turkish surgeon. We were likewise not persuaded by this defense. The clinic was owned and operated by Dr. Dervishi, who'd participated in some of the surgeries, and managed by his son Arban, who had picked some of the donors and recipients up at the airport, transported them to the clinic, and assisted them with the bogus paperwork. They both had close contact with Dr. Sonmez, who had an employee-employer relationship with the clinic.

I pointedly questioned the chief anesthesiologist about what he was thinking when he dealt with a parade of destitute foreigners who just happened to be in faraway Kosovo for kidney removals. He just shrugged and said he was only doing his job and didn't concern himself with the details. (Lutfi and Arban Dervishi refused to testify.)

Late in the trial, we learned from the war crimes prosecutor in Belgrade, Serbia, of a potential witness who also claimed there was a direct link between the *Medicus* case and the purported organ trafficking by the KLA years earlier. We were anxious to pursue this lead, but were wary of the motives of the Serbian prosecutor and this potential witness. We arranged to interview him in a closed session, without the defendants or their attorneys present, by video link from Belgrade. We would then decide whether to admit the testimony at trial.

The information he provided was bizarre in the extreme. He testified under oath that he had been a volunteer with the KLA and had undergone some basic medical training. He said he was present at the yellow house in Albania and personally participated in an organ extraction. He claimed he was ordered first to cut open the chest of a live Serbian prisoner, then crack open the ribs and extract the beating heart, which he said he did. The heart was then packed in ice and shipped off to the airport. Present during this procedure, so this person claimed, was none other than Dr. Lutfi Dervishi, the lead defendant in the *Medicus* case.

In our view, this testimony was seriously lacking in credibility, so we decided not to use it in the trial. We concluded that this witness must have been trying to gain favor for some reason with the Belgrade prosecutor, since the prosecutor would have been delighted to prove that KLA soldiers were guilty of torturing Serbians. Perhaps this was Marty's purported connection to *Medicus*. But without his testimony, we were never able to establish the link between the *Medicus* case and the alleged organ trafficking back in the day.

Before the end of the trial, during the holidays, Kristina and I returned to the US for the first time in nearly two years. For me it was a couple of weeks of home leave, but Kristina had decided to remain in Vermont. I planned to complete my tour in Kosovo shortly after the trial concluded.

Chapter 36

Completing Business

My return trip to Kosovo after a brief visit home took me through Munich, then to Pristina, or so I'd thought. However, when I arrived in Munich early in the morning, I could not find my flight to Pristina posted on any of the airport monitors. I wandered around the nearly empty airport until I located the Lufthansa counter, the airline I was scheduled on, and explained my predicament to the representative. He checked his computer, then looked up at me somewhat sheepishly and said the route had been canceled. I asked about the next flight, and he repeated that the route had been canceled. Not the flight, but the route. Lufthansa no longer flew from Munich to Pristina.

I explained that I had booked the round trip through a US travel agency, and had not been notified of any change. The agent was sympathetic, but said there was nothing he could do. After several minutes of my pleading and him fiddling with his terminal, he informed me that Lufthansa would put me up at a hotel and book a flight for the following day to Vienna, and then on to Pristina. Problem solved, although I had a frank conversation with my travel agent upon my return.

Since Kristina had decided to stay home, I notified Besim that I would be vacating the apartment and moving to a smaller, less expensive place around the corner. He was sorry to see me go, but there were other likely tenants and we remained on good terms. He told me to be careful with my new landlord who, according to him, could be a problem.

My new apartment was a one-bedroom unit above a Turkish fast food restaurant, up three flights of stairs, with a balcony overlooking the street. The landlord promised a flat-screen TV, and delivered one that was obviously used. When I turned it on, it began to smoke, then literally exploded. Perhaps this was the kind of thing Besim was warning about, but the TV was replaced promptly and I never had another problem with the landlord.

EULEX had decided that all trial judges, along with administrative staff and legal officers, would be consolidated in Pristina rather than continue to work in the regional courts, like I had in Prizren. This new arrangement was called the Mobile Unit. We all took up offices in a UN building downtown, and I shared an office with a Bulgarian judge. When cases were ready for trial, the assigned judge would drive from Pristina to the court, wherever it might be, for the proceedings. Or, in my case, walk to the Pristina courthouse for the *Medicus* trial.

This consolidation worked out reasonably well, though not without some initial grumbling among my colleagues. Edi, my administrative assistant in Prizren, had to commute to Pristina every day and was not pleased, at least at first, since he was now one among many rather than king of his castle. However, Edi slowly advanced his way up the ladder to become chair of the local staff committee, representing the staff in dealings with the EULEX hierarchy.

The *Medicus* case was continuing in fits and starts, heading toward a conclusion. There were regular delays as we struggled with technical issues, tracked down witnesses, or accommodated other trials in progress, so I volunteered for other work.

One time I was sent to the city of Peja, about an hour away, to rule on a prosecutor's request for a detention order. The defendant was the same Kosovo prosecutor I referred to earlier, who had been charged with corruption and was in jail awaiting trial. I granted the request and returned to Pristina.

Being in Peja brought back a memory. A year or so earlier, there had been a meeting of all the international judges at a hotel downtown. Just as we were about to leave, there was an announcement of an emergency, the hotel was locked down, and we couldn't leave for a while. We later learned there had been a murder right in front of the hotel, which had become a crime scene.

During down time, I also wrote regulations for the use of cameras in the courtroom, which, up to that time, had not been allowed. Indeed, at one point during the *Medicus* trial, a camera crew from Canada showed up at the courthouse to film the proceedings for an HBO documentary on organ trafficking. We had to explain that cameras were not permitted, so the best they could do was film the defendants and judges entering the courtroom.

Now, however, there was new legislation authorizing cameras in the courtroom, and regulations implementing the law had to be written. Since I was familiar with the subject, I volunteered for the task. The regulations were modeled after those in Vermont. I presented the regulations at a meeting of all the international judges, and they approved. I then submitted them to the local judicial authorities and they were formally adopted, a major step forward in the interest of transparency.

Since Kristina was no longer in Kosovo, I spent a good part of each weekend preparing to write the decision in the *Medicus* case, even though we had not yet completed the trial. As the only native English speaker on the panel, this responsibility fell primarily to me, with the assistance of my competent legal officer, this one from Denmark. I had to review the testimony of dozens of witnesses, study reams of medical and forensic evidence, review all of our rulings, organize all of the boxes of materials into some semblance of order, and create an outline for the decision—an arduous and time-consuming task.

Chapter 37

Medicus Verdict and Appeals

At the conclusion of all the evidence and closing arguments, the three of us on the trial panel retired to chambers to begin our deliberations, which continued over two or three days. We announced our unanimous verdict orally in open court on April 29, 2013, and I read a fifteen-page statement I had written summarizing our reasoning in detail. The defendants sat motionless and tense, and their lawyers listened intently, hoping for the best but expecting the worst. Prosecutor Ratel swiveled around in his chair, facing the defendants behind him so he could assess their reactions.

We found the two main defendants, Lutfi Dervishi and his son Arban, guilty of organ trafficking and organized crime, and ordered them to serve prison sentences of eight years and seven years, three months, respectively.

Announcing the verdict. Photo ©EULEX.

We found Sokol Hajdini, the chief anesthesiologist, guilty of causing grievous bodily harm by participating in illegal kidney transplants, and sentenced him to three years in prison. These two doctors, Lutfi and Sokol, were also prohibited from practicing their profession for two years and one year, respectively. The two other anesthesiologists who carried out Hajdini's orders were also found guilty of causing grievous bodily harm, and given one-year sentences, which were suspended.

The two government officials were acquitted: Ilir Rrecaj, as mentioned above, and Driton Jilta, a health inspector employed by the Organization for Security and Cooperation in Europe. We determined that Jilta was aware of the transplants but did not report them as required by his job description. However, there was no evidence he had received "material benefit," as required by the operative criminal law.

Prosecutor Ratel was ecstatic with the verdict; all his efforts over several years had come to fruition. A colleague of mine heard him say that we (the trial panel) had hit it out of the park. Ours was the first decision throughout the world that found medical doctors guilty of organ trafficking, and was covered in news outlets globally.

The *New York Times* ran a story on April 29, 2013, "5 Are Convicted in Kosovo of Organ Trafficking." The article described the verdict:

> PARIS—Five people were convicted Monday in Pristina, the capital of Kosovo, in connection with an elaborate organ trafficking network that lured poor people to the country to sell their kidneys and other organs to wealthy transplant recipients from Israel, Canada and Germany. Organs sold for as much as $130,000 each.
>
> The defendants, all Kosovars, were tried before a panel of two European judges (sic) and one Kosovar judge. A special prosecutor for the union, Jonathan Ratel, called the case a landmark because doctors had been convicted.[72]

Our verdict was also the subject of an article in the *New Yorker*, by Nicholas Schmidle, on April 29, "An Organ-Trafficking Conviction in Kosovo."[73] I had met with Schmidle in Kosovo when he was researching another article about President Hashim Thaçi and his possible involvement in organ trafficking, which was published in the May 6 edition, and titled, "Bring Up the Bodies."[74] The Canadian documentary for HBO, called *Tales from the Organ Trade*,[75] was broadcast in fall 2013.

My tour of duty ended shortly after we announced the verdict, and I returned to the US in mid-May 2013. I was able to complete some of our 125-page decision before leaving Kosovo, but did not finish until several weeks after I returned home. The defendants promptly appealed our verdict, remaining free on bail pending appeal.

Shortly after our return, Kristina and I were interviewed by a columnist for the *Stowe Reporter*, who wrote a monthly column for the paper sharing his perceptive observations about local and national affairs. He was a screenwriter and also an attorney, who coincidentally had been legal counsel for Vermont Governor Howard Dean, who succeeded Gov. Snelling when Snelling died unexpectedly in 1991 after returning to office earlier that year. The column, dated May 30, 2013, and titled "Vt. Judge's 'Retirement' Leads to Kosovo,"[76] was an excellent summary of our international trajectory after both Kristina and I had retired from our primary jobs in Vermont. The column helped us reintroduce ourselves to our many friends with whom we had been out of touch, and we were grateful.

After an inordinate delay of two years following our verdict in April 2013, the Kosovo Court of Appeals, in a well-reasoned decision, generally upheld the verdict (organized crime and trafficking) against the two main perpetrators, Lutfi and Arban Dervishi. However, the court found Sokol Hajdini, the chief anesthesiologist, who had been convicted by us of committing grievous bodily harm, guilty of the more serious crimes of organized crime and trafficking, like the Dervishis. The two subordinate anesthesiologists were acquitted.

While the reasoning of the Court of Appeals differed from our reasoning on several important points, and while some of our findings were rejected or amended, the important thing was that our findings of guilt were upheld, at least as to the seven illegal transplants for which there was direct evidence in court.

The sentence of eight years for Lutfi Dervishi was upheld; the sentence for Arban was increased by nine months, to eight years; and the sentence for Sokol was increased from three years to five. Immediately after this decision, Lutfi and Arban fled the country rather than reporting to prison to serve their sentences. Sokol Hajdini, who did not flee, appealed the decision against him to the Kosovo Supreme Court, which issued its ruling in September 2016. The Court disagreed about organized crime and trafficking, as had been determined by the Court of Appeals, and reinstated the conviction for causing grievous bodily harm, the same as our verdict in the trial court. The Supreme Court also modified the sentence back to three years in prison, using the same rationale we had used in our verdict.

Importantly, in each of these appeals, the panels consisted of a majority of international judges, which was mandated in high-profile EULEX cases. Unfortunately, the case was not over yet. There is a procedure in Kosovo law that allows a last-gasp appeal, called "protection of legality." This appeal was heard by another panel of Supreme Court judges, this panel consisting of two local Kosovar judges and only one international judge, something that was not supposed to happen, particularly in a case like this. My understanding is that the EULEX Special Prosecution Office handed the last phase of this case over to local authorities as part of its downsizing process, probably assuming that nothing untoward would happen, since the case had been reviewed multiple times.

In December 2016, the two local judges completely reversed the convictions of Lutfi and Arban Dervishi and Sokol Hajdini, and ordered a retrial, claiming there had been procedural errors during the trial which were serious enough to undo all the years of work that had gone into this case, regardless of the overwhelming evidence of guilt. A key error, so they decided, was that Judge Arek had acted in a pretrial capacity and should not have been on the trial panel, despite the ruling that there was absolutely no evidence of any bias. Indeed, this panel did not even look for bias; it was a purely rote decision based on a strict reading of the procedure code. The EULEX judge issued a vigorous dissent, explaining the legal folly of the decision.

To say I was angry would be a gross understatement. In January 2017, I wrote a detailed analysis of why I thought this decision was a travesty of justice, and circulated it widely in Kosovo, including to the Special Prosecutor's Office, the president of the EULEX Assembly of Judges, and the EULEX Press Office.

There was then another appeal, this one by the prosecutor's office, attempting to get the ruling on protection of legality overturned, which was decided by yet another panel in May 2017, all to no avail. Thus, the case would have to be retried, and the retrial began in July 2017.

Lutfi Dervishi was back in Kosovo by then, so he was one of the defendants along with Sokol Hajdini. Arban Dervishi was still among the missing, so was not part of this retrial. While the retrial was still in progress in 2018, I wrote an article which was published on May 2, by *Balkan Insight*, titled "Kosovo's Medicus Case: Bad Omen for Rule of Law."[77] I summarized the original *Medicus* trial and presented many of the same arguments I'd made in my open letter a year and a half earlier. I concluded the article as follows:

> The *Medicus* case was one of the most important cases undertaken by EULEX during its tenure, and this shameful ruling summarily negated six years of prosecutorial and judicial efforts to adjudicate this highly complicated and ground-breaking case, and to deliver justice for the exploited victims.
>
> The case is now being retried in the Basic Court of Pristina, an extraordinary waste of time and resources in an over-taxed judicial system. But more importantly, the decision undermined the rule of law. Kosovo's judiciary has struggled with this concept, and has had considerable difficulty showing that it can deliver justice free from incompetence, corruption and political influence. Regrettably, the *Medicus* decision raises serious concerns about the future of the rule of law in Kosovo after EULEX departs this summer.

Then, on May 28, 2018, the retrial concluded. To my great satisfaction, the court determined that Lutfi Dervishi and Sokol Hajdini were guilty of organ trafficking and organized crime, just as we had. Of course, there was then another appeal, as always seems to be the case in Kosovo. And on November 28, 2018, I received an email from Jonathan Ratel, the original prosecutor in the case, with whom I have stayed in occasional contact, which said only "Good God," and attached a link to another article from that date in *Balkan Insight*, "Kosovo Orders Second Retrial for Organ-Trading Defendants."[78] To the best of my knowledge, the case is still rumbling through the courts and has not yet been finally decided. I don't believe that the defendants have ever served a day of their sentences, and perhaps they never will.

Chapter 38

Conclusion

Sometime after I returned to Vermont following my two and a half years in Kosovo, Kristina and I were hosting a German friend, Gert, and his family for dinner at our home. Gert was very inquisitive and skeptical about our experience abroad, and asked me pointedly if I thought that promoting the rule of law internationally made any real difference. He then asked directly if I thought I personally had accomplished anything significant in this regard.

I pondered the questions momentarily, and responded, "I can only answer based on my own experience, but yes, I think so, both generally and personally. But, frankly, it all depends." What I explained was that success or failure (and progress overall) really depended on the particular circumstances of each country, of each task or case, the resources involved, the receptivity of the various stakeholders, personal relationships, whether there was ongoing reinforcement, and many other factors. And for me, the factors were different in all four countries.

Generally speaking, when foreign colleagues in legal and judicial spheres, wherever they might be, are introduced to new ideas or different ways of doing things, the result can be positive. However, even when the seed is planted, change can be hard. It may take time, renewed effort, follow-up, and the right mix of factors before there is a positive payoff. And there may not be a positive payoff at all. The other side may simply go through the motions and revert to the comfortable ways of doing things after you or your program leave the country. This is not uncommon.

At the risk of sounding chauvinistic, I think being an American is helpful in promoting the rule of law, especially through such entities as the

American Bar Association Rule of Law Initiative and the many American NGOs that spring up throughout the world. In my experience, Americans are generally respected and considered good role models, practitioners, and tutors abroad, even in the former Soviet republics. (I don't wish to imply that representatives from other countries are not also well qualified and effective, but Americans may have an edge.) And our democratic and legal systems are admired worldwide, although I fear this is changing rapidly as our problems at home proliferate.

Regardless, as I said at the outset of this book, international rule of law work does not proceed in a linear fashion, and occasional gratification and success can often be muted by frustration and failure, as I hope I have demonstrated.

In Russia, for example, our project (and many others) was forced to end when Russia expelled USAID from the country. But before the project shut down, it grew from the single Vermont–Karelia partnership to partnerships involving eleven states and eleven Russian regions, stretching all the way from Petrozavodsk in northwestern Russia to Tomsk in south central Russia. The history of the project has not been written, but I am convinced there was valuable cross-pollination in many subject areas which, hopefully, has withstood the test of time.

In Kazakhstan, I participated in an international conference as an American jury trial expert, just as Kazakhstan was set to begin jury trials. I strongly promoted jury trials in my speech as a means of enhancing the independence of the judiciary and eliminating political interference. The audience of judges, lawyers, court personnel, members of the media, and other international experts was very receptive, as were the judges during the workshop the following day. Jury trials began as scheduled and continue to this day, although I can only take slight credit, if any.

In Georgia, turf battles and squabbles between US agencies impeded my work as a jury trial expert, the position for which I had been hired. And unexpected events, like an international military crisis, not only interfered with my work but placed me and others in harm's way. Moreover, the Judicial Reform Index soured our relations with the Georgian Supreme Court.

Yet I believe that the Georgia assignment was relatively successful in other respects. My accomplishments were primarily in the realm of outreach, where I represented the ABA in working with the Georgian legal profession and judiciary, as well as the public at large, in such subjects as fair elections, domestic violence, legal and judicial ethics, judicial independence, bench/bar relations, and, to a limited extent, jury trials. And the study tour to the US was otherwise very successful, despite the debacle in the jury trial we observed. Moreover, the ABA project continued long after I departed, so continuity and reinforcement were mainstays.

In Kosovo, my longest international assignment by far, there were numerous obstacles to success, some of which were overcome, others not. Corruption and political interference were always lurking in the background when it came to trials involving the KLA, though I came away unaffected in this regard. While it was obvious that EULEX and Kosovo's benefactors, like the EU and the US, wanted convictions, and KLA interest groups wanted acquittals, I was never pressured to deliver a particular verdict, though certain colleagues of mine have claimed they were pressured. And it was obvious in war crimes cases that witnesses often had amnesia or claimed other problems, like inaccurate translations or police coercion, to avoid implicating war heroes, likely having been pressured.

The trials often had a never-ending quality to them, with verdicts being appealed, followed by a retrial, followed by another appeal, and on and on it went—the *Kabashi* case, and particularly the *Medicus* case, being examples. It sometimes seemed that the appellate courts were primarily interested in simply finding fault with the trial courts.

Yet those cases were successful in another sense. Ultimately, Kabashi, after two trials and two appellate proceedings, was convicted of a war crime and sent to prison. And the *Medicus* case was the first one in the world to result in convictions, at the trial level, of medical professionals—indeed twice—and brought worldwide attention to human organ trafficking, even though the case is still pending in the courts.

The Daka murder case, despite its tragic end, brought about reforms to practices by the police and prosecutor following the trial panel's dismissal of the case based on an illegal search of Daka's premises. In the first *Limaj* case, I am gratified that my dissenting opinion resulted in the trial going forward, following the Supreme Court's decision which adopted my reasoning.

The Puka insurance case was also successful, and brought to light an elaborate scam which affected twenty-four victims and sent a corrupt judge to prison. I was also able to negotiate a noteworthy plea agreement in the *Fortuna* international drug smuggling case, a novel accomplishment at the time, saving time and expense and bringing about a just result.

Having local Kosovar judges sitting on the bench, participating as equal members of three-judge trial panels, was also an excellent way to mentor them in best courtroom practices, both American and European. It was also enlightening, if challenging, to work with judges, legal officers, and court staff from numerous, mostly European, countries with different legal traditions and procedures; we all learned from each other.

This exposure caused me to rethink some basic assumptions of our common law legal system. For example, is a jury trial really the best way to bring about justice as opposed to a trial with just professional judges making the decision?

Of course, I participated many times on trial panels with only professional judges, since there were no juries, and believe our decisions were mostly correct and well-reasoned. But, without a doubt, I prefer the jury system because I think decisions by a jury of one's peers enhance the independence of the judiciary and result in greater trust and confidence in the judicial system by members of the public.

And in Kosovo, like Georgia, it was personally enriching to live among the local citizens and experience their culture, history (as difficult as it has been), resilience, and friendliness.

In sum, serving as a judge in these four countries was the capstone of my judicial career, and I like to think that my efforts to enhance the rule of law were occasionally productive and successful.

Epilogue

New War Crimes Court in The Hague

More than a year after our verdict in the *Medicus* case, and nearly three years after the initiation of the Special Investigative Task Force, Ambassador Williamson issued a report of its findings: *Statement of the Chief Prosecutor of the Special Investigative Task Force,* July 29, 2014.[79] The report states:

> As a result of this investigation, we believe that SITF will be in a position to file an indictment against certain senior officials of the former Kosovo Liberation Army.
>
> Information compiled by SITF indicates that certain elements of the KLA intentionally targeted the minority populations with acts of persecution that included unlawful killings, abductions, enforced disappearances, illegal detentions in camps in Kosovo and Albania, sexual violence, other forms of inhumane treatment, forced displacements of individuals from their homes and communities, and desecration and destruction of churches and other religious sites.

On the subject of organ trafficking, Williamson reported that,

> . . . there are compelling indications that this practice did occur . . . and that a small number of individuals were killed for the purpose of extracting and trafficking their organs. This conclusion is consistent with what was stated in the Marty

Report, namely that a "handful" of individuals were subjected to this crime. The use of the word "handful" by Senator Marty was intentional and it was meant literally. . . . Statements that have been made by some implying that hundreds of people were killed for the purpose of organ trafficking are totally unsupported by the information we have and that Dick Marty had.

Williamson said that "in order to prosecute such offenses, however, it requires a level of evidence that we have not yet secured." But, like the allegations advanced by Del Ponte and Marty, those in the SITF report concerning organ trafficking grabbed the attention of the media. For example, the online outlet EURACTIV ran this headline on July 29, the day the report was released: "KLA Guerrillas Harvested Murdered Serb's Organs, Say EU Investigators."[80]

The SITF report went on to say, and this is critical, "In regard to those crimes for which SITF has prosecutable evidence, the filing of an indictment will not occur until the specialist court designated to hear these cases is established—hopefully early next year," meaning early 2015.[81] It was not to be.

Why was a "specialist court" necessary, by which Williamson meant a totally new court completely separate from EULEX, located out of Kosovo and staffed 100 percent by internationals? EULEX already had a fully functioning international judicial system in Kosovo, and had prosecuted high-profile perpetrators of war crimes and other serious offenses, including organ trafficking, as I have described in detail. Further, the EU was about to open a brand-new Palace of Justice in Pristina in 2015, with state-of-the-art technology and security.

But Kosovo's benefactors, like the EU and US, agreed with Williamson about the necessity for a new court. First, the proceedings against high-level KLA veterans had to be seen as independent and not influenced in any way by the strong negative sentiment in Kosovo against prosecuting war heroes, or be subject to political interference. Also, the integrity of the SITF had to be protected from adverse influences. Moreover, there could be security problems for judges, prosecutors, and court staff despite the new Palace. Thus, the perceived need for a neutral location outside of Kosovo.

In addition, the judicial apparatus created by EULEX in Kosovo was deemed to be inadequate. The international community was not satisfied with EULEX's track record in war crimes cases—not enough investigations of difficult cases, too many acquittals, too many appeals and retrials. And the "big fish" identified in the Marty report, such as Hashim Thaçi and Kadri Veseli, had not yet been held accountable.

There was great concern for witness protection. It was considered just too dangerous to expect witnesses to testify in a Kosovo courtroom against high-level Kosovo war heroes, as doing so could put themselves and their families in great danger. It was believed that many witnesses would simply refuse to testify if the proceedings were conducted in Kosovo. The suicide of the key prosecution witness in the *Limaj* case may have been a driving force for enhanced witness protection. Conducting the proceedings in a neutral country far away from Kosovo, with vigorous witness protection and support, could mitigate some of these concerns.

In order to provide the legal framework for the new court, the Kosovo Parliament had to be persuaded to pass constitutional amendments and a law creating the court. This finally occurred in August 2015, but only because of intense international pressure. This was a difficult task, as described by *Balkan Insight* on August 6, 2015:

> The . . . Law . . . which was negotiated between the EU and Kosovo, was finally passed this week by the Kosovo Parliament after months of bitter arguments, street protests, frenzied media speculation and delays caused by political opposition to the legislation that will see former KLA guerrillas—who are seen as heroes of the liberation struggle in Kosovo—put on trial.[82]

Henceforth, the new court, which would be part of the Kosovo judicial system rather than a separate, freestanding entity, would be known by the cumbersome name of the Kosovo Specialist Chambers and Specialist Prosecutor's Office. Its exclusive mandate is to prosecute war crimes, crimes against humanity, and other serious crimes, such as the organ trafficking committed during 1998–2000 by members of the KLA. However, crimes committed by Serbians are not included within the court's jurisdiction, a point of intense contention within segments of Kosovo society who believe the court is biased against the KLA by definition.

Following the passage of the necessary legal enactments, the job of actually setting up the court had to be tackled, a major bureaucratic undertaking that took two full years. The task required entering into a host state agreement with the Netherlands; refurbishing a large building in The Hague; hiring a whole new court staff including administrators, IT personnel, translators, security experts, and victim support services; recruiting and hiring a cadre of international judges and legal officers; establishing rules of procedure and evidence; and developing a witness protection program, all of which was time-consuming, labor intensive, and expensive, much of which was duplicative of EULEX's justice system in Kosovo.

David Schwendiman, an internationally experienced and respected American prosecutor, who succeeded Clint Williamson as the head of SITF, was appointed as the first chief prosecutor of the Specialist Prosecutor's Office (SPO) in September 2016, as SITF was merged with the SPO. The investigation continued into all of the crimes identified in the SITF report, presumably including organ trafficking.

The new court finally declared itself open for business in July 2017. The expectation was that indictments would be filed immediately upon opening the court, but such was not the case, and time passed with no indication from the SPO when the indictments would be filed. Then, in March 2018, Schwendiman surprised the international legal community by announcing his resignation. No indictments had been filed by the time he left. Regardless, he deserves credit for his service.

I was initially a supporter of the new court based on my understanding (and that of everyone else) that the court would be up and running quickly, fulfilling its basic function of adjudicating indictments without further delay. Williamson expected the new court to be functioning in early 2015, at which time the indictment he referred to in his report could have been filed. I changed my opinion, however, for reasons outlined in an article I wrote for *Balkan Insight*, published online on March 21, 2018, just before Schwendiman left office. The essence of my argument was as follows:

> [T]he new court's evolution stands as a stark example of international criminal justice in slow motion—good intentions gone awry and the rule of law stuck in quicksand. Today, the court has yet to receive any indictments to adjudicate, despite a

multi-year birthing process and a massive budget of 41 million euros. The tragedy of delay is two-fold. First, alleged perpetrators of heinous crimes have been allowed to go about their lives with impunity.

But more importantly, and I can't emphasize this point enough, the victims and their families have been forced to twist in the wind of uncertainty far too long, waiting for justice to be served. And the 1600 missing persons, many of whose photos are posted outside the Parliament building, have not been vindicated for their suffering. Even if the court started adjudicating cases tomorrow, the years of delay, uncertainty, and anguish could never be recouped.

Staying the course with EULEX, which had a fully functioning justice component, would have been a far better choice than starting anew. True, EULEX had its problems, but these problems could have been ameliorated, if not solved, if a concerted effort had been made to do so.

Accountability for crimes by members of the KLA, and justice for the victims and their families, are important goals in international law that cannot be forgotten by the passage of time. But the passage of time makes it more and more difficult to achieve these goals as we are seeing. Witnesses die or disappear, witnesses forget, witnesses are threatened or killed, family members die, perpetrators die or disappear, key personnel resign, evidence is lost, stories change.

It is now nearly 10 years since Del Ponte's allegations, over six years since Marty's report, nearly four years since Williamson's benchmark report, two and a half years since the court was approved by Parliament, nine months and counting since the court became fully operational.

Yet the court sits idle like a ghost court, at least in terms of its essential function—adjudicating cases. If indictments had been filed with EULEX in 2014 when Williamson had enough evidence to do so, the cases would probably be nearing completion by now. Instead, the victims and their families continue to wait and hope for justice to be served.[83]

Another experienced and respected American prosecutor, Jack Smith, replaced Schwendiman and was sworn in on September 11, 2018. Again, expectations ran high that indictments would soon be filed, but the new chief prosecutor needed time to get up to speed, and more time passed with no charges being laid. While waiting for indictments, the Specialist Chambers grew exponentially, with authorized expenditures increasing to over 200 million euros, and a staff of approximately two hundred, from twenty-seven different countries, although none from Kosovo.

Finally, by the end of 2020, twelve years after Del Ponte's allegations against the KLA, the chief prosecutor filed indictments in four separate cases, each of which was confirmed by the pretrial judge. The most important of the four cases is the indictment against Hashim Thaçi, who promptly resigned as president of Kosovo; Kadri Veseli, the former Speaker of the Assembly; and two other prominent KLA war veterans, for war crimes, crimes against humanity, and other serious offenses from March 1998 through September 1999. (An amended indictment was filed on April 29, 2022, charging additional crimes.)

Trials commenced in two of the four cases in the fall of 2021, neither involving the "big fish," Thaçi and Veseli, whose cases are still in the pretrial phase. A verdict in one of these two cases was announced on May 18, 2022, finding the two defendants guilty of intimidating witnesses. This was the first verdict issued by this court since it was created in 2015. It is anticipated that it will take years to process all these cases, and more indictments are likely to be filed.

Notably, none of the indictments makes any mention whatsoever of organ trafficking. So the explosive claims made by Del Ponte, and the findings made by Marty and Williamson, although dramatically moderated, have all come to naught in this regard, even though these claims and findings were responsible in part, perhaps in large part, for creation of the Specialist Court.

Indeed, the significance of the organ trafficking allegations has been emphasized by Clint Williamson, author of the 2014 SIFT report. In an interview in November 2020 with Bronwyn Jones, an American journalist living in Kosovo, Williamson indicated that the court might never have been created without these allegations. He said:

And I think there was also a part to play because of the more sensational allegations about organ trafficking that garnered the attention of the wider outside world. I'm not sure, if that had not happened, if there would have been as much momentum behind this process.[84]

We may never know for certain whether organ trafficking did occur during wartime and immediately thereafter, and if so whether there was any connection to the *Medicus* case. Regardless, despite agonizing delays and exorbitant cost, the alleged perpetrators of heinous crimes are finally being held to account, at least in the eyes of the international community.

Predictably, however, it appears the court has very little legitimacy in Kosovo: It was imposed on Kosovo by Kosovo's international benefactors; it is located far away, in the Hague; there are no Kosovars among the judges or staff; the mandate of the court focuses exclusively on veterans of the KLA, viewed as war heroes and liberators; and the jurisdiction of the court does not include Serbian war criminals who decimated Kosovo during the war. Any hope that the verdicts issued by the court will bring about reconciliation within Kosovo's society is doubtful.

Medicus Case, Ongoing Interest

The *Medicus* case continues to arouse interest. It is still the only case I am aware of where medical doctors have been convicted of organ trafficking—indeed, twice—at least at the trial court level. As such, it has been the subject of scholarly research: by Frederike Ambagtsheer in a study titled, "Understanding the Challenges to Investigating and Prosecuting Organ Trafficking: A Comparative Analysis of Two Cases," published in *Trends in Organized Crime*, June 3, 2021.[85]

Also, Roos Bugter's master's thesis at Erasmus University Rotterdam, titled, "Legal Actors in Illegal Organ Trade: A Crime Script of the Logistical Process of Illegal Organ Transplants and the Legal Actors Involved in the *Medicus* Case," September 2020.[86]

And, by Diana Santos and Eduardo Salcedo Albaran, in a study titled, "The 'Medicus Case': Organ Trafficking Network in Kosovo," published in the *Global Observatory of Transnational Criminal Networks*, No. 14 (2017).[87]

In January 2021, I was contacted by a representative of RTV1, a nongovernmental satellite channel in Russia (not affiliated with RT, the state-run station) which broadcasts to a Russian-speaking audience around the world. I was asked to participate in a video interview about the *Medicus* case, as many of the kidney donors were Russian-speaking. The station was preparing a documentary on the international organ trade. The interview was conducted on February 8, and the documentary, including my interview, is now available on YouTube; English subtitles can be superimposed.[88]

The Kosovo Precedent and the 2022 Russia-Ukraine Conflict[89]

As the world recoiled in horror in late February 2022, Russia, without legitimate provocation, invaded Ukraine, a sovereign country, while the Western powers found common cause against Russia under the aegis of the North Atlantic Treaty Organization (NATO). This crisis was a long time in the making, with important historical antecedents, such as the fact that Ukraine was a republic within the former Soviet Union, and President Putin's long-held ambition to recreate "Mother Russia." But it is also important to understand that more recent history also plays an important part, in particular the war between Serbia and Kosovo and its aftermath, which has influenced Russia's geopolitical strategy since the war ended in 1999.

In 1999, under the leadership of President Bill Clinton and Secretary of State Madeleine Albright, NATO intervened with an intensive bombing campaign in the brutal internecine war between Serbia, a sovereign country, and its breakaway province of Kosovo, in which Serbia engaged in ethnic cleansing of the Albanian Kosovar majority. After seventy-eight days, NATO prevailed and the war ended in June 1999, following which the UN took control of Kosovo, but its legal status vis-à-vis Serbia remained in limbo until 2008. Russia strongly opposed NATO's intervention and has been Serbia's staunch ally to this day. And NATO continues to maintain a peacekeeping force in Kosovo, called KFOR (Kosovo Force), in which the US participates. These events planted the seeds for the "Kosovo precedent," which would rise up several years later.

At the time of the NATO incursion, Vladimir Putin was the secretary of the Russian Security Service, and in August 1999 was appointed prime minister. Then the political merry-go-round began. Putin was elected president in May 2000, and served two terms until May 2008, when he was succeeded by Dmitry Medvedev, who served until 2012. During Medvedev's term, Putin was again the prime minister until he was reelected president in 2012, and has served in that office ever since. Medvedev was recycled back to prime minister in 2012 until 2020. However, it has never been in doubt who held the real power.

In February 2008, just before Putin's second four-year presidential term ended, Kosovo unilaterally declared its independence from Serbia with the support of the US, the EU, and other countries. This watershed event infuriated Putin, and he vowed that it created a precedent which would circle back to harm the West. And it did so in short order.

Just several months later, in August 2008, after Medvedev had become president and Putin prime minister, Russia invaded the country of Georgia, a former Soviet republic which was leaning toward NATO and the EU, under the pretext that Russian speakers and passport holders in the breakaway province of South Ossetia were being threatened by the Georgian military. Russian tanks and military personnel quickly poured through the Roki Tunnel separating the two countries as if they had been waiting for this moment, and Russian forces quickly overwhelmed the Georgian military. Russia then recognized the independence of South Ossetia and another rebellious province, Abkhazia, and continues to do so to this day, although only a handful of other countries have joined in recognition. Thus, the Kosovo precedent was fully implemented.

In 2010, the International Court of Justice, in a legal challenged brought by Serbia, ruled that Kosovo's unilateral declaration of independence did not violate international law. Russia would argue that this result would apply equally to South Ossetia and Abkhazia.

Then in 2014, during Putin's return to the presidency, a restive province of Ukraine, Crimea, declared its independence from Ukraine following a welcomed incursion by Russian soldiers and a popular referendum by the citizens of Crimea. The written declaration of independence actually cites the Kosovo precedent (unilaterally declaring independence) as one of the justifications for breaking away from Ukraine. Crimea was subsequently incorporated into the Russian Federation.

In early January 2022, peaceful protests began in Kazakhstan, also a former Soviet republic, over the rise in gas prices, but quickly devolved into violence amid rising dissatisfaction with the autocratic government and economic inequality. The government cracked down brutally, but could not control the violence and called for assistance from Russia under their military alliance. Putin responded quickly and sent Russian soldiers to help quell the disturbance, resulting in over two hundred dead and thousands of arrests. While this situation was not directly related to the Kosovo precedent, it clearly demonstrated that Putin was willing to use military force to prop up his fellow autocrats within the former Soviet Union and to crush any popular dissent, or liberalization as has occurred in Ukraine.

During the last eight years, Russian separatists have fought the Ukrainian military in the Donbas region of Ukraine, and the separatists have received support from Russia just across the border. One of Putin's first acts after the invasion of Ukraine began in February 2022 was to recognize the independence of Donetsk People's Republic and the Luhansk People's Republic, utilizing the Kosovo precedent as solidified during the war with Georgia.

There is an ongoing debate as to whether the events in Kosovo actually established a precedent under international law. Many argue that Kosovo was a unique situation, a one-off, because it was initiated and justified as a humanitarian mission limited to stopping the bloodbath and ethnic cleansing. But the concept remains alive at least in the mind of Vladimir Putin.

Endnotes

Chapter One

1   Ratner, "Goldfinger Buys a Library."

2   Hays, "Library Won't be Called Englehard."

3   "Discard the Bad Regulations."

4   Goddard, "Snelling Subpoena is Quashed."

5   Slater, "Judge Quashes Snelling Subpoena."

6   "Judicial Board Should Name Female Candidates."

7   "Put a Woman on the Bench."

Chapter Two

8   Clifford, "Troopers Crack Child Abuse Sect."

9   "Children of Sect Seized in Vermont."

10   Nickerson, "Vermont Seizes 112 Children from Sect."

11   Brown, "At Dawn, Officials Moved In."

12   Brown, "Judge Blocks State."

13   "Judge Sends Sect's Children Home."

14   Watkin, "From Left, Right, Lawyers Rap Raid."

15   Brown, "Officials Defend Church Raid as Routine."

16   Quoted in Watkin, "Mahady: Raid 'Grossly Unlawful,'" *Rutland Herald*, June 27, 1984

17   Snelling, "State Took Action to Protect Children and the Constitution."

18   Smith, "Secrets from Island Pond's Chilling Raid."

19   Slater, "Pineles Grilled on Church Raid."

20   "Raid Raises Questions about Pineles' Judgment."

21   "Raid on Sect Raises Doubts About Pineles."

22   Johnson, "Pineles Lauded by Witnesses at Confirmation Hearing."

23   Brown, "Pineles Presents Witnesses to 'Protect My Reputation.'"

Dean B. Pineles

24   Johnson, "Support Voiced for Judge Pineles."

Chapter Three

25   Costello, "Rapist Gets 22–50 Years for Series of Rampages."
26   Flood, "Vermont Rape Victims Kept Waiting for Justice."
27   Campbell, "Percy Rape Trial Begins."
28   Johnson, "Insanity is Key to Defense."
29   Campbell, "Victim Describes Rape in Percy Case."
30   Johnson, "War Stress Detailed at Rape Trial."
31   Campbell, "Witness tells of life in Vietnam."
32   Campbell, "Witness Says Percy Suffered Flashback."
33   Campbell, "Accused Rapist is Called Sane."
34   Campbell, "Percy Guilty Again."
35   Campbell, "Percy Receives 40–60 years."
36   Quote of the Week.
37   State v. Russell, unpublished Entry Order, No. 2001-217, January Term 2002.
38   Roth, "Crowd Led by Priests Attacks Gay Rights Marchers in Georgia."

Chapter Twelve

39   "Jury Duty and Rule 20."

Chapter Fifteen

40   Haxhiaj, "Kosovo's Forensic Investigators: 'We are the Voice of the Dead.'"
41   *An Overview of War Crime Trials in Kosovo in the Period 1999–2018.*
42   "Corruption Perceptions Index."
43   Bami, "Kosovo's Courts Struggle to Hold Corrupt Officials to Account."
44   Higgins, "In a Land Dominated by Ex-Rebels."
45   Bami, "Fearful Witness in Kosovo Serb Politician's Murder Trial Changes Testimony."
46   "Head of the EU Office in Kosovo Tomas Szunyog said…"

Chapter Sixteen

47   Higgins, "Not the Worst Hotel in the World, Perhaps, but 'the World is Very Big.'"

Chapter Twenty-One

48   Attewell, "Kosovo Bomb Blast Kills Two."

Chapter Twenty-Two
49   Pineles, Ruling on Confirmation of Indictment, GJPP 281/11, PPS 29/11, and 47/12, District Court of Pristina, May 18, 2012.
50   Quoted in Pineles, Ruling on Confirmation of Indictment, KA No. 44/12, Municipal Court of Pristina, May 3, 2012. *Infopress* is a now-defunct daily newspaper that operated in Kosovo for approximately twelve years, until 2015. Archives for the newspaper are unavailable, and all *Infopress* article quotes in this chapter are taken from the ruling cited here.
51   Quoted in Pineles, Ruling on Confirmation of Indictment, KA No. 44/12, Municipal Court of Pristina, May 3, 2012.
52   Quoted in Pineles, Ruling on Confirmation of Indictment, KA No. 44/12, Municipal Court of Pristina, May 3, 2012.
53   Quoted in Pineles, Ruling on Confirmation of Indictment, KA No. 44/12, Municipal Court of Pristina, May 3, 2012.

Chapter Twenty-Three
54   Bilefsky, "In Albanian Feuds, Isolation Engulfs Families."
55   Bytyci, "High-Profile War Crimes Suspects Escape Kosovo Hospital."

Chapter Twenty-Six
56   Morina, "24 Charged over Kosovo Ex-Guerrilla's Prison Breaks."

Chapter Twenty-Nine
57   Brumwasser, "Death of War Crimes Witness Casts Cloud on Kosovo."
58   "Kosovo Court Orders Retrial of Ex-Rebel for War Crimes."

Chapter Thirty-Four
59   Ristic, "Kosovo Organ Trafficking."
60   Del Ponte and Sudetic, *Madame Prosecutor. Confrontations with Humanity's Worst Criminals and the Culture of Impunity.*
61   Traynor, "Former War Crimes Prosecutor Alleges Kosovan Army Harvested Organs From Serb Prisoners."
62   Whitmore, "Balkans: Allegations of Organ Trafficking in Del Ponte Memoir Spark Scandal."

63   Quoted in Ristic, "Kosovo Organ Trafficking."

64   Marty, "Inhuman Treatment of People and Illicit Trafficking in Human
      Organs in Kosovo."

65   Marty, "Inhuman Treatment."

66   Marty, "Inhuman Treatment."

67   Lewis, "Kosovo PM is Head of Human Organ and Arms Ring."

68   "Factsheet," Special Investigative Task Force.

Chapter Thirty-Five

69   Marty, "Inhuman Treatment of People and Illicit Trafficking in Human
      Organs in Kosovo."

70   "European Envoy to Testify in Kosovo Organ Case."

71   Pineles, Arkadiusz Sedek and Vahid Hilili, Decision and Judgment Order,
      P309/10 and 340/10, Basic Court of Pristina, April 29, 2013.

Chapter Thirty-Seven

72   Bilefsky, "5 Are Convicted in Kosovo of Organ Trafficking."

73   Schmidle, "An Organ-Trafficking Conviction in Kosovo."

74   Schmidle, "Bring Up the Bodies."

75   *Tales from the Organ Trade.*

76   Rocchio, "Vt. Judge's 'Retirement' Leads to Kosovo."

77   Pineles, "Kosovo's Medicus Case: Bad Omen for Rule of Law."

78   Morina, "Kosovo Orders Second Retrial for Organ-Trading Defendants."

Epilogue

79   Williamson, *Statement of the Chief Prosecutor of the Special Investigative Task
      Force.*

80   Crisp, "KLA Guerrillas Harvested Murdered Serb's Organs."

81   Williamson, *Statement of the Chief Prosecutor of the Special Investigative Task
      Force.*

82   Ristic, "Kosovo's New War Crimes Court, How Will it Work?"

83   Pineles, "'Ghost Court' Delays Justice for Kosovo War Victims."

84   Jones, unpublished interview with Clint Williamson.

85   Ambagtsheer, "Understanding the Challenges to Investigating and Prose-
      cuting Organ Trafficking."

86   Bugter, "Legal Actors in Illegal Organ Trade."

87   Santos, "The 'Medicus Case'"

88   RTV1, interview with Dean Pineles.

89   Pineles, "How the 'Kosovo Precedent' Shaped Putin's Plan to Invade Ukraine," *Balkan Insight*, March 9, 2022.

BIBLIOGRAPHY

Ambagtsheer, Frederike. "Understanding the Challenges to Investigating and Prosecuting Organ Trafficking: A Comparative Analysis of Two Cases." *Trends in Organized Crime*. June 3, 2021.

An Overview of War Crime Trials in Kosovo in the Period 1999–2018. Humanitarian Law Center in Kosovo. October 2018.

Attewell, Fred. "Kosovo Bomb Blast Kills Two." *The Guardian*. September 4, 2007.

Bami, Xhorxhina. "Kosovo's Courts Struggle to Hold Corrupt Officials to Account." *Balkan Insight*. March 5, 2021.

Bami, Xhorxhina. "Fearful Witness in Kosovo Serb Politician's Murder Trial Changes Testimony." *Balkan Insight*. November 24, 2021.

Bilefsky, Dan. "In Albanian Feuds, Isolation Engulfs Families." *New York Times*. July 10, 2008. h

Bilefsky, Dan. "5 Are Convicted in Kosovo of Organ Trafficking." *New York Times*. April 29, 2013.

Brown, Leslie. "At Dawn, Officials Moved In." *Burlington Free Press*. June 23, 1984.

Brown, Leslie. "Judge Blocks State." *Burlington Free Press*. June 23, 1984.

Brown, Leslie. "Officials Defend Church Raid as Routine." *Burlington Free Press*. June 26, 1984.

Brown, Leslie. "Pineles Presents Witnesses to 'Protect My Reputation.'" *Burlington Free Press*. March 21, 1985.

Brumwasser, Matthew. 'Death of War Crimes Witness Casts Cloud on Kosovo." *New York Times*. October 6, 2011.

Bugter, Roos. "Legal Actors in Illegal Organ Trade: A Crime Script of the Logistical Process of Illegal Organ Transplants and the Legal Actors Involved in the *Medicus* Case" (master's thesis). Erasmus University, Rotterdam. September 2020.

Campbell, Lori. "Percy Rape Trial Begins. Potential Jurors Hear Description of 10-Year-Old Case." *Burlington Free Press*. October 16, 1990.

Campbell, Lori. "Victim Describes Rape in Percy Case. She Says She Expected to Die." *Burlington Free Press*. October 19, 1990.

Campbell, Lori. "Witness Tells of Life in Vietnam. Percy Jury Hears of Horror, Constant Drug Use." *Burlington Free Press*. October 20, 1990.

Campbell, Lori. "Witness Says Percy Suffered Flashback." *Burlington Free Press*. October 23, 1990.

Campbell, Lori. "Accused Rapist is Called Sane." *Burlington Free Press*. October 24, 1990.

Campbell, Lori. "Percy Guilty Again." Headline. *Burlington Free Press*. October 26, 1990.

Campbell, Lori. "Percy Receives 40–60 years. Sentence Ends Tortuous 10-Year Rape Case." *Burlington Free Press*. February 7, 1991.

"Children of Sect Seized in Vermont." *New York Times*. June 23, 1984.

Clifford, Timothy, and Joe Sciacca. "Troopers Crack Child Abuse Sect, 112 Kids Rescued." *Boston Herald*. June 23, 1984.

"Corruption Perceptions Index." Transparency International. January 2022.

Costello, Stephen. "Rapist Gets 22–50 Years for Series of Rampages." *Rutland Herald*. 1989.

Crisp, James. "KLA Guerrillas Harvested Murdered Serb's Organs, Say EU Investigators." EURACTIV. July 29, 2014.

Del Ponte, Carla, and Chuck Sudetic. *Madame Prosecutor. Confrontations with Humanity's Worst Criminals and the Culture of Impunity*. New York: Other Press, 2009.

"Discard the Bad Regulations and Enforce the Good Ones." Editorial. *Burlington Free Press*. March 23, 1981.

"European Envoy to Testify in Kosovo Organ Case." EUbusiness. April 4, 2012.

"Factsheet," Special Investigative Task Force.

Flood, Royal. "Vermont Rape Victims Kept Waiting for Justice. Two Cases Have Dragged On for Nearly 10 Years." *Boston Sunday Globe.* September 2, 1990.

Goddard, Kevin. "Snelling Subpoena is Quashed." *Rutland Herald.* September 2, 1983.

Haxhiaj, Serbeze. "Kosovo's Forensic Investigators: 'We are the Voice of the Dead.'" *Balkan Insight.* November 29, 2021.

Hays, Laurie. "Library Won't be Called Engelhard." *Boston Globe.* May 12, 1979.

Higgins, Andrew. "In a Land Dominated by Ex-Rebels, Kosovo Women Find Power at the Ballot Box." *New York Times.* March 6, 2021.

Higgins, Andrew. "Not the Worst Hotel in the World, Perhaps, but 'the World is Very Big'" *New York Times.* March 1, 2018.

Johnson, Sally. "Support Voiced for Judge Pineles." *The Rutland Herald.* March 21, 1984.

Johnson, Sally. "Pineles Lauded by Witnesses at Confirmation Hearing." *Times Argus.* March 20, 1985.

Johnson, Sally. "Insanity is Key to Defense." *Rutland Herald.* October 18, 1990.

Johnson, Sally. "War Stress Detailed at Rape Trial." *Rutland Herald.* October 20, 1990.

Jones, Bronwyn. Unpublished interview with Clint Williamson. 2020.

"Judge Sends Sect's Children Home." Headline. *Times Argus.* June 23, 1984.

"Judicial Board Should Name Female Candidates." Editorial. *Burlington Free Press.* June 7, 1983.

"Jury Duty and Rule 20." Editorial. *Caledonian Record.* December 9, 1986.

"Kosovo Court Orders Retrial of Ex-Rebel for War Crimes." EUbusiness. November 21, 2012.

Lewis, Paul. "Kosovo PM is Head of Human Organ and Arms Ring, Council of Europe Reports." *The Guardian.* December 4, 2010.

Marty, Dick. *Inhuman Treatment of People and Illicit Trafficking in Human Organs in Kosovo.* Committee on Legal Affairs and Human rights,

Parliamentary Assembly of the Council of Europe, Paris. December 16, 2010.

Morina, Dia. "24 Charged over Kosovo Ex-Guerrilla's Prison Breaks." *Balkan Insight*. November 17, 2017.

Morina, Dia, and Blerta Iberdemaj. "Kosovo Orders Second Retrial for Organ-Trading Defendants." *Balkan Insight*. November 28, 2018.

Nickerson, Colin, and John Donnell. "Vermont Seizes 112 Children From Sect." *Boston Globe*. June 23, 1984.

Pineles, Dean. "'Ghost Court' Delays Justice for Kosovo War Victims." *Balkan Insight*. March 21, 2018.

Pineles, Dean. "Kosovo's Medicus Case: Bad Omen for Rule of Law." *Balkan Insight*. May 2, 2018.

Pineles, Dean. "The Kosovo Precedent and the 2022 Russia-Ukraine Conflict." *Balkan Insight*. March 9, 2022.

"Put a Woman on the Bench." Editorial. *Brattleboro Reformer*. June 10, 1983.

Quote of the Week. *Burlington Free Press*. February 10, 1991.

"Raid Raises Questions about Pineles' Judgment." Editorial. *Burlington Free Press*. February 22, 1985.

"Raid on Sect Raises Doubts About Pineles." Editorial. *Burlington Free Press*. March 14, 1985.

Ratner, Jonathan D. "Goldfinger Buys a Library." *Harvard Crimson*. October 13, 1978.

Ristic, Marija. "Kosovo's New War Court, How Will it Work?" *Balkan Insight*. August 6, 2015.

Ristic, Marija. "Kosovo Organ Trafficking: How the Claims Were Exposed." *Balkan Insight*. September 4, 2015.

Rocchio, David. "Vt. Judge's 'Retirement' Leads to Kosovo." *Stowe Reporter*. May 30, 2013.

Roth, Andrew. "Crowd Led by Priests Attacks Gay Rights Marchers in Georgia." *New York Times*. May 17, 2013.

RTV1 (Russian TV station in New York). Interview with Dean Pineles regarding *Medicus* case. February 8, 2021.

Santos, Diana, and Eduardo Salcedo Albaran. "The 'Medicus Case': Organ

Trafficking Network in Kosovo." *Global Observatory of Transnational Criminal Networks*. No. 14 (2017).

Schmidle, Nicholas. "An Organ-Trafficking Conviction in Kosovo." *The New Yorker*. April 29, 2013.

Schmidle, Nicholas. "Bring Up the Bodies." *The New Yorker*. May 6, 2013.

Slater, Elizabeth. "Judge Quashes Snelling Subpoena." *Times Argus*. November 10, 1983.

Slater, Elizabeth. "Pineles Grilled on Church Raid." *Times Argus*. February 20, 1985.

Smith, Robin. "Secrets from Island Pond's Chilling Raid." *Caledonian Record*. August 5, 2017.

Snelling, Richard. "State Took Action to Protect Children and the Constitution." *Burlington Free Press*. June 30, 1984.

"Szunyog: Violence Against Women, a Terrible Reality in Kosovo." *RTK Live*. November 30, 2021.

Tales From the Organ Trade. HBO. 2013.

Traynor, Ian. "Former War Crimes Prosecutor Alleges Kosovan Army Harvested Organs From Serb Prisoners." *The Guardian*. Friday, April 11, 2008.

Watkin, Tom. "From Left, Right, Lawyers Rap Raid." *Times Argus*. June 23, 1984.

Watkin, Tom. "Mahady: Raid 'Grossly Unlawful.'" *Rutland Herald*. June 27, 1984.

Whitmore, B. "Balkans: Allegations of Organ Trafficking in Del Ponte Memoir Spark Scandal." *Radio Free Europe*. April 23, 2008.

Williamson, Clint. *Statement of the Chief Prosecutor of the Special Investigative Task Force*. July 29, 2014.

Acknowledgments

Upon my return to Vermont after twenty-eight months in Kosovo in 2013, I presented a series of lectures about my experiences in international rule of law work in Russia, Kazakhstan, Georgia, and Kosovo. Out of these lectures, along with strong encouragement from several friends, evolved my manuscript, which now includes a Vermont section. I worked in fits and starts over a period of years, and not infrequently considered quitting the project all together. But my wife, Kristina Stahlbrand, who was my companion in these overseas adventures, gave me constant, unwavering support, and was able to talk me off the cliff on many occasions. And as an inveterate reader, critic, and tireless grammarian, her advice and guidance were invaluable. Without her, there would be no book, and she has my enduring love and gratitude.

Many other people have given me assistance along the way, which came in a variety of forms from both home and abroad, such as ongoing verbal encouragement, suggesting themes, content and structure, reading and commenting on the entire manuscript or discrete sections, fact checking, editorial help, offering blurbs for publication, and more. As an expression of my gratitude I will list them here: Jeffery Amestoy, Pamela Aronson, Kim Cheney, Matthew Collin, Michael Cuniff, Phil Cykon, John Dooley, William Gilbert, David Goodman, Aidan Hehir, Witold Jakimko, Bronwyn Jones, Edward P. Joseph, Philip Kearney, Garry Ledbetter, William Mares, Michael McShane, Edi Nimani, Larry Novins, Mark Oettinger, Erika Pineles-Mark, Gillian Randall, Jonathan Ratel, David Rocchio, Charles Smith III, Dirk VanSusteren, Clint Williamson, and Ronald Wolfson.

This is the first book I have written and I found myself in unfamiliar territory. While I have written many articles for publication, both in Vermont and the Balkans, I have never gone through the process of working with a book publisher. I was very fortunate to be referred to Rootstock Publishing in Montpelier, Vermont, and its co-publisher Stephen McArthur, who expressed immediate enthusiasm about my manuscript. I have since worked closely with Stephen and members of his staff, including Samantha Kolber and Marisa Keller, as well as copy editor Jim Higgins, proofreader Courtney Jenkins, and photo consultant Paul Hislop, all of whom have been very professional, skillful, and helpful. I couldn't have done it without them.

Thank you all!

About the Author

Dean Pineles grew up in Hamilton, Massachusetts, where he attended school through sophomore year, then enrolled in Mount Hermon School, graduating in 1961. He then attended Brown University (1965) and Boston University School of Law (1968), following which he served in the US Army and then in the US Justice Department in Washington, D.C.

In 1973, Dean and his wife, Kristina Stahlbrand, returned to New England, and Dean became an assistant attorney general in Vermont, representing the Department of Social Welfare. He presented one of his legal cases to the US Supreme Court. He then furthered his education at the Harvard Kennedy School, receiving a master's degree in public administration in 1979, following which he became deputy commissioner and general counsel with the Vermont Department of Health.

In 1981, he was appointed by the governor as commissioner of labor and industry, and then in 1982 as the governor's legal counsel. In 1984, he was appointed to a judgeship on the Vermont District Court and served for twenty-one years, until 2005.

Following his retirement, Dean became actively involved in international rule of law work, serving short-term assignments as a legal adviser in Russia and Kazakhstan, and a year-long residential assignment in the country of Georgia with the American Bar association Rule of Law Initiative (2008–09).

He was then appointed to an international criminal judgeship with the European Union Rule of Law Mission in Kosovo where he served for two and a half years (2011–13). There, he adjudicated cases involving war crimes, judicial corruption, narcotics trafficking, murder, and human organ trafficking.

Since his return from Kosovo, he has lectured and written extensively about his experiences in that country. He and Kristina live in Stowe, Vermont.

Also Available from Rootstock Publishing:

The Atomic Bomb on My Back by Taniguchi Sumiteru

Pauli Murray's Revolutionary Life by Simki Kuznick

Blue Desert by Celia Jeffries

China in Another Time: A Personal Story by Claire Malcolm Lintilhac

Collecting Courage: Anti-Black Racism in the Charitable Sector
Edited by Nneka Allen, Camila Vital Nunes Pereira, & Nicole Salmon

An Everyday Cult by Gerette Buglion

Fly with A Murder of Crows: A Memoir by Tuvia Feldman

Horodno Burning: A Novel by Michael Freed-Thall

I Could Hardly Keep from Laughing by Don Hooper & Bill Mares

The Inland Sea: A Mystery by Sam Clark

Intent to Commit by Bernie Lambek

Junkyard at No Town by J.C. Myers

The Language of Liberty: A Citizen's Vocabulary by Edwin C. Hagenstein

A Lawyer's Life to Live by Kimberly B. Cheney

Lifting Stones: Poems by Doug Stanfield

The Lost Grip: Poems by Eva Zimet

Lucy Dancer Story and Illustrations by Eva Zimet

Nobody Hitchhikes Anymore by Ed Griffin-Nolan

Preaching Happiness: Creating a Just and Joyful World by Ginny Sassaman

Red Scare in the Green Mountains: Vermont in the McCarthy Era 1946-1960
by Rick Winston

Safe as Lightning: Poems by Scudder H. Parker

Street of Storytellers by Doug Wilhelm

Tales of Bialystok: A Jewish Journey from Czarist Russia to America
by Charles Zachariah Goldberg

To the Man in the Red Suit: Poems by Christina Fulton

Uncivil Liberties: A Novel by Bernie Lambek

Venice Beach: A Novel by William Mark Habeeb

The Violin Family by Melissa Perley; Illustrated by Fiona Lee Maclean

Walking Home: Trail Stories by Celia Ryker

Wave of the Day: Collected Poems by Mary Elizabeth Winn

Whole Worlds Could Pass Away: Collected Stories by Rickey Gard Diamond

You Have a Hammer: Building Grant Proposals for Social Change by Barbara Floersch

CPSIA information can be obtained
at www.ICGtesting.com
Printed in the USA
BVHW062354030722
641185BV00001B/4

9 781578 690886